Outline of Classical Chinese Grammar

CW00802042

Outline of Classical Chinese Grammar is a comprehensive introduction to the syntactical analysis of Classical Chinese. Focusing on the language of the high classical period, which ranges from the time of Confucius to the unification of the empire by Qin in -221, the book pays particular attention to the *Mencius*, the *Lúnyu*, and, to a lesser extent, the *Zuŏzhuàn* texts.

Renowned for his work in Classical Chinese, Edwin Pulleyblank opens the book with a brief historical overview and a discussion of the relationship between the writing system and the phonology. This is followed by an outline of the overall principles of word order and sentence structure. He then deals with the main sentence types – nominal predicates, verbal predicates, and numerical expressions, which constitute a special type of quasiverbal predication. The final section covers topics such as subordinate constituents of sentences, nondeclarative sentence types, and complex sentences.

Clear and well organized, *Outline of Classical Chinese Grammar* is an authoritative study and will be an invaluable resource tool for anyone involved in Chinese language studies.

Edwin G. Pulleyblank is professor emeritus of the Department of Asian Studies at the University of British Columbia. He is the author of *Lexicon of Reconstructed Pronunciation in Early Middle Chinese, Late Middle Chinese, and Early Mandarin* (1991) and *Middle Chinese: A Study in Historical Phonology* (1984).

Edwin G. Pulleyblank

Outline of Classical Chinese Grammar

UBC PRESS / VANCOUVER

Printed in Canada on acid-free paper ∞

ISBN 0-7748-0505-6 (hardcover)
ISBN 0-7748-0541-2 (paperback)

Canadian Cataloguing in Publication Data

Pulleyblank, Edwin G. (Edwin George), 1922-
  Outline of classical Chinese grammar

  Includes bibliographical references and index.
  ISBN 0-7748-0505-6 (bound).
  ISBN 0-7748-0541-2 (pbk.)

  1. Chinese language – Grammar, Historical. 2. Chinese language – to 600. I. Title.

PL1101.P84 1995   495.I'5   C95-910219-1

This book has been published with the help of a grant from the Canadian Federation for the Humanities, using funds provided by the Social Sciences and Humanities Research Council of Canada.

Financial assistance was also provided by the Chiang Ching-kuo Foundation for International Scholarly Exchange.

UBC Press also gratefully acknowledges the ongoing support to its publishing program from the Canada Council, the Province of British Columbia Cultural Services Branch, and the Department of Communications of the Government of Canada.

UBC Press
University of British Columbia
6344 Memorial Road
Vancouver, BC V6T 1Z2
(604) 822-3259
Fax: (604) 822-6083

Contents

Preface /xiii
Abbreviations /xv

I.   Introduction /3
     1. Historical Outline /3
     2. Sound /4
        (a) *Fǎnqiè* 反切 /5
        (b) Tones /6
     3. Symbol /7
     4. Syllable and Word /8
     5. Morphology /10
II. Some Basic Principles of Classical Chinese Syntax /12
     1. Word Classes /12
     2. Subject and Predicate /13
     3. Word Order /14
III. Noun Predication /16
     1. Verbless Noun Predication /16
        (a) Questions /16
        (b) Pronouns and Particles with Verbless Noun Predicates /17
        (c) Verbless Comparisons with *Yóu* 猶 /18
        (d) Omission of *Yě* 也 /18
        (e) The Aspect Particle *Yǐ* 已 after Verbless Noun Predicates /19
        (f) Other Meanings of *Yě* 也 /20
     2. The Copula Verb *Wéi* 為 /20
     3. The Copula *Yuě* 曰 /21
     4. The Preclassical Copula *Wéi* 唯 /22
IV. Verbal Predicates /23
     1. Classes of Verbs /23
     2. Adjectives /24
     3. Nouns Used as Verbs /25
     4. Intransitive Verbs /26
     5. Transitive Verbs — Active and Passive /27
     6. Verbs of Motion and Location — Intransitive and Transitive /28

7. The Verbs *Yǒu* 有 'have; there is/are' and *Wú* 無 'not have; there is/are not' /30
8. Transitive Verbs with Two Objects /31
9. Passive Constructions /35

V. Compound Verbal Predicates /39
1. Coordination /39
2. Clause Objects — Verb Phrases as Objects of Transitive Verbs /39
3. Pivot Constructions — The Causative /40
4. Verb Phrases as Complements to Adjectives /42
   (a) Adjectives That Make a Following Verb Passive /42
   (b) Other Adjectives That Take Verb Phrases as Complements /44
5. Verbs in Series /44
   (a) The Construction in General — The Particle *Ér* 而 /44
   (b) *Dé (ér)* 得 (而), *Shuài (ér)* 率 (而), etc. /46
6. Coverbs /47
   (a) Transitive Verbs Corresponding to Prepositions /47
      (i) *Yǐ* 以 'take, use; with, by means of' /47
      (ii) *Yòng* 用 'use; with' /50
      (iii) *Yǔ* 與 'accompany; give; with; and' /50
      (iv) *Wèi* 為 'for, on behalf of, for the sake of' /51
      (v) *Zì* 自 , *Yóu* 由 , *Cóng* 從 'follow from' /52
   (b) Coverbs of Place /53
      (i) *Yú* 于 'go; to, at' /53
      (ii) *Yú* 於 'in, at, to, from, than, etc.' /53
      (iii) *Hū* 乎 /54
      (iv) Locative complements /54
      (v) Omission of the coverb in locative complements /55
      (vi) Pronominal substitutes *yuán* 爰 and *yān* 焉 /56
      (vii) X *zhī yú* 之 於 Y /56
   (c) Descriptive Complements with *Rú* 如 and *Yóu* 猶 /57
   (d) Coverbs as Subordinating Conjunctions /57

VI. Numerical Expressions /58
1. As Predicates /58
2. As Complements /58
3. As Modifiers of Nouns /59
4. *Yòu* 有 'and' /60

VII. Noun Phrases and Nominalization /61
1. Coordination and Subordination of Nouns /61

(a) Coordination /61
(b) Subordination /61
2. Nominalization /62
(a) Unmarked Nominalization /62
(b) Marked Nominalization by Inserting *Zhī* 之 /64
(c) *Zhě* 者 /66
(d) *Suǒ* 所 /68
VIII. Topicalization and Exposure /69
1. Exposure of an Element That is Not the Subject /69
2. Exposure of the Subject /71
3. *Zé* 則 Marking Exposure /72
4. *X zhī yú* 之 於 Y /73
5. Other Particles Marking Topicalization or Contrastive Exposure /73
(a) *Yě* 也 /73
(b) *Wéi* 唯 /74
(c) *Zhě* 者 /74
(d) *Fú* 夫 /74
(e) *Ruò fú* 若 夫 /75
IX. Pronouns and Related Words /76
1. Personal Pronouns /76
(a) First Person /76
(b) Second Person /77
(c) Third Person /78
(d) Reflexive Personal Pronoun /83
(e) Personal Pronouns with Negative Particles /84
2. Demonstratives /85
(a) *Shì* 是 /85
(b) *Cǐ* 此 /86
(c) *Bǐ* 彼 /86
(d) *Sī* 斯 /88
(e) *Zī* 茲 /88
(f) *Shí* 實, *Shí* 寔 /89
(g) *Shí* 時 /89
(h) *Fú* 夫 /89
(i) *Ěr* 爾 /90
(j) *Ruò* 若 /90
3. Interrogatives /91
(a) (i) *Shuí* 誰 /91

        (ii) *Shú* 孰 /92
        (iii) *Chóu* 疇 /93
    (b) (i) *Hé* 何 /93
        (ii) *Xī* 奚 /95
        (iii) *Hú* 胡 /95
        (iv) *Hé* 曷 /95
        (v) *Hé* 盍 /95
    (c) (i) *Yān* 焉 , *ān* 安 /96
        (ii) *Wū hú* 惡乎 , *wū* 惡 , *wū* 烏 /96
  4. Indefinite Pronouns /97
    (a) *Tuō* 他 /97
    (b) *Mǒu* 某 /97
    (c) *Rén* 人 /97
X. Adverbs /99
  1. Adverbial Use of Nouns /99
  2. Adjectives as Adverbs /100
  3. Verbs as Adverbs /101
  4. Numerical Expressions as Adverbs /101
  5. Expressive Adverbs in *Rán* 然 , *Rú* 如 , etc. /102
XI. Negation /103
  1. P/f Negatives /103
    (a) *Bú* 不 /103
    (b) *Fǒu* 否 /103
    (c) *Fú* 弗 /104
    (d) *Fēi* 非 /106
    (e) *Pǒ* 叵 /106
    (f) *Hé* 盍 /107
  2. M/w Negatives /107
    (a) *Wú* 毋 , *wú* 無 and *wú* 无 /107
        (i) *Wú* 無 as prohibitive particle /107
        (ii) *Wú* 無 'not have.' See Section IV.7
    (b) *Wù* 勿 'do not' /108
    (c) *Wáng* 亡 /109
    (d) *Wǎng* 罔 /109
    (e) *Mò* 莫 /109
    (f) *Wèi* 未 /109
    (g) *Wéi* 微 /110
    (h) *Mǐ* 靡 /110

(i) *Miè* 滅 /110

(j) *Mò* 末 /111

XII. Aspect, Time, and Mood /112

  1. Verbal Aspect — Preverbal Particles /112

    (a) *Jì* 既 /113

    (b) *Wèi* 未 /114

    (c) Preverbal *Yǐ* 已 /115

  2. Sentential Aspect — Sentence Final Particles /116

    (a) *Yǐ* 矣 /116

    (b) *Yě* 也 /118

    (c) *Yǐ* 已 (*Yě yǐ* 也已, *Yě yǐ yǐ* 也已矣) /118

  3. Time Words /119

    (a) Time Expressions in Topic Position /119

    (b) *Cháng* 嘗 /119

    (c) *Céng* 曾 /119

    (d) *Jiāng* 將 /120

    (e) *Qiě* 且 /121

    (f) *Fāng* 方 /121

    (g) *Shǐ* 始 /121

    (h) *Chū* 初 /122

  4. Modality /122

    (a) *Qí* 其 /123

    (b) *Dài* 殆, *Shū jī* 庶幾 /124

    (c) *Gài* 蓋 /124

    (d) *Wú* 毋, *Wú* 無, and *Wù* 勿 /124

    (e) *Níng* 寧 /125

XIII. Adnominal and Adverbial Words of Inclusion and Restriction /126

  1. Words of Inclusion /126

    (a) *Zhū* 諸 'all; members of the class of' /126

    (b) *Fán* 凡 'all' /127

    (c) *Jiē* 皆, *Jǔ* 舉 'all' /127

    (d) *Jū* 俱 'both, together' /129

    (e) *Gè* 各 'each' /130

    (f) *Měi* 每 'every (time), always; whenever' /130

    (g) Words of Verbal Origin /131

  2. Restriction /131

    (a) *Wéi* 唯 'only' /131

      (i) Introducing the subject or an exposed element /131

          (ii) Introducing a noun predicate /132

          (iii) In adverbial position restricting the predicate /132

      (b) *Dú* 獨 'only' /133

      (c) Other Similar Words /133

      (d) Restriction by Final Particles /134

   3. Some, None /134

      (a) *Huò* 或 'some one; some' /134

      (b) *Mò* 莫 'no one; none' /136

   4. Reflexive and Reciprocal Pronominal Adverbs /136

      (a) *Zì* 自 'oneself' /136

      (b) *Xiāng* 相 'each other, mutually' /136

      (c) *Shēn* 身 'body, person, self' /137

      (d) *Jiāo* 交 'in exchange, mutually'; *Hù* 互 'mutually'/137

XIV. Imperative, Interrogative and Exclamatory Sentences /138

   1. Imperative Sentences /138

      (a) Unmarked /138

      (b) *Qǐng* 請 'I beg of you; please' /138

      (c) Prohibition. See XI.2

      (d) Modal *Qí* 其 in Imperative Sentences. See XII.4a.

   2. Interrogative Sentences /139

      (a) Simple Questions /

          (i) The final particle *Hū* 乎 /139

          (ii) *Yě hū* 也乎, *yú* 與 (歟), *yé* 邪 (耶) /139

          (iii) *Zhū* 諸 /140

          (iv) *Fǒu* 否. See XI.1b.

          (v) Interrogative pronouns. See IX.3

      (b) Rhetorical Questions /140

          (i) Negative questions requiring affirmative answers /140

          (ii) *Qí* 其 in rhetorical questions /142

          (iii) *Qǐ* 豈 /142

          (iv) *Yōng* 庸, *Jù* 詎, *Qú* 渠, *Yōng jù* 庸遽, etc. /144

          (v) *Wú* 無 in rhetorical questions /144

          (vi) *Fú* 夫 'is it not' /145

          (vii) Rhetorical questions with interrogative pronouns /145

          (viii) *Kuàng* 況 'how much the more' /146

   3. Exclamatory Sentences /146

      (a) *Zāi* 哉 /146

      (b) Inversion of Subject and Predicate /147

XV. Complex Sentences /148
  1. Parataxis and Hypotaxis /148
  2. Conditional Clauses /149
     (a) Parataxis /149
     (b) Subordination by a Particle in the If-Clause /150
         (i) *Ruò* 若, *Rú* 如, *Ér* 而 /150
         (ii) *Shǐ* 使, *Líng* 令, etc., 'supposing' /151
         (iii) *Gǒu* 苟 /152
         (iv) *Chéng* 誠, *Xìn* 信 /153
         (v) *Jí* 即 /153
         (vi) *Fēi* 非 /154
         (vii)*Wēi* 微 /154
     (c) Subordination by a Particle in the Main Clause /154
         (i) *Zé* 則 'then' /154
         (ii) *Sī* 斯 'then' /155
         (iii) *Jí* 即 'then' /155
  3. Concessive Clauses /156
     (a) *Suī* 雖 'although, even if' /156
     (b) *Suī ... ér ...* 雖 ... 而 ... /157
     (c) *Fēi ... ér ...* 非 ... 而 ... /157
     (d) *Zòng* 縱 /158
  4. Temporal Clauses /158
     (a) Verbs in Series /158
     (b) Aspect Particles in the First Clause /158
     (c) *Jí* 及 'when' /158
     (d) *Simultaneity* — Dāng 當, Fāng 方, ... shí 時 /160
     (e) Topic Phrases /161
     (f) *Ér hòu* 而後, *Rán hòu* 然後 /161
  5. Cause, Reason /161
     (a) The Coverb *Yǐ* 以 /161
     (b) *Gù* 故 'reason' /162
     (c) Explanatory Noun Predicate after Main Clause. See VII.2a.ii
         and XII.3c)
Notes /163
Sources of Examples /169
Bibliography /171
Index of Chinese Vocabulary Items /175
General Index /189

Preface

This *Outline of Classical Chinese Grammar* has grown out of notes prepared over the years for teaching Classical Chinese to undergraduates at the University of Cambridge and the University of British Columbia, as well as at summer schools in Bloomington, Indiana, Columbus, Ohio, and Minneapolis, Minnesota, in the 1960s. When I began the study of this language at the end of the Second World War, there were very few textbooks or other learning aids available. There was, in fact, still a widespread belief that Chinese, especially the classical language, had no grammar and that the only way to learn it was by a kind of osmosis. By reading texts with a teacher, preferably a native speaker of a modern spoken form of the language, one was supposed to absorb a facility at guessing at the meanings of passages by piecing together the meanings of successive words as provided in a dictionary.

There had, of course, been pioneering works by western sinologists in the nineteenth century, particularly noteworthy being Georg von der Gabelentz, *Chinesische Grammatik* (1881), but these were held in little regard. Rather more heed was paid to the contributions of Bernhard Karlgren, whose work had first put the study of Middle and Old Chinese pronunciation on a scientific basis and who had also made many insightful observations on the grammar of the classical language. There were others, like my old teacher, Walter Simon, at the School of Oriental and African Studies, or George Kennedy at Yale and Harold Shadick at Cornell, who were trying to apply modern linguistic theory to Classical Chinese. Nevertheless, it would be true to say that there was nothing approaching a coherent analysis of the syntax of the language available. I felt this lack even more acutely when, all too soon, I found myself in the position of having to teach the language myself. Along with other contemporaries, like William Dobson and Angus Graham, I found myself pushed into doing research in this area. After publishing two or three papers on grammatical questions, I concentrated my publication more on historical phonology but I continued to think about questions of syntax and to prepare teaching notes for my students. The *Outline* that I offer here is the end result of this process.

The world has, of course, changed greatly in the half century since I began to study Chinese, not least in linguistic theory, which has been revolutionized by the theories of Noam Chomsky and his followers. While this has inspired much recent work on Modern Chinese grammar, it has, unfortunately, had comparatively little impact so far on the study of the classical language. We are still at the stage of struggling to work out the basic patterns of Classical Chinese syntax. Perhaps some students will be inspired by the unsolved problems that they find in this book to apply new theoretical tools and bring the grammar of Classical Chinese into the linguistic mainstream instead of being in a rather esoteric backwater. Meanwhile, I am encouraged by the reactions of those who have seen and used earlier versions both at the University of British Columbia and elsewhere to think that students and teachers will continue to find it a useful introduction to the language.

It is impossible in a short work of this kind to argue fully for all the positions taken, let alone discuss the views of other scholars who agree or differ from them. I have endeavoured in the endnotes to acknowledge major contributions of my predecessors and contemporaries but I am only too aware that the references I have made are far from complete in this regard. I can only hope that my colleagues will forgive me, bearing in mind my primarily pedagogical aim.

In preparing this work for publication I have been greatly assisted by a generous grant from the Social Sciences and Humanities Research Council of Canada. The grant was provided for a *Concise Dictionary of Classical Chinese*, of which the *Outline of Classical Chinese Grammar* was to serve as an introduction. In the end it has seemed better to publish the *Outline* separately. The *Dictionary* exists in the form of a preliminary draft on computer but will still require much work before it is in publishable form.

Among those whom the grant has enabled me to employ, Dr. Gary Arbuckle must be specially mentioned for his help in preparing the computerized text of this book. I should also like to thank Mr. Jingtao Sun and the copy editor of the UBC Press who have proofread the text with great care and caught many errors. Errors that remain are of course my own responsibility.

I also acknowledge with gratitude the publication grants which the book has received from the Humanities Federation of Canada and the Chiang Ching-kuo Foundation.

Abbreviations

EM	Early Mandarin
EMC	Early Middle Chinese
Gōng	*Gōngyáng zhuàn* 公羊傳
Guǎn	*Guǎnzǐ* 管子
GY	*Guóyǔ* 國語
HF	*Hán Fēizǐ* 韓非子
LMC	Late Middle Chinese
LY	*Lúnyǔ* 論語
Mèng	*Mèngzǐ* 孟子
Mò	*Mòzǐ* 墨子
OC	Old Chinese
Shī	*Shījīng* 詩經
Shū	*Shū jīng* 書經
Xún	*Xúnzǐ* 荀子
ZGC	*Zhànguó cè* 戰國策
Zhuāng	*Zhuāngzǐ* 莊子
Zuǒ	*Zuǒzhuàn* 左傳

I. Introduction

1. Historical Outline

Chinese was the principal vehicle of culture and civilization for the whole of East Asia for many centuries and today is spoken by more people than any other language. The earliest known examples of written Chinese are the so-called 'oracle bones,' records of divination from the last capital of the Shāng 商 dynasty at Ānyáng 安陽. They date from approximately -1300 to -1050. From the following centuries, after the founding of the Zhōu 周 dynasty, come inscriptions on bronze vessels recording royal donations and other such events. The earliest of the Chinese classics — parts of the *Book of Changes* (*Yìjīng* 易經), the *Book of Documents* (*Shūjīng* 書經), and the *Book of Odes* (*Shījīng* 詩經) — also date from the early centuries of the Zhōu dynasty. All these texts are written in an archaic form of Chinese referred to as preclassical.

The classical period proper begins with Confucius 孔子 (-551 to -479) and continues through the Warring States period to the unification and founding of the empire by Qín 秦 in -221. This was the period of the major philosophers and also of the first works of narrative history. Though all the productions of the period are in Classical Chinese, there is considerable linguistic diversity among them. This is, no doubt, partly the result of the geographical disunity and decentralization of the country, which allowed various regional dialects to become the vehicles of literature in their own areas. It is also the result of historical evolution. Exhaustive studies of these differences have yet to be made, but one can distinguish at least the following: (a) a rather archaic form of literary language, showing features in common with the *Shījīng* and probably based on a central dialect, used in historical texts such as the *Zuǒzhuàn* 左傳 and *Guóyǔ* 國語; (b) a Lǔ 魯 dialect used in the Confucian *Analects* (*Lúnyǔ* 論語; more archaic) and Mencius (*Mèngzǐ* 孟子; more evolved); (c) a Chǔ 楚 dialect used in the *Lí Sāo* 離騷 and other early poems of the *Chǔcí* 楚辭; and (d) a third-century dialect found in texts such as *Zhuāngzǐ* 莊子, *Xúnzǐ* 荀子, and *Hán Fēizǐ* 韓非子, showing an evolution towards a common literary standard but still with marked differences between different texts.

With the imperial unification under Qín and Hàn 漢, the movement towards a common literary standard was accelerated, not only by the centralization of the government, but also by the increasing tendency towards imitation of classical models in preference to the living spoken language. An important influence in this respect was the triumph of Confucianism which made the Confucian classics the basis for education and for advancement in government service. In a comparatively early text like the *Records of the Historian* (*Shǐjì* 史 記) one can still detect influence from the spoken language, but as time went on Literary Chinese (*wén yán* 文 言) became increasingly a dead language, playing a role like that of Latin in Western Europe, from which the current spoken language increasingly diverged.

Literary Chinese was never completely static and uniform. Different styles were fashioned by successive literary movements and for special purposes such as government documents or Buddhist writings. There was no development of a prescriptive grammar and people learned to write by imitating earlier models rather than by obeying explicit rules as in the case of Latin. The spoken language always had some influence even in belles lettres and poetry, and still more in writings of a more practical nature. The result is that even those well versed in classical texts may have difficulty when they first encounter later material, such as official documents of the Qīng 清 dynasty.

2. Sound

Chinese characters are sometimes referred to as if they directly represent ideas. This is a fallacy. Even though many of them are pictorial or otherwise iconic in origin, in their use as a system of writing they are conventional symbols for particular spoken words. Thus synonyms (words that are the same in meaning but different in sound) are normally written with different characters, while homophones (words that are the same in sound but different in meaning) may be written with the same character. For example, *quǎn* 'dog' is written 犬, based on a pictogram for 'dog,' but *gǒu*, which also means 'dog,' is written 狗, with a distorted form of 犬 + *gǒu* 句 'hook' to represent the sound. On the other hand, *ān* 'how? where?' and *ān* 'peace' are both written 安.

Since in Chinese, as in every other language, the spoken form is primary, it is desirable to get back, as closely as possible, to the actual sounds that underlie the characters. Unfortunately, since the characters represent whole syllables and give no direct phonetic information, and since the sounds have changed greatly over the centuries, this is only possible through a difficult process of reconstruction. The most widely used system of reconstruction is that of Bernhard Karlgren as published in *Grammata Serica Recensa* (1957). This gives two reconstructions, one for what he calls Ancient Chinese, based on the *Qièyùn* 切韻, a rhyme dictionary of +602, and one for what he calls Archaic Chinese, based on the rhymes of the *Shījīng,* relevant to a period terminating around -600.

A revised system of reconstruction for the *Qièyùn,* called Early Middle Chinese (EMC), together with a reconstruction for Late Middle Chinese (LMC) of the Táng period, which together replace Karlgren's Ancient Chinese, is published in Pulleyblank, *Lexicon of Reconstructed Pronunciation in Early Middle Chinese, Late Middle Chinese and Early Mandarin* (1991), which also contains a new reconstruction of Early Mandarin (EM) of the Yuán 元 period.

The reconstruction of stages earlier than EMC is a much more difficult problem since the available evidence is more fragmentary. While the rhyme patterns of the *Shījīng,* worked out by scholars of the Qīng period, and the rhyming of poets at various periods between then and the *Qièyùn* provide evidence for the evolution of the finals, that is the rhyming parts of syllables, comparable systematic evidence for the non-rhyming parts, the initial consonants or groups of consonants, is lacking. Anything that purports to be a complete reconstruction of Old Chinese (OC), such as Karlgren's Archaic Chinese, is bound to be somewhat illusory at the present time. In this *Outline,* reconstructed readings in EMC or LMC will be given from time to time for illustrative purposes. Tentative reconstructions in OC will also sometimes be given, marked with an asterisk *.

Apart from systems of reconstruction which propose actual phonetic values, there are some traditional methods used by commentators for indicating how characters should be read that readers of classical texts should be aware of. These are the traditional spelling system known as *fǎnqiè* and the system of indicating the four ancient tones by small circles at the four corners of characters.

(a) Fǎnqiè
This term, literally 'turning-cutting,' combines two alternative terms, *fǎn* 反 'turn' and *qiè* 切 'cut,'[1] for a method invented by commentators of the Later Hàn period for spelling the sound of one word by means of two others, one of which had the same initial and the other of which had the same final. For example, *dōng* 東 'east' might be spelled *dé* 德 'virtue' +

gōng 工 'work.' In the course of time, such spellings became the basis for rhyme dictionaries which classified words by rhymes and then, within each rhyme, by homophone groups with the same non-rhyming parts. The earliest of these dictionaries that is (partially) extant is the *Qièyùn* 切 韻, completed in +601 by Lù Fǎyán 陸 法 言. It went through many revisions and enlargements culminating in the *Guǎngyùn* 廣 韻 of +1008, which is still extant. Though the *Qiè yùn* has not survived in its original form, extensive manuscript fragments have been recovered from Dunhuang and there are also partial or complete manuscripts of some of the intermediate recensions. It is important to realize that, as the language changed, *fǎnqiè* spellings became out of date. *Fǎnqiè* spellings contained in such dictionaries as the *Kāngxī zìdiǎn* 康 熙 字 典, the *Cíyuán* 辭 源, and Morohashi's *Dai Kanwa jiten* 大 漢 和 辭 典 are mostly taken from dictionaries of the Táng 唐 and Sòng 宋 periods and may give erroneous results if interpreted in terms of modern Pekingese.

(b) *Tones*

Middle Chinese had a system of four 'tones' (*sì shēng* 四 聲) which, according to tradition, were first recognized and named by Shěn Yuē 沈 約 in the +5th century. They are called *píng* 平 'level,' *shǎng* 上 'rising,' *qù* 去 'departing,' and *rù* 入 'entering.' Though they are the same in number as the four tones of Pekingese, they do not correspond one for one. The old 'level' tone has split into Pekingese tones 1 and 2, depending on whether the initial consonant was originally voiceless or voiced. Words in the old 'rising' tone with voiceless initials or with initial liquids or nasals have Pekingese tone 3. Words in the old 'departing' tone and words in the 'rising' tone with originally voiced stops or fricatives have tone 4 in Pekingese. Words in the Middle Chinese 'entering' tone originally ended in -p, -t, or -k, still preserved in Cantonese. These endings have been lost in Pekingese and the words in question may have any of the four Pekingese tones.

Since many characters have more than one reading, often differing in tone, commentators had to indicate which reading was to be followed. One method was to give a *fǎnqiè* spelling. Another was to place a small circle or half circle at one of the four corners of the character in question, starting at the lower left. Usually the most common reading of the character was left unmarked. Thus the word *wáng* 王 'king,' in the 'level' tone, is not marked but the word *wàng* 王 'to be king,' in 'departing' tone, is marked 王 in texts using this system.

Throughout this book the pronunciation of Chinese characters is indicated in the modern standard language known as *pǔtōnghuà* 普 通 話 'common speech' in the new standard romanization, *pīnyīn* 拼 音. Teachers of Classical Chinese have sometimes preferred to use a spelling system based on a reconstruction of ancient pronunciation but, while this has the advantage of focusing attention on the fact that the ancient language was pronounced very differently from the modern language and may seem justified from a purist point of view, in the present uncertainties and absence of agreement about ancient pronunciation it seems to place an artificial and unnecessary burden on the learner. Instead, ancient pronunciation will only be referred to as seems necessary for explanatory purposes. There are still problems, however. One of the most serious is that in current usage colloquial pronunciations have largely replaced special literary readings that were still regularly followed in the reading of classical texts as late as the first half of the present century and are still in use among conservative scholars in Táiwān 臺 灣 and elsewhere. This sometimes has the unfortunate consequence of obscuring important distinctions that were still transparent when the system of reading pronunciations was in vogue. In the present work I have followed the principle adopted in my *Lexicon* (1991) of adhering to older reading pronunciations in such cases. Words to which this decision has been applied include (C. = Colloquial): *chí* 治 'to govern' (C. *zhì*), *guō* 過 'to pass' (C. *guò*), *jū* 俱 (C. *jù*), *qí* 期 (C. *qī*), *tuō* 他 (C. *tā*), *wéi* 微 (C. *wēi*), *wéi* 危 (C. *wēi*), *yì* 曳 (C. *yè*).

3. Symbol

Xǔ Shèn 許 慎, who compiled the first etymological dictionary of Chinese characters, the *Shuōwén jiězì* 説 文 解 字 (*Explanations of Graphs and Analysis of Characters*), around the beginning of the +2nd century, classified Chinese characters into six types: (a) *zhǐ shì* 指 事 'pointing to things,' that is, graphs that directly symbolize ideas, for example, *shàng* 上 'up,' *xià* 下 'down'; (b) *xiàng xíng* 象 形 'imitating shapes,' that is, graphs derived from pictograms, such as *rì* 日 'sun' and *yuè* 月 'moon'; (c) *xíng shēng* 形 聲 'form and sound,' that is, graphs that combine two simpler graphs, one representing the sound and one referring to the meaning, for example, *jiāng* 江 'river' and *hé* 河 'river' — in each case the element on the left, derived from the pictogram for 'water,' is combined with another element which has nothing to do with the meaning but stands for a word that was similar in sound to the particular word that was being written; (d) *huì yì* 會意 'combined meanings,' for example *míng* 鳴 'cry,' composed of 'mouth' + 'bird'; (e) *zhuǎn zhù* 轉 注 'transferred notation,' an uncommon category, apparently meaning cases where words of different sound but similar meaning are written with similar graphs, for example, *lǎo* 老 'old' and *kǎo* 考 'old'; and (f) *jiǎjiè* 假借 'borrowing,' where a character used for another word of the same or similar sound, for example, *ān* 安 'peace,' is used to write the interrogative pronoun *ān* 'where? how?'

Of these six types, (a), (b), (d) and (e) are non-phonetic, that is, the meaning is directly represented in an iconic way without reference to the sound. Types (c) and (f) are based on a phonetic principle and together they account for the great majority of characters. There is no hard and fast line between (c) and (f). With the addition of a semantic determinant ('signific' or 'radical'), a *jiǎjiè* becomes a *xíng shēng*, for which the more usual term is *xiéshēng* 諧聲. The addition of significs was very fluid before the Hàn dynasty. Thus, the graph 女, which originated as a pictogram for *nǚ* 'woman,' was borrowed (*jiǎjiè*) for *rǔ* 'you' at an early period. Later the graph 汝, which has the element 'water' as signific and originated as a *xiéshēng* graph for the name of the Rǔ River in Hénán, was borrowed as the standard graph for *rǔ* 'you.' The choice of significs could also be variable. Thus the graph 說, with the 'speech' signific, which was later confined to the readings *shuō* 'explain; explanation; doctrine, theory; story; (later) say' and *shuì* 'persuade,' is often used for *yuè* 'be pleased' in pre-Hàn texts, for which the standard graph eventually became 悅, with the 'heart' signific.

The printed forms of the characters that were standard until the recent official script simplification, and that are still standard in Taiwan, are in a style known as *kǎishū* 楷書. This style evolved during the Former Hàn dynasty out of the earlier 'clerical style,' *lìshū* 隸書, which, in turn, was based on the 'Small Seal,' *xiǎo zhuàn* 小篆, which came into being as a result of Lǐ Sì's 李斯 script reform under the First Emperor of Qín. In Hàn times the obsolete forms of writing of the pre-Qín period were known as *gǔ wén* 古文 'ancient script.' An earlier form of script, traditionally attributed to Zhòu 籀, the Grand Scribe of King Xuān 宣 of Zhōu (r. -827 to -782), was known as 'Large Seal' *dà zhuàn* 大篆.

4. Syllable and Word

In general the syllable, written with a single character, and the word correspond in Classical Chinese, but there are a few exceptions which may be classified as follows:

(a) Bound compounds, that is, words whose meanings cannot be deduced simply from the separate morphemes of which they are composed, for example *jūnzǐ* 君 子 'gentleman, superior man; gentlemanly,' composed of *jūn* 君 'ruler, lord' + *zǐ* 子 'son'; *shùjī* 庶 幾 'almost; probably,' composed of *shù* 'many' + *jī* 'few' (compare modern *duōshǎo* 多 少). In Classical Chinese such bound compounds are not numerous and, in general, when two morphemes are used in combination, the meaning of the whole can be readily deduced from the meanings of the parts.

(b) Disyllabic expressions formed by total or partial reduplication of monosyllables, e.g., *xūyú* 須 臾 'a moment,' derived from *xū* 須 'wait.' These often form expressive adjectives or adverbs, e.g., *zhuó zhuó* 濯 濯 'glistening' (describing the plumage of birds), *hú sù* 觳 觫 'trembling, frightened.' Names of insects and small animals are often formed in this way, e.g., *táng láng* 螳 螂 'praying mantis,' *xī shuài* 蟋 蟀 'cricket' (EMC sit ṣwit).

(c) Polysyllabic foreign loanwords, e.g., *shā mén* 沙 門 'Buddhist monk,' from Sanskrit *śramaṇa*, *tuó tuó* 橐 駝 or *luò tuo* 駱 駝 'camel,' borrowed in early Hàn from an unknown foreign language, probably Xiōngnú 匈 奴 . Clearly identifiable words of this kind are not found before the Hàn dynasty.

(d) In some cases two monosyllables have contracted into a single syllable written with one character. This is like the modern *bié* 別 'don't,' from *bù yào* 不 要 , or English *don't* from *do not*. Among the contractions of this kind in Classical Chinese are:

    (i) *zhū* 諸 = *zhī hū* 之 乎 , where *zhī* is the object pronoun and *hū* is either the final question particle or a variant of the coverb *yú* 於 'in, at, to, from' (see Section IV) (*zhū* is also a separate word meaning 'all, the class of')

    (ii) *zhān* 旃 = *zhī yān* 之 焉 (rare)

    (iii) *ěr* 耳 = *ér yǐ* 而 已 'only'

    (iv) *hé* 盍 = *hú pù* 胡 不 'why not'

    (v) *yú* 與 (also written 歟) = *yě hū* 也 乎

    (vi) *yé* 邪 (also written 耶) = *yě hū* 也 乎 , probably a dialect variant of (v).

(e) In other cases a monosyllabic particle is bimorphemic, that is, it is equivalent in meaning to two morphemes, even though one of the elements cannot be identified as a separate word. Thus the postverbal particle *yān* 焉 is equivalent in meaning to an expected **yú zhī* 於 之 'in it, to it, etc.'

which is never found. A similar formation is found in some other words, like *rán* 然, equivalent to *rú zhī* 如 之 '(it) is like that, (it) is so,' with various specialized grammatical usages, and *yún* 云 'says (so)' related to *yuē* 曰 'say' (see IX.1c.vii below).

5. Morphology

In Modern Chinese there is very little morphology, that is, changes in the forms of words to convey differences in meaning, apart from noun suffixes, such as *-men* 們, which forms plurals of pronouns and is used in certain circumstances with nouns referring to persons treated as collective groups, and *-zi* 子 and *-r* 兒, which originally formed diminutives, and verb suffixes such as the aspect markers *-le* 了 and *-zhe* 著. There are, however, still words which are clearly related in both sound and meaning. Sometimes it is a case of one character having two different pronunciations, such as, *hǎo* 好 'good,' also pronounced *hào* in the sense of 'to like, love,' or *cháng* 長 'long,' also pronounced *zhǎng* in the sense of 'grow; elder.' In other cases the words are written with different characters which share the same phonetic element, for example, *zhāng* 張 'stretch,' *zhàng* 脹 or 漲 'to swell' (originally also written 張) and *zhàng* 帳 'curtain, tent' (that is, 'something stretched'), which are all semantically related to *cháng* 'long'; or *xìng* 性 '(inborn) nature' and *xìng* 姓 'clan name, surname,' which are related in sound and sense to *shēng* 生 'be born, live, alive' and have it as the phonetic part of their graphs.

In the classical language there were many more cases of this kind, and also cases in which obviously related words are written with totally unrelated graphs, for example, the first person pronouns *wú* 吾 and *wǒ* 我 (EMC ŋɔ and ŋaʾ), or the second person pronouns *ěr* 爾 (EMC ȵiǎʾ), *rǔ* 汝 (EMC ȵiǎʾ), *ruò* 若 (EMC ȵiak). These have been called word families. As our understanding of the phonology of Old Chinese improves, it is becoming possible to explain some of this morphology in terms of affixes of various kinds. The following are some of the most important patterns.

(a) There are many cases in which a word in departing tone is clearly derived from a word in one of the other three tones. This probably reflects an Old Chinese suffix *-s, cognate to the suffix *-s* in Tibetan. In some cases the derived word is a verb, e.g., *wàng* 王 'to be king,' derived from *wáng* 王 'king'; *hào* 好 'to like' derived from *hǎo* 好 'good,' *wù* 惡 'to hate,' derived from *è* 惡 'bad' (EMC ʔak, entering tone). In other cases it is a noun, e.g., *shèng* 乘 'vehicle,' from *chéng* 乘 'to ride (in a vehicle)'; *zuò*

坐 (EMC dzwa', rising tone) 'sit,' *zuò* 座 (EMC dzwa[h], departing tone) 'seat'; *duó* 度 (EMC dak, entering tone) 'to measure,' *dù* 度 (EMC dɔ[h], departing tone) 'a measure; degree.' And several other semantic relationships may be involved.[2]

(b) Alternation between Middle Chinese voiceless and voiced initials is often found in verbs with transitive and intransitive or neuter meaning respectively, e.g., *jiàn* 見 (EMC kɛn[h]) 'see,' also read *xiàn* (EMC ɣɛn[h] < *g-) 'appear' (now written 現 in this meaning); *zhǔ* 屬, 囑 (EMC tɕuawk) 'to attach, enjoin,' *shǔ* 屬 (EMC dʑuawk) 'be attached, belong.' This probably reflects a prefix *a-, cognate to Tibetan *ḥa-čhuṅ* and Burmese *ʔă-*.[3]

(c) Alternation, or ablaut,[4] between the vowel /ə/ and the vowel /a/ in Old Chinese may convey a similar semantic contrast, e.g., *tán* 譚 (EMC dəm) 'talk (about something),' *tán* 談 ((EMC dam) 'talk (intransitive); conversation.'
Other traces of morphology, including a prefix *s- and an infix (or prefix) *r-, can also be found.[5]

Even in the limited state of knowlege that has been achieved so far, it is important to be aware of morphological patterns of this kind. It is especially important to be aware that the same character can stand for two or more different, though related, words and to pay attention to readings given by ancient commentators which differentiate such words.

II. Some Basic Principles of Classical Chinese Syntax

1. Word Classes

In spite of the traces of morphology that can be discerned, words in Classical Chinese are not formally marked for grammatical function. Nevertheless, in their syntactical behaviour they do fall into distinct classes that correspond to such categories as nouns, verbs, and adjectives in other languages.

Traditional Chinese usage distinguishes between full words (*shízì* 實 字) and empty words (*xūzì* 虛 字). The former, also called content words, correspond to nouns, verbs, and adjectives that carry the main semantic content, and the latter to particles whose main function is to show grammatical relationships. Another traditional word for grammatical particles is *cí* 詞 .

The basic division among content words is between nouns and verbs. They are distinguished by the types of syntactical constructions in which they appear. Verbs are by nature predicating words that require one or more nouns or noun phrases to complete their meaning. Thus, an intransitive verb like *lái* 來 'come' implies that someone or something 'comes' and a transitive verb like *shā* 殺 'kill' implies that someone or something 'kills' someone or something. By contrast, nouns like *mǎ* 馬 'horse,' *shí* 石 'stone,' and noun phrases (see Section VII) stand alone in terms of their meaning and require special constructions to function as predicates, e.g., the final particle *yě* 也 and the special negative *fēi* 非 (see Section III). For nominalization, constructions which allow verbs and verb phrases to play the roles of nouns in sentences see Section VII.2. On the use of nouns as verbs, see Section IV.3.

Adjectives form a separate category of content words in many languages, including English. In Chinese they are a subcategory of verbs, though, as we shall see, they have some peculiar properties that make them somewhat noun-like. Numerals and expressions of quantity also behave syntactically like verbs. Words that correspond to English prepositions are verbs of a special type, called coverbs.

As in other languages, words can be transferred from one grammatical category to another. Rules for deriving verbs from nouns and nouns from verbs, as well as for deriving transitive verbs from intransitive verbs and

adjectives and causative verbs from transitive verbs, will be given below. It
is not true, however, as is sometimes alleged, that words in Chinese can be
used indifferently in any grammatical category.

2. Subject and Predicate

As in English, Chinese sentences can, in general, be divided into two main
parts, a subject and a predicate, although the subject may sometimes be
unexpressed.

The subject is typically, and most commonly, a noun or noun phrase
and the predicate a verb, as in

> **1.** Mèngzǐ | jiàn   Liáng Huì Wáng   (*Mèng* 1A/1)
> 孟子 | 見   梁惠王
> Mencius | saw   King Huì of Liáng
> Subject | Predicate

In general, English declarative sentences require an explicit subject.
Hence the dummy subject *it* has to be inserted with impersonal verbs, as in
It is raining, or an expletive *there* has to occupy the subject position in
front of the verb *be*, when it predicates existence, as in *There are evil men
in the world*. On the other hand, the second person subject pronoun *you* is
normally omitted before a verb in the imperative and, if inserted, carries
special emphasis — *You open the door!* versus *Open the door!* In Classical
Chinese the subject is normally unexpressed in declarative sentences: (a)
when it is understood from the context, (b) when it is indefinite, and (c)
when it is impersonal (that is, when it is to be understood as the
environment or the world in general), as in the following examples:

> **2.** Yì yǒu rén yì ér yǐ yǐ 亦有仁義而已矣
> [I] surely have benevolence and righteousness (to offer you) and
> that's all. (*Mèng* 1A/1)

The subject 'I' is understood from the context because Mencius is answering
a question addressed to himself.)

> **3.** Bù wéi nóng shí 不違農時
> [If one] does not go against the proper seasons of agriculture,
> (*Mèng* 1A/3)

The indefinite 'one' is not expressed in Chinese. This is especially common
in subordinate clauses.

> **4.** Wèi yǒu rén yì ér yí qí qīn zhě yě 未有仁義而遺其親
> 者也

There has never been one who was benevolent and righteous yet
abandoned his parents. (*Mèng* 1A/1)

The verb *yǒu* 有 'have' is used impersonally to predicate existence, like *il y a* in French.

In imperative sentences, on the other hand, a second person subject is commonly expressed without implying any special emphasis. This means that only the context can distinguish declarative from imperative sentences (see Section XIV.1).

The predicate may be a noun or noun phrase instead of a verb, in which case it takes a special form (see Section III). Conversely, the subject may be a nominalized verb phrase (see Section VII).

3. Word Order

The basic rules of word order in Classical, as well as Modern, Chinese are: (a) the subject precedes the predicate, (b) a modifier (adjective, possessive noun, relative clause, adverb) precedes the word it modifies, (c) the verb precedes its object. All these rules have certain exceptions, as follows:

(a) The normal subject-predicate order is inverted in exclamatory sentences (see Section XIV.3).

(b) The object of a verb, or some other postverbal element, may be placed in exposed position in front for purposes of topicalization, contrast, or emphasis (see Section VIII).

(c) In certain cases pronoun objects precede the verb in Classical Chinese even when not exposed. Two rules which apply throughout the classical period are: (i) interrogative pronoun objects precede the verb (see Section IX.3); and (ii) when a verb is negated, unstressed personal pronouns are placed between the negative particle and the verb (see Section IX.1e). In the *Shījīng* and comparatively early texts of the classical period, such as the *Zuǒzhuàn* and *Guóyǔ,* an exposed object is regularly recapitulated by a pronoun, most often *zhī* 之 or *shì* 是, which is also placed in front of the verb. Later the rule is that the recapitulating pronoun takes its normal position after the verb, except in certain stereotyped expressions which preserve the earlier order (see Section VIII.1).

Note that in Classical Chinese there is a clear relationship between the rule that the subject precedes the verb and the rule that the modifier precedes the modified, since, when a verb phrase is nominalized, the particle of noun subordination, *zhī* 之 , is placed between the subject and the verb (see Section VII). That is, the subject is treated as a modifier of the nominalized verb.

III. Noun Predication

1. Verbless Noun Predication

When a noun or noun phrase forms the predicate of a sentence in Classical Chinese, there is normally no copula, like the verb 'to be' in English, or *shì* 是 in Modern Chinese. The rule in such cases is that the sentence ends in the final particle *yě* 也. There is also a special negative *fēi* 非 instead of the regular verbal negative *bù* 不. Thus we can set up the formula: A (*fēi* 非) B *yě* 也: 'A is (not) B.'

> **5.** Fēi wǒ yě, bīng yě 非 我 也 ， 兵 也
> It was not I, it was the weapon. (*Mèng* 1A/3)

Frequently the predicate in such a sentence is a verb phrase treated as a noun (unmarked nominalization — see Section VII.2a) or a relative clause with its head replaced by *zhě* 者 'that which, one who, etc.' (see Section VII.2c).

> **6.** Shì bù wéi yě, fēi bù néng yě 是 不 為 也 ， 非 不 能 也
> This is not-doing, it is not not-being-able. (*Mèng* 1A/7)

> **7.** Wèi tiān zhě yě 畏 天 者 也
> '... is one who fears Heaven. (*Mèng* 1B/3)

Note that *zhě* may be omitted when the relative clause contains *suǒ* 所 'that which' standing for the object of the verb in the clause (see Section VII.2d).

> **8.** Sǒu zhī suǒ zhī yě 叟 之 所 知 也
> It is what your reverence well knows. (*Mèng* 1A/7)

(a) *Questions*

In the early form of Classical Chinese found in the *Zuǒzhuàn* the interrogative particle *hū* 乎 is added after *yě* 也 to make a question. In later texts, *yě hū* 也 乎 is replaced by *yú* 與 (also written *yú* 歟) or *yé* 邪 (also written *yé* 耶), which are probably dialect variants of one another and both phonetic fusions of *yě hū* 也 乎. The Lǔ 魯 texts, represented by *Lúnyǔ*, and *Mèngzǐ* have exclusively *yú* 與, while *yé* 邪 predominates in other Warring States texts.[6]

> **9.** Fú fēi jìn rén zhī zǐ yú 夫 非 盡 人 之 子 與
> Are we not all the sons of some man? (*Mèng* 7A/36)

10. Qí zhèng sè yé 其 正 色 邪

Is it its true colour? (*Zhuāng* 1/4)

In some cases, especially in the *Lúnyǔ*, we find *yě yú* 也 與 instead of the simple fused form *yú* 與. This is difficult to explain purely in phonetic terms and may represent a partial restoration of the unfused form in the course of oral transmission of the text.

The final particle *fú* 夫 'is it not?,' which is equivalent in meaning to modern *ba* 吧, and may be a fusion of *bù hū* 不 乎 (see Section XIV.2b.vii), can also follow a noun predicate with *yě* 也.

11. Rán ér zhì cǐ jí zhě, mìng yě fú 然 而 至 此 極 者 ，命 也 夫

That nonetheless I have reached this extremity, is fate, is it not? (*Zhuāng* 6/97)

(b) Pronouns and Particles with Verbless Noun Predicates

As in example **6**, the subject of a noun predicate may be resumed by a demonstrative pronoun, such as *shì* 是 'this, that,' *cǐ* 此 'this,' *sī* 斯 'this.'

12. Cǐ Wén Wáng zhī yǒng yě 此 文 王 之 勇 也
This was King Wén's courage. (*Mèng* 1B/3)

13. Shì yì zǒu yě 是 亦 走 也
This was also running away. (*Mèng* 1A/3)

Note that in Classical Chinese *shì* 是 is not itself a copula, with the meaning 'to be,' as in Modern Chinese. Its frequent occurrence as a resumptive pronoun introducing a noun predicate was no doubt influential in giving it this meaning, which it had acquired in the colloquial language by the Hàn period.

If the subject is plural, it is resumed by *jiē* 皆 'all.' Compare modern *dōu* 都.

14. Jiē gǔ shèng rén yě 皆 古 聖 人 也
They were all sages of old. (*Mèng* 2A/2)

The particles *nǎi* 乃 and *jí* 即, both of which also occur with verbal predicates in the sense of 'then, thereupon' (see Section XV), add emphasis to a noun predication, but are not copulas.

15. Shì nǎi rén shù yě 是 乃 仁 術 也
This indeed is the technique of (= used by) *rén*. (*Mèng* 1A/7)

16. Nǎi fū zǐ yě. wú kuàng zǐ. 乃 夫 子 也 。 吾 贶 子

It was you (and no one else). I will reward you. (*Zuǒ* Dìng 9/5)

Jí is comparatively uncommon in this usage in texts of the classical period. In the following example it emphasizes the truth of something previously mentioned:

17. Jí bù rěn qí húsù, ruò wú zuì ér jiù sǐ dì, gù yǐ yáng yì zhī yě
即 不 忍 其 觳 觫 ， 若 無 罪 而 就 死 地 ， 故 以 羊
易 之 也

It was indeed that I could not bear its trembling, like an innocent person going to the place of execution, and so changed it for a sheep. (*Mèng* 1A/7)

Other sentence adverbs that can be used with verbless noun predicates include *bì* 必 'necessarily,' *chéng* 誠 'truly, really,' *gù* 固 'definitely, certainly,' *dài* 殆 'almost, probably,' *yì* 亦 'also,' *yòu* 又 'again, also.'

18. ... bì ruò Jié Zhòu zhě yě 必 若 桀 紂 者 也

... will necessarily be one like Jié or Zhōu. (*Mèng* 5A/6)

19. Zǐ chéng Qí rén ye 子 誠 齊 人 也

You are truly a man of Qí. (*Mèng* 2A/1)

20. Gù suǒ yuàn yě 固 所 願 也

It is certainly what I want. (*Mèng* 2B/10)

(c) *Verbless Comparisons with* Yóu 猶

The particle *yóu* 猶, which means 'still, yet' with verbal predicates, has the meaning of 'like' when it introduces a verbless noun predicate with *yě* 也.

21. Jīn zhī yuè yóu gǔ zhī yuè yě 今 之 樂 猶 古 之 樂 也

The music of today is like the music of old (from the point of view of the argument). (*Mèng* 1B/1)

Note that *yóu* is not a verb. It cannot be negated by *bù* like the verbs *rú* 如 and *ruò* 若, which also mean 'like.' It is a sentence adverb that changes the force of the noun predicate. Like *rú*, it can, however, be used to add a descriptive complement to another verb (see Section V.6c).

(d) *Omission of* Yě 也

The final particle *yě* 也 is occasionally omitted even in the classical period.

22. Wàn shèng zhī guó, shì qí jūn zhě, bì qiān shèng zhī jiā 萬
乘之國，弒其君者，必千乘之家
The one who murders the ruler of a country of ten thousand
chariots will certainly be (the head of) a family of a thousand
chariots. (*Mèng* 1A/1)

Such sentences are comparatively rare and the circumstances under which
they occur have not been worked out. It is possible that the presence of the
sentence adverb *bì* 必 plays a role here.

(e) *The Aspect Particle* Yǐ 已 *after Verbless Noun Predicates*
The perfect aspect particle, *yǐ* 矣, commonly found with verbal predicates
(see Section XII.2a), is never found after *yě* 也. We do, however, find *yǐ*
已, sometimes enlarged to *yě yǐ* 也已 or *yě yǐ yǐ* 也已矣, after noun
predicates and in other cases where *yě* 也 can occur, apparently combining
the functions of *yě* 也 and *yǐ* 矣.

23. Shì luàn guó yǐ 是亂國已
One can tell that this is a disordered country. (*Xún* 10/89)

The author claims that when entering the borders of a country one can tell
the state of its government by observable signs, such as the way in which
the border guards carry out their duties, the condition of the fields, etc. As is
often the case with sentence final *le* 了 in Mandarin, *yǐ* 已 here does not
imply an objective change of state, but only a change in knowledge about
it.

24. Jūn zǐ yuē, cǐ yì wàng rén yě yǐ yǐ 君子曰，此亦妄
人也已矣
The gentleman will say, 'I now realize that this is indeed a wild,
reckless fellow. (*Mèng* 4B/28)

The context is that the 'gentleman,' that is, the man of cultivated moral
sensibilities, who has received outrageous treatment from someone else will
first examine his own conduct to see whether he has been at fault, but if, in
spite of his best efforts, the outrageous behaviour continues, he will come
to a point at which he will have to conclude that the other person is no
better than an animal and that his failure to respond casts no reflection on
the gentleman himself. In this case too the 'change of state' marked by *yǐ*
已, indicated in the translation by the phrase 'I now realize that,' is not a
change in the person who is the subject of the noun predication, but in the
attitude of the speaker.

In this usage yǐ 已 appears to be a phonetic fusion of yě yǐ 也 矣 and must be distinguished from the preverbal particle yǐ 已 'already' (see Section XII.1c) and the phrasal particle ér yǐ 而 已 '(then stop =) only' after verbal predicates (see Section XIII.2d), both derived from the full verb yǐ 已 'stop, finish.' The enlarged forms yě yǐ 也 已 and yě yǐ yǐ 也 已 矣 may be compared to yě yú 也 與 instead of yú 與 alone noted above.[7]

(f) *Other Meanings of* Yě 也

Though its most salient use in Classical Chinese is as a mark of noun predication, yě 也 is not a copula. Some of its other uses seem to be related to its use as a mark of noun predication. Thus we find it after nominalized verb phrases which are the topic of a sentence or the object of a verb or coverb (see Sections VII.2b, XV.4), and also a marker of proper nouns (see Section VII.3). In other cases, however, it occurs after purely verbal predicates. On its use in contrast to yǐ 矣 as a mark of continuing state, see Section XII.2b below.

2. The Copula Verb *Wéi* 為

Apart from the verbless noun predicate construction, the verb wéi 為 'make, do' can be used as a copula in the sense of 'to be.' Thus, wéi is used, like zuò 作 in modern Chinese, to indicate a temporary role.

25. Mèngzǐ wéi qīng yú Qí 孟 子 為 卿 於 齊

Mencius was a minister of state in Qí. (*Mèng* 2B/6)

A formal difference between wéi 為 'do, make' and wéi 為 'be' is that an interrogative pronoun must precede the former as its object by the general rule for such pronouns with transitive verbs (see Section IX.3), while an interrogative pronoun follows the latter as its subjective complement.

26. Zǐ wéi shuí 子 為 誰

sir make who = Who are you? (*LY* 18/6)

One may ask why wéi shuí 為 誰 is used here in place of shuí yě 誰 也, which also occurs. The answer is probably that the expected answer here is the person's name, that is, identification among persons already known, or possibly known, rather than further descriptive information.[8]

Wéi 為 is used instead of the verbless construction if the aspect particle yǐ 矣 or certain verbal auxiliaries are required.

27. ... bù wéi bù duō yǐ 不 為 不 多 矣

not make not many PERFECT = is (already) not not-many. (*Mèng* 1A/1)

Bù duō 'not many' is a verb phrase which is the complement of *wéi*, hence an example of unmarked nominalization (VII.2a). If the perfect aspect marked by *yǐ* 矣 were not required, the meaning 'is not not-many' would be expressed as *fēi bù duō yě* 非 不 多 也 .

28. Rén jiē kě yǐ wéi Yáo Shùn 人 皆 可 以 為 堯 舜

Men can all be a Yáo or Shùn. (*Mèng* 6B/2)

On the auxiliary *kě (yǐ)* '可〔以〕is possible,' which requires a verb as its complement, see Section IV.1. One could also translate this sentence as 'It is possible for all men to *become* a Yao or Shun.' That is, there is an element of (potential) change through time involved, not just the timeless equation that is implied by verbless noun predication. This comes from the meaning of *kě yǐ*, however, not from anything semantically inherent in *wéi*, which, in itself, is quite colourless as far as mood or aspect are concerned. The simplest way of accounting for the presence of *wéi* is by the formal requirement that *kě yǐ* must take a verb as its complement. Neither *kě* nor *kě yǐ* can be followed by a bare noun.

As with many other problems of Classical Chinese syntax, much more study is needed to determine all the circumstances under which *wéi* is used in the sense of 'to be' instead of the verbless noun predicate construction.

3. The Copula *Yuē* 曰

Yuē 曰, which, as a verb, means 'say,' introducing quoted speech, is used as a copula, that is, with a subjective complement rather than an object, in the sense of 'be called.'

29. Lǎo ér wú qī yuē guān 老 而 無 妻 曰 鰥

To be old and without a wife is called 'guān.' (*Mèng* 1B/5)

In this sense *yuē* 曰 can also introduce a complement after a main verb of 'calling.'

30. Gōng yuē, shì qí shēng yě yǔ wú tóng wù. Mìng zhī yuē Tóng 公 曰 , 是 其 生 也 與 吾 同 物 。 命 之 曰 同

The duke said, 'This one in his birth is of the same substance as me.' He named him Tóng ('Same'). (*Zuǒ Huán* 6/5)

4. The Preclassical Copula *Wéi* 唯 (隹 , 惟 , 維)

In the preclassical language the noun predicate construction with *yě* 也 does not occur. Instead the particle *wéi* 唯 (also written 惟 or 維 , and simply 隹 on inscriptions) is used as a copula introducing a noun predicate. In spite of the coincidence in modern pronunciation, it is totally unrelated to *wéi* 為 'do, make; be.' In EMC it was jwi, while the latter was wiǎ. Preclassical *wéi* 唯 has other uses as a noun marker that resemble those of *yě* 也 and the two words may be etymologically related. In the classical language it survives with the specialized meaning 'only,' while retaining vestiges of its preclassical syntactic behaviour.[9]

31. Suǒ lín wéi xìn 所 臨 唯 信

What they (the spirits) attend is only good faith. (*Zuǒ* Xiāng 9/6)

Note the absence of final *yě* 也 which would otherwise be expected in an equational sentence of this kind in the *Zuǒzhuàn*.

32. Wéi yì suǒ zài 惟 義 所 在

It is only where right behaviour lies (that a great man places his words and conduct). (*Mèng* 4B/11)

In *Mencius*, however, it is more usual to have *yě* 也 even after *wéi* 唯 'only.'

The negator of nouns *fēi* 非 is probably a fusion of *bù wéi* 不 唯 . Other related words are *wěi* 唯 'yes' and *suī* 雖 'although' (see Section XV.3).

IV. Verbal Predicates

Unlike nouns, verbs are inherently predicating words and can form predicates without any particle or copula. They take the simple particle of negation *bù* 不, while nouns require *fēi* 非 . They also differ from nouns as predicates in being able to take the perfect aspect particle *yǐ* 矣 and the nonperfective aspect negative *wèi* 未 .

1. Classes of Verbs

Adjectives, e.g., *shān gāo* 山 高 'the mountain is high,' form the first major subdivision that needs to be distinguished among naturally predicating words in Chinese. Though, as words that form predicates without the addition of a particle, they belong with verbs rather than nouns, they differ from verbs proper in their syntactical behaviour in a number of ways. They are sometimes called 'stative verbs' but there are objections to this, since transitive verbs such as *zhī* 知 'know' also denote a state rather than an action. A possible alternative would be 'quality verb,' but as a class they correspond closely in meaning to adjectives in other languages and we shall continue to use this traditional term.

Among verbs proper the main distinction is between intransitive verbs, which require a single noun to complete their meaning, e.g., *wáng lái* 王 來 'the king comes,' and transitive verbs, e.g., *wáng shā rén* 王 殺 人 'the king kills a man,'*wáng yǔ zhī dāo* 王 與 之 刀 'the king gives him a knife,' which require two or more nouns. The equational or copula verb *wéi* 為 (see Section III.2) is transitive in syntactical form, although it takes a subjective complement rather than an object.

One can distinguish these four main classes of verbs on the basis of their behaviour with the verbal auxiliary *kě* 可 'is possible' (itself a predicate adjective)[10]. Only transitive verbs may follow *kě* 可 'possible' directly, in which case they must be understood as passive; that is, the subject of *kě* is the object (or patient) of the verb — *rén kě shā* 人 可 殺 'the man is possible to kill' = 'the man may be killed.' A transitive verb in an active sense, or an intransitive verb requires *kě yǐ* 可 以 , rather than *kě* alone — *wáng kě yǐ shā rén* 王 可 以 殺 人 'it is possible for the king to kill a man' or 'the king can kill a man'; *wáng kě yǐ lái* 王 可 以 來 'it is possible for the king to come' or 'the king can come.' In this construction *yǐ* 以 , which as a verb means 'use' and as a coverb (or preposition) is used for the instrument, fills the role of passive transitive verb complement to *kě*. That is, the meaning of instrument is extended to include agency: 'the king may be used to' → 'the king may be the agent to.'

Like nouns (example **28**), adjectives require the copula verb *wéi* 為 after *kě yǐ* 可 以 .

> **33.** ... kě yǐ wéi měi hū ... 可 以 為 美 乎
>
> ... could [Ox Mountain] be (i.e., remain) beautiful [when its trees were all cut down to supply wood for the nearby city]? (*Mèng* 6A/8)

2. Adjectives

Adjectives must be classed as verbs in Classical, as well as Modern Chinese, since they form predicates without a copula or final *yě* 也, are negated by *bù* 不, and take the aspect markers *yǐ* 矣 and *wèi* 未. Nevertheless, as their behaviour with *kě* 可 shows (see previous section), they differ from intransitive verbs in their syntax and have certain resemblances to nouns.

As the traditional English name implies, adjectives are typically found, not as predicates, but as modifiers of nouns. This is also true in Chinese — *gāo shān* 高 山 'high mountain' versus *shān gāo* 山 高 'the mountain is high.' As a syntactical form, however, this can be regarded as simply a special case of the general rule that verbs and verb phrases can modify nouns (see Section VII.1b), e.g., *liú shuǐ* 流 水 'flowing water.' Monosyllabic adjectives and monosyllabic verbs used attributively in this way are commonly directly followed by the noun they modify, but adjectival phrases of more than one syllable are generally followed by the particle of noun modification, *zhī* 之 .

> **34.** Ruò fú háo jié zhī shì ... 若 夫 豪 傑 之 士
>
> As for heroic knights ... (*Mèng* 7A/10)

Comparative degree is expressed by the coverb *yú* 於, which takes on the special meaning 'than.'

> **35.** ... zé wú wàng mín zhī duō yú lín guó yě 則 無 望 民 之 多 於 鄰 國 也
>
> ... then do not hope that your people will be more than [those of]

the neighbouring countries. (*Mèng* 1A/3)

The copula verb *wéi* 為 can be used with an adjective to give a superlative sense.

36. Wù jiē rán, xīn wéi shèn 物 皆 然 ， 心 為 甚

Things are all like that and the heart is most so. (*Mèng* 1A/7)

A general characteristic of adjectives is that they can be made into transitive verbs either in a causative sense or in a denominative sense — *měi zhī* 美 之 'make it beautiful' or 'call it beautiful' — simply by moving the subject into the object position after the verb and supplying another subject as agent.

37. Wáng qǐng dà zhī 王 請 大 之

I beg Your Majesty to make it great. (*Mèng* 1B/3)

38. Sǒu, bù yuǎn qiān lǐ ér lái 叟 ， 不 遠 千 里 而 來

You have come, sir, not regarding 1,000 *lǐ* as too far. (*Mèng* 1A/1) (This regular transformational use of *yuǎn* 遠 'far' to mean 'call far, regard as far' must be distinguished from the derived verb *yuàn* 遠 'keep at a distance, avoid,' with change of tone. See example **287**.)

Apart from these causative and denominative constructions, which apply to adjectives in general, some predicate adjectives can be followed by nouns which look like objects but which are semantically like oblique cases in a language like Latin or prepositional phrases in English. One of these is *ān* 安 'peaceful, content.'

39. Bǎi xìng ān zhī 百 姓 安 之

The common people were peaceful under him. (*Mèng* 5A/5)

Note than *ān* 安 can also be used transitively in a causative sense in the normal way.

40. ... zé bù néng ān Zǐsī 則 不 能 安 子 思

... then he could not make Zǐsī content. (*Mèng* 2B/11)

3. Nouns Used as Verbs

Like adjectives, nouns can be used as verbs in a causative sense.

41. Gù Tāng zhī yú Yīyǐn, xué yān ér hòu chén zhī 故 湯 之 於 伊 尹 ， 學 焉 而 後 臣 之

Thus Táng's [behaviour] towards Yīyǐn was to learn from him and afterwards make him his subject. (*Mèng* 2B/2)

42. Ěr yù Wú Wáng wǒ hū 爾 欲 吳 王 我 乎

Do you want to King-of-Wú me (= treat me in the way the King of
Wú was treated)? (*Zuǒ* Dìng 10/7)

Nouns of status are also sometimes used as intransitive verbs in the
sense of 'act the part of.'

43. Jūn jūn, chén chén, fù fù, zǐ zǐ 君 君 ，臣 臣 ， 父
父 ，子 子

Let the ruler act as a ruler should, the minister as a minister, the
father as a father, the son as a son. (*LY* 12/11)

44. Wéi chén ér jūn ... wáng zhī běn yě 為 臣 而 君 ⋯ 亡 之
本 也

For one who is a minister to act as a ruler ... is the root of
perdition. (*Zuǒ* Xiāng 7/7)

Apart from such constructions, which, although not very common,
must be regarded as part of the syntactical possibilities of nouns in general,
particular nouns have acquired special meanings as verbs which must be
treated as separate lexical items, for example: *lǐ* 禮 'treat with ceremony,'
from *lǐ* 'ceremony, ritual'; *chéng* 城 'wall a city,' from *chéng* 'wall'; *jūn*
軍 'encamp,' from *jūn* 'army.' The compound word *jūnzǐ* 君 子
'gentleman' is used in the *Lúnyǔ* as an adjective meaning 'gentlemanly,' as
in *jūnzǐ rén* 君 子 人 'gentlemanly man.' In such cases there is no
morphological change when a verb is derived from a noun. There are also,
of course, many examples of verbs derived from nouns and nouns from
verbs by morphological processes (see Section I.5 above).

4. Intransitive Verbs

With intransitive verbs only one noun is involved in the action and it
occupies the subject position.

45. Yī lái 醫 來

The physician came. (*Mèng* 2B/2)

46. Jī míng ér qǐ ... zhě 雞 鳴 而 起 ⋯ 者

He who gets up when the cock crows ... (*Mèng* 7A/25)

Intransitive verbs resemble adjectives in that, in general, they can be
made transitive in a causative sense by transferring the subject to the object
position and supplying another subject as agent. Unlike adjectives,
however, they cannot be used denominatively in this way.

47. Gù yuǎn rén bù fú, zé xiū wén dé yǐ lái zhī 故 遠 人 不
服 ， 則 脩 文 德 以 來 之
Therefore, if distant people do not submit, cultivate civil virtue so
as to *make them come.* (*LY*16/1)

Many other verbs besides *lái* are commonly used either intransitively, or
transitively in a causative sense, in this way, e.g.: *xíng* 行 'go, proceed;
put into motion, operate, carry out,' *qǐ* 起 'rise up; raise, start,' *shēng* 生
'live; give life to, bear,' *zuò* 作 'arise, appear; cause to arise, create, make.'
Intransitive verbs made transitive in this way differ from inherently
transitive verbs in that they revert to their intransitive meaning when they
are used without an expressed object. Inherently transitive verbs either retain
their active, transitive meaning with an indefinite or implied object, or
become passive (see Section IV.5 below).

Like adjectives, some intransitive verbs can take complements that
look on the surface like the objects of transitive verbs but correspond to
oblique cases or prepositional phrases in other languages.

48. ... zé miáo bó rán xīng zhī yǐ 則 苗 勃 然 興 之 矣
... then the sprouts suddenly spring up in response to it [the rain].
(*Mèng* 1A/6)

49. Wú yǒu sī sǐ zhě sān shí sān rén ér mín mò zhī sǐ yě 吾 有
司 死 者 三 十 三 人 而 民 莫 之 死 也
Thirty-three of my officers died and none of the people was willing
to die for them. (*Mèng* 1B/12)

The verb *sǐ* 死 'die' is quite commonly used in this way with an indirect
object meaning a person of higher status for the sake of whom someone is
willing to offer his or her life.

5. Transitive Verbs — Active and Passive

Transitive verbs require at least two nouns, an agent and a patient, to
complete their meaning. When the agent (if expressed) is in the subject
position in front of the verb and the patient (if expressed) is in the object
position (normally after the verb but with certain exceptions in the case of
pronouns), the verb is active.

50. Qī shí zhě yì bó shí ròu 七 十 者 衣 帛 食 肉
When seventy year olds *wear* silk and *eat* meat ... (*Mèng* 1A/3)

If the patient is in the subject position, the verb is passive.

51. Shī xíng ér liáng shí 師 行 而 糧 食

The host proceeds and supplies *are eaten*. (*Mèng* 1B/4)

Note that, unlike an intransitive verb used causatively, an inherently transitive verb like *shí* 'eat' can be used actively without an object expressed when the object is indefinite.

52. Xián zhě yǔ mín bìng gēng ér shí 賢 者 與 民 並 耕 而 食

The worthy plough and eat together with the common people. (*Mèng* 3A/4)

The agent of a passive verb may be left unexpressed, as in **51**, or may be introduced by the coverb *yú* 於.

53. Láo xīn zhě chí rén, láo lì zhě chí yú rén, chí yú rén zhě sì rén, chí rén zhě sì yú rén 勞 心 者 治 人 ， 勞 力 者 治 於 人 ， 治 於 人 者 食 人 ， 治 人 者 食 於 人

Those who labour with their minds [literally: labour their minds] rule others, those who labour with their strength are ruled by others. Those who are ruled by others feed others, those who rule others are fed by others. (*Mèng* 3A/4)

Note that 食 is to be read here as *sì* 'feed,' not *shí* 'eat.' The character 治 should also properly be read *chí* in the transitive meaning 'to rule,' instead of *zhì*, which is a derived adjective 'well-governed.' The reading *chí* is sometimes still recognized as a reading pronunciation but has become obsolete in ordinary usage, which uses *zhì* for both meanings. They were originally two separate words, however, and must be distinguished in reading classical texts.

Besides the simple passive by inversion with transitive verbs, there are special devices by which any verb can be marked as passive (see below).

6. Verbs of Motion and Location — Intransitive and Transitive

Some verbs of motion are primarily used to refer to a kind of activity without reference to a destination. In such cases if a destination is mentioned it must be expressed as a locative complement introduced by *yú* 於 (see Section V.6b.ii). Among such verbs are *lái* 來 'come,' *wǎng* 往 'go,' *xíng* 行 'go, proceed,' *fēi* 飛 'fly,' *zhǐ* 止 'stop.'

54. Chú ráo zhě wǎng yān 芻 蕘 者 往 焉

The gatherers of hay and firewood went there (*yān* = **yú zhī*) .
(*Mèng* 1B/2)

Other verbs of motion imply a destination as part of their meaning and take it as a direct object. They are thus syntactically transitive, though the object is not semantically the patient or recipient of the action. Examples of such verbs are *zhī* 之 'go (to a place),' *jiù* 就 'go up to.'

55. ... jiāng zhī Chǔ 將之楚
... was going to go to Chǔ. (*Mèng* 3A/1)

56. Jiù zhī ér bù jiàn suǒ wèi yān 就之而不見所畏焉
Going up to him, I did not see anything to fear (= awesome) in him. (*Mèng* 1A/6)

There are also verbs, like *jí* 及 'reach,' *dá* 達 'extend to,' which can take the destination either as a direct object or as a locative complement without any apparent difference in meaning.

57. Jué jǐng jiǔ rèn ér bù jí quán 掘井九軔而不及泉
To dig a well to a depth of nine *rèn* (seventy-two feet) and not reach the spring ... (*Mèng* 7A/29)

58. Gù jí yú nàn 故及於難
Therefore he encountered calamities. (*Zuǒ* Mǐn 2/*fù* 2 — but simply *jí nàn* in *Zuǒ* Xī 24/*fù* 1)

Verbs of location, like *jū* 居 'dwell,' *zài* 在 'be at (a place)' similarly express the location either as a direct object or as a locative complement.

59. Xī zhě Tài Wáng jū Bīn. Dí rén qīn zhī. Qù zhī Qí shān zhī xià, jū yān 昔者大王居邠，狄人侵之，去之岐山之下，居焉
In former times King Tài dwelt in Bīn. The Dí invaded it and he left and went to beneath Mount Qí and dwelt there. (*Mèng* 1B/14)

In the first sentence *jū* 居 'dwell' is followed directly by the place name Bīn but in the second it is followed, not by *zhī* 之 'it,' but by *yān* 焉 'in it.' Since *yú* 於 can be deleted in all its senses, it might be argued that this has occurred before Bīn. In other passages where the place is pronominalized, however, we sometimes find *jū zhī* 居之 instead of *jū yān* 居焉, e.g., *Mèng* 3B/9, 3B/10. This shows that the verb itself can be construed in two different ways. Similarly, though neither *zài yān* 在焉 nor *zài zhī* 在之 is common, examples of both can be found in the sense of 'be there.'

7. The Verbs *Yǒu* 有 'have; there is/are' and *Wú* 無 'not have; there is/are not'

When these verbs have personal subjects, they are ordinary transitive verbs meaning 'have' and 'not have.'

60. Yì yǒu rén yì ér yǐ yǐ 亦 有 仁 義 而 已 矣

(I) surely have only benevolence and righteousness [to offer you]. (*Mèng* 1A/1)

61. Rén zhě wú dí 仁 者 無 敵

The man of benevolence has no match. (*Mèng* 1A/5)

The same verbs are also commonly used impersonally to predicate existence, like *il y a* in French.

62. Wèi yǒu yì ér hòu qí jūn zhě yě 未 有 義 而 後 其 君 者 也

There has never been one who was righteous and put his ruler last. (*Mèng* 1A/1)

63. Wú jūnzǐ, mò chí yě rén, wú yě rén, mò yǎng jūnzǐ 無 君 子，莫 治 野 人，無 野 人，莫 養 君 子

If there were no gentlemen, there would be no one to rule the rustics; if there were no rustics, there would be no one to support the gentlemen. (*Mèng* 3A/3)

As impersonal existential verbs, *yǒu* 有 and *wú* 無 have no subjects but there is often a noun or noun phrase in front providing a kind of pseudo-subject. In one common type, which is paralleled in Modern Chinese, it is a locative phrase that fulfils this role.

64. Tú yǒu è piǎo 塗 有 餓 莩

On the roads there are people dying of hunger. (*Mèng* 1A/3)

This is equivalent to: *yǒu è piǎo yú tú* 有 餓 莩 於 塗. The coverb *yú* 於 is omitted when the phrase is placed in front as a pseudo-subject. This is different from exposure of such a phrase for contrast or emphasis, in which *yú* 於 may be retained and the phrase is recapitulated after the verb by *yān* 焉.

65. Yú wǒ xīn yǒu qī qī yān 於 我 心 有 戚 戚 焉

In *my* heart there was a responsive feeling. (*Mèng* 1A/7)

Compare also example **229** in Section VII.1, where the exposed phrase omits *yú* 於 but is still recapitulated by *yān* 焉.

In another common type the position of pseudo-subject is taken by the subject of a relative clause with *zhě* 者 as head. (On this construction, see Section VII.2c below.)

> **66.** Wáng zhī chén yǒu tuō qí qī zǐ yú qí yǒu ér zhī Chǔ yóu zhě
> 王之臣有託其妻子於其友而之楚遊者
> [Suppose that] there was one of Your Majesty's ministers who entrusted his wife and children to a friend and travelled to Chǔ ...
> (*Mèng* 1B/6)

This is equivalent to: *yǒu wáng zhī chén zhī tuō qí qī zǐ yú qí yǒu ér zhī Chǔ yóu zhě* 有王之臣之託其妻子於其友而之楚遊者. Since this construction has no parallel in the modern language, the pseudo-subject is often misinterpreted as a locative phrase. The partitive implication of *yǒu* 有 is like that of the cognate particle *huò* 或 'some one, some.' (See Section XII.3a)

In the following example a modifying phrase rather than the head is moved to the front as if it were the subject of the existential verb.

> **67.** Jiāo lín guó yǒu dào hū 交鄰國有道乎.
> Is there a way for dealing with neighbouring countries? (*Mèng* 1B/3)

This is equivalent to: *yǒu jiāo lín guó zhī dào hū* 有交鄰國之道乎

On the expressions *yǒu yǐ* 有以 'have whereby to. ..; have the means to ...' and *wú yǐ* 無以 'not have whereby to ...; not have the means to ...' see Section V.6 below.

On *yǒu* 有 used adverbially in the sense of 'some' see Section XIII.3.

8. Transitive Verbs with Two Objects

(a) Verbs of giving, telling, teaching and the like take two objects. The first, usually personal, corresponds to the indirect object in English and the second corresponds to the direct object.

> **68.** ... néng yǔ rén guī jǔ 能與人規矩
> ... can give a man a compass or a square ... (*Mèng* 7B/5)

> **69.** ... shòu Mèngzǐ shì 授孟子室
> ... to give Mencius a house ... (*Mèng* 2B/10)

> **70.** Hòu Jì jiào rén jià sè 后稷教人稼穡
> Hòu Jì taught the people sowing and reaping. (*Mèng* 3A/4)

In English one can, in general, replace an indirect object by a prepositional phrase introduced by 'to' — 'give a house to Mencius,' etc. In Chinese it is more usual to replace the direct object by a phrase introduced by *yǐ* 以 'with, by means of.' Compare this with English 'to present someone with something.'

71. Yáo yǐ tiānxià yǔ Shùn 堯以天下與舜
Yáo with the world gave Shùn = Yáo gave the world to Shùn (*Mèng* 5A/5)

The phrase introduced by *yǐ* 以 can either precede the main verb or follow it.

72. ... jiào rén yǐ shàn 教人以善
... teaching others goodness ... (*Mèng* 3A/4)

As always, the object pronoun *zhī* 之 is omitted after *yǐ* 以 (see Section V.6a), which, in this case, must precede the main verb.

73. Yǐ gào Mèngzǐ 以告孟子
He told it to Mencius. (*Mèng* 6A/5)

It is also possible with some of these verbs to replace the indirect object by a locative phrase introduced by *yú* 於.

74. ... bù gào yú Wáng 不告於王
... without reporting it to the king ... (*Mèng* 2B/8)

Both objects may also be replaced by prepositional phrases.

75. Nán Shì shēng nán, zé yǐ gào yú jūn yǔ dà fū ér lì zhī 南氏生男，則以告於君與大夫而立之
If Lady Nán should give birth to a male child, I would announce it to the ruler and the great officers and establish him [as heir]. (*Zuǒ Ai* 3/6)

(b) The verb *duó* 奪 'rob, deprive' takes two objects, the first, or indirect, object being the person deprived and the second, or direct, object being the thing that is taken away.

76. ... duó zhī shí 奪之食
... by robbing him of his food' (*Mèng* 6B/1)

With this verb neither object can be replaced by a coverbal phrase.

(c) The verb *wén* 聞 'hear' takes what is heard as the direct object and the source as a locative phrase after the direct object.

77. Wú cháng wén dà yǒng yú fūzǐ yǐ 吾 嘗 聞 大 勇 於 夫 子 矣

I once heard about great courage from the master. (*Mèng* 2A/2)

As with other locative phrases, the coverb may be omitted.

78. Chén wén zhī Húhé yuē ... 臣 聞 之 胡 齕 曰 …

I heard it from Húhé that ... (*Mèng* 1A/7).

The related verb *wèn* 問 'ask' may take the same construction or may take the person asked as its first object, like verbs of telling.

79. Huò wèn hū Zēng Xī yuē ... 或 問 乎 曾 西 曰 …

Someone asked Zēng Xī ... (*Mèng* 2A/1 — here *hū* 乎 is a variant of *yú* 於, see Section V.6b.iii.)

80. Huò wèn zhī yuē ... 或 問 之 曰 …

Someone asked him ... (*Mèng* 2B/8 — note the use of *zhī* rather than *yān*..)

(d) The verb *wéi* 為 'do, make' can take a personal indirect object as well as a direct object.

81. Zhòng wéi zhī lǐ ér guī zhī 重 為 之 禮 而 歸 之

He treated him with great ceremony and sent him home. (*Zuǒ Chéng* 4/*fù* 1 — literally: 'greatly made for him ceremony')

In the sense of 'act as, be,' *wéi* can also take an indirect object.

82. Qiú yě wéi Jì Shì zǎi 求 也 為 季 氏 宰

Qiú was steward for the Jì clan. (*Mèng* 4A/15)

As will be shown below, this construction is the source of one type of passive formation.

(e) The so-called 'pivot construction' after verbs such as *shǐ* 使 'send; make, cause,' *lìng* 令 'order; make, cause,' and *zhù* 助 'help' is a double object construction in which the first object, usually personal, is, at the same time, the subject of an embedded clause which constitutes the second object (see Section V.3).

(f) The verb *wèi* 謂 'say, tell, call' can similarly be used in a pivot construction in the sense of 'tell someone to do something.'

83. Rén jiē wèi wǒ huǐ míng táng 人 皆 謂 我 毀 明 堂

People all tell me to destroy the Hall of Light. (*Mèng* 1B/5)

In its more common meaning 'call,' *wèi* 謂 takes as its second object an embedded noun predicate, of which the first object is the subject: 'one calls A [A is B]' → 'one calls A B.' In this sense, the second object is optionally introduced by *yuē* 曰 say.'

84. Wèi qí tái yuē líng tái 謂其臺曰靈臺

They called his tower the spirit tower. (*Mèng* 1A/2)

A still more common use of *wèi* 謂 is in the sense of 'say,' with the person spoken to as the first, indirect, object, and followed by what is said introduced by *yuē*.

85. Mèngzǐ wèi Qí Xuān Wáng, yuē ... 孟子謂齊宣王，曰

Mencius said to King Xuān of Qí ... (*Mèng* 1B/6)

(g) The verbs *ruò* 若 and *rú* 如, which both mean 'like,' have an idiomatic double object construction in which the second object is the interrogative pronoun *hé* 何 'what.' *Ruò* 若 X *hé* 何 and *rú* 如 X *hé* 何 mean, roughly, 'what is one to do about X? how is one to deal with X?' Syntactically *ruò* 若 and *rú* 如 are like *wèi* 謂 'call.' That is, they have to be interpreted causatively: 'make X [X is like what]' → 'make X like what.' The choice between *rú* and *ruò* seems to be a matter of dialect. In the *Zuǒzhuàn* and *Guóyǔ* one finds exclusively *ruò* 若. In the *Shījīng, Lúnyǔ* and *Mèngzǐ* one finds *rú* 如. In *Mòzǐ, Zhuāngzǐ* and *Xúnzǐ rú* 如 is rare, *ruò* 若 occurs occasionally, but more often one finds *nài* 奈, which may be a fusion of *ruò zhī* 若之.

In the *Zuǒzhuàn* X in the formula is often a noun or noun phrase which may be quite long.

86. Zǐ ruò guó hé 子若國何

What are you, sir, going to do about the country? (*Zuǒ* Xī 23/3)

87. Wú ruò zhū hóu zhī shǔ rǔ zài guǎ jūn zhě hé 無若諸侯之屬辱在寡君者何

We have no way of providing for the retinues of feudal lords who condescend to visit us. (*Zuǒ* Xiāng 31/*fù* 3)

X may also be replaced by the pronoun *zhī* 之, in which case the noun phrase to which it refers is either understood from the context or placed after the whole phrase, in apposition.

88. Ruò zhī hé zǐ zhī bù yán yě 若之何子之不言也

What is to be done about your not speaking? (*Zuǒ* Ai 11/*fù* 2)

In later texts, such as *Mèngzǐ*, *rú zhī hé* 如之何 or *ruò zhī hé* 若

之何 is normal and it is comparatively rare to find a noun or noun phrase between *rú* 如 or *ruò* 若 and *hé* 何 .

89. Rú zhī hé qí shǐ sī mín jī ér sǐ yě 如 之 何 其 使 斯 民 飢 而 死 也

What would he have said about their causing these people to die of hunger? (*Mèng* 1A/4 — translated as 'said' here because the context is Confucius' condemnation of the person who had merely started the custom of burying human effigies in graves.)

9. Passive Constructions

The unmarked passive construction by which an intrinsically transitive verb becomes passive when its object is placed in the subject position has been illustrated above. There are also special devices for marking a verb as passive.[11]

(a) *jiàn* 見

The verb *jiàn* 見 'see,' can serve as a marker of the passive when it stands in front of another verb. It seems likely that this usage is a specialized extension of *jiàn* 見 'see' in the sense of 'meet, encounter,' but the use as a passive marker has been grammaticalized and a literal rendering in this way would be inappropriate.

90. Bǎixìng zhī bù jiàn bǎo, wèi bù yòng ēn yān 百 姓 之 不 見 保 ，為 不 用 恩 焉

The people's not being protected is because of not using benevolence towards them. (*Mèng* 1A/7)

The marking of the passive in this case is probably because the subject, *bǎixìng* 百 姓 'people,' being human, could be misinterpreted as agent for the verb *bǎo* 保 'protect.' Earlier in the same passage we find two examples of an unmarked passive: *yī yǔ zhī bù jǔ* 一 羽 之 不 舉 'one feather's not being lifted' and *yú xīn zhī bù jiàn* 輿 薪 之 不 見 'a cartload of firewood's not being seen.' In these cases the subjects, being inanimate, are unlikely to be interpreted as agents for the verbs *jǔ* 'lift' and *jiàn* 'see.' The insertion of *jiàn* as a passive marker before *bǎo* removes any possible ambiguity.

The only other example in *Mèngzǐ* is the following:

91. Pénchéng Kuò jiàn shā 盆 成 括 見 殺

Pénchéng Kuò was killed. (*Mèng* 7B/29)

Here again the subject is human.

As with the unmarked passive, agency can be expressed by the coverb *yú* 於.

92. Wú cháng jiàn xiào yú dà fāng zhī jiā 吾常見笑於大方之家

I would forever have been laughed at by masters of great accomplishment. (*Zhuāng* 17/5)

Not only inherently transitive verbs but also intransitive verbs and adjectives used transitively, and even nouns used as verbs, can be marked as passive by *jiàn* 見.

93. … ér yǐ qián suǒ yǐ jiàn xián ér hòu huò zuì zhě, ài zēng zhī biàn yě 而以前所以見賢而後獲罪者，愛憎之變也

… and the fact that he later received condemnation for that for which he had earlier been regarded as worthy, was [because of] the change of love to hate. (*HF* 12, p.65, *xián* 'regard as worthy' is derived from the adjective *xián* 'worthy,' see Section IV.2.)

94. Fú pò rén zhī yú pò yú rén yě, chén rén zhī yú jiàn chén yú rén yě, qǐ kě tóng rì ér lùn zāi 夫破人之於破於人也，臣人之於見臣於人也，豈可同日而論哉

How can overthrowing others and being overthrown by others, making others one's subject and being made subject by others be discussed at the same time? (*Shǐjì* 69.2248)

In Hàn and post-Hàn Chinese *jiàn* 見 sometimes indicates the speaker rather than the subject of the verb as patient. The verb has its agent in the normal subject position.

95. Shēng hái liù yuè, cí fù jiàn bèi 生孩六月，慈父見背

Six months after he gave me birth, I was deserted by [the death of] my loving father.' (Lǐ Mì 李密, 'Chén qíng shì biǎo 陳情事表,' *Quán Jìn wén* 70/1865)

It should be noted that *bèi* 被, used somewhat like *jiàn* 見 as a marker of the passive in Modern Chinese, is a full verb, meaning 'receive, undergo, suffer' in the classical language.

(b) *wéi* 為

The copula verb *wéi* 為 is used to form a kind of passive construction.

96. Zhǐ, jiāng wéi sān jūn huò 止 ， 將 為 三 軍 獲
If you stop, you will be captured by the Three Armies. (*Zuǒ* Xiāng 18/4)

97. Zài shàng wéi wū yuān shí, zài xià wéi lóu yǐ shí 在 上 為 烏 鳶 食 ， 在 下 為 螻 蟻 食
Above I'll be eaten by crows and kites, below I'll be eaten by mole crickets and ants. (*Zhuāng* 32/49-50)

This should not be interpreted as if the complement after *wéi* 為 were a noun phrase with the first noun to be construed as possessive — 'will be the capture of the three armies.' It would imply that the complement was a nominalized verb phrase, which would require *zhī* 之 as a marker of nominalization between the subject and the verb (VII.2b), but this is never found. Moreover, we should expect *qí* 其 as the pronoun substitute for such a subject. Instead we find the object pronoun *zhī* 之 .

98. Míng zhě wéi wéi zhī shǐ 明 者 唯 為 之 使
The bright-eyed are only ordered about by them. (*Zhuāng* 32/51)

The *wéi* 為 passive is best understood as a kind of pivot construction (see Section V.3), in which the first object is not the direct object of the governing verb, as it is with verbs of causing, ordering, etc., but an indirect, or dative, object. The embedded verb which constitutes the second object has the subject of the main verb as its patient and the indirect object as its agent — 'You will be for the Three Armies [the Three Armies] capture [you].'

In later Literary Chinese, from about the beginning of the Hàn dynasty, this construction takes on a new form, in which *suǒ* 所 is inserted in front of the embedded verb. That is, *wéi sān jūn huó* 為 三 軍 獲 would become *wéi sān jūn suǒ huó* 為 三 軍 所 獲 . As we shall see, *suǒ* 所 is the regular substitute for the object of a verb in a relative clause when this is coreferent with the head of the clause. The noun after *wéi* 為 continues to be its indirect object, not the subject of the relative clause, since it is never followed by *zhī* 之 as a mark of nominalization and since it takes the object pronoun *zhī* 之 rather than the possessive pronoun *qí* 其 as its pronoun substitute.

99. ... zhōng wéi zhī suǒ qín yǐ ··· 終 為 之 所 擒 矣
... in the end you will be captured by him. (*Shǐjì* 92.2622)

In its new form we must therefore construe our sample sentence as 'You will be for the Three Armies what [the Three Armies] capture.'

With both *wéi* 為 and *wéi suǒ* 為 所 the agency may be left unexpressed.

100. Hòu zhě wéi lù, bó zhě jiàn yí 厚者為戮，薄者見疑

In the worst case [the man] was executed, and even in the lesser case he was suspected. (*HF* 12, p.65)

101. Fǒu zhě ruò shǔ jiē qiě wéi suǒ lǔ 不者若屬皆且為所虜

If not, you fellows will all be captured [by him]. (*Shǐjì* 7.313)

In modern works on Classical Chinese grammar we usually find *wéi* 為 as a passive marker interpreted as a preposition or coverb (*jièzì* 介字), like modern *bèi* 被, which is used to gloss it. This is based on a false analogy with the modern language and is not a valid interpretation of the syntax of Classical Chinese itself. The graph is sometimes even read *wèi* in this sense, like the coverb meaning 'for, on behalf of,' but this is certainly mistaken. The best authorities retain the old level tone reading.

V. Compound Verbal Predicates

1. Coordination

Two verbs used together may be coordinate:

> **102.** Bān bái zhě bù fù dài yú dào lù yǐ 頒 白 者 不 負 戴 於
> 道 路 矣
>
> Those whose hair is streaked with white will not carry loads on
> their heads or on their backs on the ways and roads. (*Mèng* 1A/3)

The verbs *fù* 負 and *dài* 戴 have the same status in the sentence and neither
is subordinate to the other. Their order could be reversed without changing
the meaning. (The same is true of the nouns *dào* 道 and *lù* 路 .)

The particle *qiě* 且 'and, moreover' may be used between coordinate
verbs, especially adjectives.

> **103.** Bāng yǒu dào, pín qiě jiàn yān chǐ yě; bāng wú dào, fù qiě
> guì yān chǐ yě 邦 有 道 ，貧 且 賤 焉 恥 也 。邦 無
> 道 ，富 且 貴 焉 恥 也
>
> When a country has the Way, to be poor and lowly in it is
> shameful; when a country does not have the Way, to be rich and
> noble in it is shameful. (*LY* 8/13)

2. Clause Objects — Verb Phrases as Objects of Transitive Verbs[12]

Very often, however, there is a relation of dependency between two verbs in
succession. Thus, a verb phrase may be the object of a preceding transitive
verb: *wáng yù shā rén* 王 欲 殺 人 'the king wishes to kill a man.' The
verb phrase *shā rén* 殺 人 , which has *wáng* 王 as its underlying subject,
is the object of the verb *yù* 欲 'wish.' It can be replaced by a pronoun just
like a noun object: *wáng yù zhī* 王 欲 之 'the king wishes it,' *wáng suǒ
yù* 王 所 欲 'what the king wishes.'

When the subject of such an object clause is the same as that of the
main verb, it is deleted as in *wáng yù shā rén* 王 欲 殺 人 . When it is
not the same, the clause is marked as nominalized by the insertion of the
subordinating particle *zhī* 之 between the subject and the verb or replacing
the subject by the possessive pronoun *qí* 其 (see Section VII.2b below).

104. ... zé wú wàng mín zhī duō yú lín guó yě 則 無 望 民 之 多 於 鄰 國 也

... then do not hope that your people will be more numerous than [those of] neighbouring countries. (*Mèng* 1A/3)

Verbs like *yù* 欲 'wish' and *wàng* 望 'look at (in the distance); hope,' are readily translated as transitive verbs in English and readily take as their objects clauses with a different subject. The class of verbs which take clause objects also includes verbs like *néng* 能 'can, be capable of,' *kěn* 肯 'be willing to,' and *gǎn* 敢 'dare,' whose object clauses almost always have the same subject and which correspond semantically to auxiliary verbs in English.

105. Wú hūn, bù néng jìn yú shì yǐ 吾 惛 ， 不 能 進 於 是 矣

I am stupid and cannot advance to this. (*Mèng* 1A/7)

106. bǐ wū gǎn dāng wǒ zāi 彼 惡 敢 當 我 哉

How does that one dare to face me? (*Mèng* 1B/3)

Note that, although *néng* is usually followed by a verb in this way, it can also take a noun or pronoun object.

107. ... bù néng sān nián zhī sāng 不 能 三 年 之 喪

To be incapable of three years' mourning ... (*Mèng* 7A/46)

108. Bù xián ér néng zhī yú 不 賢 而 能 之 與

Could he have done it if he had not been a man of superior talent? (*Mèng* 5A/9)

3. Pivot Constructions — The Causative

Certain verbs can take two objects, the first of which is a noun or pronoun and the second of which is a clause object with the first object as its subject. This has been called a 'pivot construction' because, in its surface structure, a noun or pronoun stands between two verbs and acts as a 'pivot' between them, functioning as the object of the first and the subject of the second.

109. Wáng shǐ rén lái yuē ... 王 使 人 來 曰

The king sent someone to come and say ... (*Mèng* 2B/2)

110. Líng gǒu yǒu yuàn yú fūrén zhě bào zhī 令 苟 有 怨 於 夫 人 者 報 之

He ordered all who had any grudge against the lady to repay it.
(*Zuǒ* Ai 26/*fù* 1)

111. Yǔ zhù miáo zhǎng yǐ 予助苗長矣
I have been helping the sprouts to grow. (*Mèng* 2A/2)

112. Quàn Qí fá Yān, yǒu zhū 勸齊伐燕，有諸
Is it true that you urged Qí to attack Yān? (*Mèng* 2A/9)
The verbs *shǐ* 使 'employ; send' and *líng* 令 'order' are used in a
weakened sense as auxiliary verbs to make a causative construction.

113. Shì shǐ mín yǎng shēng sāng sǐ wú hàn yě 是使民養
生喪死無憾也
This is to let the people nourish the living and mourn the dead
without regrets. (*Mèng* 1A/3)

114. ... wú líng shuǐ lào néng rù 毋令水潦能入
... so as not to let the flood waters be able to enter. (*Mò* 61/1)
Note that the object pronoun *zhī* 之 is used as the substitute for the
'pivot' noun in the pivot construction.

115. Zhù zhī zhǎng zhě ... 助之長者
One who helps them to grow ... (*Mèng* 2A/2)
This is in contrast to the use of the possessive pronoun *qí* 其 for the
subject of a clause object (see above). In the pivot construction the pronoun
zhī 之 is directly governed as object by the main verb. A repetition of the
pronominal reference by *qí* 其 as subject of the subordinate verb is therefore
avoided. This is true even if *zhī* 之 is deleted (that is, does not appear on
the surface), as frequently happens in the elliptical style of the *Zuǒzhuàn*.
    A rare example of a clause object without a pivot after a verb of this
kind is the following:

116. Qiě gù xīng tiānxià zhī lì, chú tiānxià zhī hài, líng guójiā
bǎixìng zhī bù zhì yě, zì gǔ jí jīn wèi cháng zhī yǒu yě 且故興
天下之利，除天下之害，令國家百姓之不
治也，自古及今，未嘗之有也
Moreover it has never happened from ancient times to the present
that by deliberately producing what is beneficial to the world and
getting rid of what is harmful, one has caused the state and the
people to be not well governed. (*Mò* 25/16)

In this example, the subject of the embedded clause, *guójiā bǎixìng* 國 家 百 姓, cannot be the agent of its own state of being well or badly governed and cannot be 'ordered' even in a figurative sense to bring about such a state. It therefore cannot be the object of *líng* 令 and, as a result, is not deleted in what would normally be its second occurrence, as the subject of the embedded clause.

On pivot constructions with *wèi* 謂 'call, say' see Section IV.8f above.

4. Verb Phrases as Complements to Adjectives

(a) Adjectives That Make a Following Verb Passive[13]

Some predicate adjectives can take verb phrases as complements. An important set of these consists of the four words *kě* 可 'possible; permissible,' *zú* 足 'sufficient, worth,' *nán* 難 'difficult,' and *yì* 易 'easy.' These are followed by transitive verbs which have to be understood as passive. That is, the subject of the predicate adjective is the patient of the complement verb: *wáng kě shā* 王 可 殺 'the king is possible to kill' = 'the king may be killed.' It is interesting to note that the corresponding English adjectives take a similar construction.

117. ... tiānxià kě yùn yú zhǎng 天 下 可 運 於 掌
... the world may be revolved in the palm of your hand. (*Mèng* 1A/7)

118. Zé wén wáng bù zú fǎ yú 則 文 王 不 足 法 與
Then is King Wén not worthy of being taken as a model? (*Mèng* 2A/1)

119. Jiǔ zé nán biàn yě 久 則 難 變 也
Having lasted a long time, it was difficult to change. (*Mèng* 2A/1)

120. Sān nián xué, bù zhì yù gǔ, bù yì dé yě 三 年 學 ， 不 至 於 穀 ， 不 易 得 也
To study for three years and not arrive at goodness is not easy to achieve. (*LY* 8/12)

As noted in IV.1 above, when an active verb, transitive or intransitive, is used as a complement to one of these adjectives, it is necessary to insert *yǐ* 以 : *wáng kě yǐ shā rén* 王 可 以 殺 人 'the king can kill a man,' *wáng kě yǐ lái* 王 可 以 來 'the king can come.'

121. Wǔ shí zhě kě yǐ yì bó yǐ 五十者可以衣帛矣
The fifty year olds will be able to wear silk. (*Mèng* 1A/3)

122. Wú lì zú yǐ jǔ bǎi jūn ér bù zú yǐ jǔ yī yǔ 吾力足以舉
百鈞而不足以舉一羽
My strength is sufficient to lift 3000 catties but is not sufficient to
lift one feather. (*Mèng* 1A/7)

Yǐ 以, which as a full verb means 'take, use,' is to be understood in
this construction as a transitive verb made passive by the governing
adjective. This is readily translatable into English if the subject is not
personal, that is, if it is an instrument rather than an agent: *dǎo kě yǐ shā
rén* 刀可以殺人 'a knife is possible to use to kill a man' = 'a knife
may be used to kill a man' = 'a knife can kill a man.' In Chinese, a
personal agent is treated in the same way: 'the king is possible to use to
kill a man' = 'the king can kill a man.' This is a grammatical device which
is impossible in English. Instead English uses an impersonal construction.
That is, when the verb is active it treats the complement phrase of an
adjective as the real subject, replacing it by the dummy *it* in the subject
position: 'it is possible to kill a man,' 'it is possible to come.' In such
cases the subject of the complement verb is expressed by a prepositional
phrase: 'it is possible *for the king* to kill a man,' etc.

A similar impersonal active construction is occasionally found in
Classical Chinese where *kě* 可 is followed by an active verb with the object
pronoun *zhī* 之 referring back to something earlier in the discourse.

123. Hé rú sī kě wèi zhī shì yǐ 何如斯可謂之士矣
What must one be like before it is possible to call him one of the
gentry? (*LY* 13/20)

124. Yǐ bù rěn rén zhī xīn, xíng bù rěn rén zhī zhèng, chí tiān xià
kě yùn zhī zhǎng shàng 以不忍人之心，行不忍人
之政，治天下可運之掌上
With a merciful heart practising merciful government, ruling the
world was [as if] it was possible to turn it in the palm of one's
hand. (*Mèng* 2B/6)

Verbs like *wèi* 謂 and *shǐ* 使 that take two objects can also be found
in the normal way with the subject made passive by *kě* 可, as in:

125. Kě shǐ zhì tǐng yǐ tà Qín Chǔ zhī jiān jiǎ lì bīng yǐ 可使
制梃以撻秦楚之堅甲利兵矣

They may be made to fashion clubs with which to strike the hard
armour and sharp weapons of Qín and Chǔ. (*Mèng* 1A/5)

126. … kě wèi xiào yǐ 可 謂 孝 矣
… it may be called filial. (*Mèng* 3A/2)

It should be noted that *kě* 可 can also occur in front of active verbs
meaning 'should, ought' in a hortatory or injunctive sense. This usage is
rare in texts of the classical period but is found in the preclassical period in
the *Shūjīng* and re-emerges in Hàn.

127. Wǒ bù kě bù jiàn yú Yǒu Xià 我 不 可 不 監 于 有 夏
We must not fail to take Xià as our mirror. (*Shū* 32:460 Shàogào)

128. Qín nǚ jué měi, wáng kě zì qǔ 秦 女 絕 美 ， 王 可 自
取
The woman of Qín is extremely beautiful, Your Majesty should
take her for yourself. (*Shǐjì* 66.2171)

(b) *Other Adjectives That Take Verb Phrases as Complements*
There are also adjectives that take verbs or verb phrases as complements
without making the verb passive. Among them are *yí* 宜 'fitting, proper,
right' and *shàn* 善 'good (at).'

129. Shì yǐ, wéi rén zhě yí zài gāo wèi 是 以 ， 惟 仁 者 宜
在 高 位
Therefore, only one who is benevolent is fit to be in a high
position. (*Mèng* 4A/1)

130. Wǒ shàn yǎng wú hàorán zhī qì 我 善 養 吾 浩 然 之
氣
I am good at nourishing my overflowing breath. (*Mèng* 3A/1)

5. Verbs in Series

(a) *The Construction in General — The Particle* Ér 而
Two or more verbs or verb phrases may occur in a series in which they
form a narrative or logical sequence.

131. Téng Wén Gōng wéi shì zǐ, jiāng zhī Chǔ , guō Sòng, ér
jiàn Mèng zǐ 滕 文 公 為 世 子 ， 將 之 楚 ， 過 宋 ，
而 見 孟 子

When Duke Wén of Téng was Crown Prince, he passed through
Sòng on his way to Chǔ and saw Mencius. (Mèng 3A/1 — More
literally: Duke Wén of Téng was Crown Prince, was going to go
to Chǔ, passed through Song and saw Mencius.)

Such constructions (in English as well as Chinese) differ from true
coordinate constructions in that the order cannot be changed without
changing the meaning. 'I opened the door and walked in' does not mean the
same thing as 'I walked in and opened the door.' In spite of the conjunction
'and,' which is also used in English for coordination, there is an implication
of temporal sequence corresponding to the order of the verbs in the two
sentences. In Chinese, such serial verb constructions are very common even
where English uses various kinds of more explicit subordination, as in the
idiomatic translation of **131**. The particle *ér* 而 is used as a connective
between verbs in such constructions, usually being omitted except between
the last two verbs in the series, where it serves to mark the end of the
sequence. It may be translated as 'and,' but it must be noted that it cannot
occur between nouns. Etymologically it appears to be an unstressed form of
nǎi 乃 'then.'

It is often convenient to show the relationship between verbs in series
in translation by using English participles in *-ing:* 'Duke Wén of Téng,
being the Crown Prince and about to go to Chu, and passing through Sòng,
saw Mencius.'

Though it is usual to find *ér* before the last verb in a series, this is not
obligatory. Compare the two successive sentences:

> **132.** Yóu yuán mù ér qiú yú yě ... Yuán mù qiú yú, suī bù dé yú,
> wú hòu zāi 猶 緣 木 而 求 魚 也 … 緣 木 求 魚 ， 雖
> 不 得 魚 ， 無 後 災
> It is like climbing a tree to hunt for fish ... If one climbs a tree to
> hunt for fish, even though one does not get fish, there is no
> disaster afterwards. (*Mèng* 1A/7)

In the second case, *ér* 而 is omitted without any alteration in the meaning.

The semantic relationships between verbs in a series can be quite
varied. Apart from a simple narrative sequence, as in **131**, there can be an
implication of purpose, as in **132**. In other cases, the action of a preceding
verb or verbs is considered to be simultaneous with that of the final verb,
which they serve to describe.

133. Qì jiǎ yì bīng ér zǒu 棄甲曳兵而走

Throwing down their armour and dragging their weapons, they run away. (*Mèng* 1A/3)

Besides its use in the serial verb construction, *ér* 而 is used as a conjunction after concessive clauses (see Section XV.3) and between sentences in the sense of 'but.' The graph is also used to write two homophonous words, the second person pronoun *ér* 而 'you, your' (see Section IX.1b), and *ér* 而 as a variant form of *rú* 如 'if' (see Section XV.2a.i). On the final particle *ér yǐ* 而已 'only' see Section XIII.2d.

(b) Dé (ér) 得 (而), Shuài (ér) 率 (而), etc.

The verb *dé* 得 'get' is used as an auxiliary verb in the sense of 'get to, manage to, be able to, can,' but instead of taking a object clause construction like *néng* 能 'be capable of, can,' it has a serial verb construction: 'get and do (something).' This is shown both by the fact that one can optionally insert *ér* 而 between the two verbs and by the fact that, after *kě* 可, both *dé* 得 and its following verb are made passive.

134. Shèng dé zhī shì, jūn bù dé ér chén, fù bù dé ér zǐ 盛德之士，君不得而臣，父不得而子

A scholar of complete virtue, the ruler is not able to treat as subject and the father is not able to treat as son. (*Mèng* 5A/4)

135. Jū xià wèi èr bù huò yú shàng, mín bù kě dé ér chí yě 居下位而不獲於上，民不可得而治也

If one occupies a lower position and does not obtain the confidence of the ruler, the people cannot be ruled. (*Mèng* 4A/13)

136. Kě dé wén hū 可得聞乎

May I hear about it? (*Mèng* 1A/7 — Literally: May it be got and heard?)

From the point of view of their English translations, verbs such as *shuài* 率 'lead' and *qū* 驅 'drive' might be expected to take a pivot construction, like *shǐ* 使, but they too take a serial verb construction, as shown by the insertion of *ér* 而 in examples like the following.

137. Cǐ shuài shòu ér shí rén yě 此率獸而食人也

This is leading animals to eat people. (*Mèng* 1A/4)

138. Rán hòu qū ér zhī shàn 然 後 驅 而 之 善
Afterwards you may drive [the people] to go towards goodness.
(*Mèng* 1A/7)

In both examples, the subject of the verb following *ér* 而 is the object of
the verb which precedes it. Instead of pivot constructions, however, they
must be interpreted as serial verb constructions in which there is a change of
subject for the second verb: 'lead animals and they eat people,' 'drive [the
people] and they go towards goodness.'

6. Coverbs

(a) *Transitive Verbs Corresponding to Prepositions*
The free serial verb construction, in which any and all verbs may be found,
gives rise to various special constructions, in which particular verbs lose
their independent status and serve as markers of grammatical functions, such
as showing case relationships of nouns to the main verb. Coverb is a term
that has been applied to such verbs in Chinese. Most coverbs can also occur
as independent verbs but they have special grammaticalized meanings as
coverbs. They are not normally joined to the main verb by *ér* 而 . The
following are the most important transitive verbs that correspond to
prepositions in English.

(i) *Yǐ* 以 'take, use; with, by means of'
In an example like the following *yǐ* 以 is a main verb:

139. Wǒ cí lǐ yǐ, bǐ zé yǐ zhī 我 辭 禮 矣 ， 彼 則 以 之
I declined the ritual; *they* used it. (*Zuǒ* Xiāng 10/2)

The coverbal meanings of *yǐ* 以 are quite varied. A simple extension
of the full verb meaning is its use to indicate the instrument of an action.

140. Xǐng, yǐ gē zhú Zǐfàn 醒 ， 以 戈 逐 子 犯
When he revived, he chased Zǐfàn with a halberd. (*Zuǒ* Xī 23/*fù* 2)

141. Shā rén yǐ tǐng ... 殺 人 以 梃
To kill a man with a club ... (*Mèng* 1A/4)

Note that the phrase introduced by *yǐ* 以 can either precede or come after
the main verb. This is a predictable consequence of the interpretation of
coverbs as a specialized type of verbs in series. Thus 'use halberd pursue

person' and 'kill person use club' (i.e., 'in killing a person use a club') differ only in the main focus of attention, which falls on the last verb in the series. In Modern Chinese, however, such freedom of word order has been lost and, except for special cases, where they are treated as complements of the main verb, coverb phrases are confined to preverbal position, like modifiers in general.

Besides indicating the means or instrument by which an action is performed, yǐ 以 can be used to indicate such things as the reason for an action, the time of an action, the basis for a judgement, etc.

> **142.** Yǐ wǔ shí bù xiào bǎi bù zé hé rú 以 五 十 步 笑 百 步 則 何 如
>
> If because of [only running] fifty paces they laughed at [those who ran] one hundred paces, how would it be? (*Mèng* 1A/3)

> **143.** Fǔ jīn yǐ shí rù shān lín 斧 斤 以 時 入 山 林
> If axes enter the hills and woods at the proper season ... (*Mèng* 1A/3)

> **144.** Yǐ wèi, zé zǐ jūn yě, wǒ chén yě 以 位 ， 則 子 君 也 ， 我 臣 也
>
> On the basis of rank, you are the ruler and I am the subject. (*Mèng* 5B/7)

An important characteristic of yǐ 以 as a coverb is that it is almost never followed by the object pronoun zhī. Instead yǐ 以 alone is used anaphorically with the meaning 'with it, therewith' as if it included the pronoun.

> **145.** Rù yǐ shì qí fù xiōng, chū yǐ shì qí zhǎng shàng 入 以 事 其 父 兄 ， 出 以 事 其 長 上
>
> Going in they will therewith serve their fathers and elder brothers; going out, they will therewith serve their elders and superiors. (*Mèng* 1A/5)

Anaphoric yǐ 以 is often used to express purpose: 'and thereby' = 'in order to.'

> **146.** Kě shǐ zhì tǐng yǐ tà Qín Chǔ zhī jiān jiǎ lì bīng yǐ 可 使 制 梃 以 撻 秦 楚 之 堅 甲 利 兵 矣
>
> They may be made to fashion clubs in order to strike the hard armour and sharp weapons of Qín and Chǔ. (*Mèng* 1A/5)

In such cases *yǐ* 以 must not be construed as governing the following verb as its object. For the omission of *zhī* 之 when it would be expected in front of *yǐ* 以 recapitulating a preposed object, see Section VIII.1, example **236**.

Anaphoric *yǐ* 以 marks the point of departure for spatial and temporal phrases like *yǐ lái* 以 來 (therewith come =) 'and afterwards, since,' *yǐ xià* 以 下 (therewith down =) 'and downwards.'

> **147.** Fǒu, zì shēng mín yǐ lái, wèi yǒu Kǒngzǐ yě 否 ， 自 生 民 以 來 ， 未 有 孔 子 也
> No, since the birth of mankind, there has never been [another] like our Confucius. (*Mèng* 2A/2)

> **148.** Qīng yǐ xià bì yǒu guī tián 卿 以 下 必 有 圭 田
> From the high ministers downward, they had to have their sacrificial land. (*Mèng* 3A/3)

Note the phrases *yǒu yǐ* 有 以 and *wú yǐ* 無 以 in the sense of *yǒu suǒ yǐ* 有 所 以 'have that by which; have whereby,' and *wú suǒ yǐ* 無 所 以 'not have that by which; not have whereby.' The omission of *suǒ* 所 in these expressions is comparable to the regular omission of the object pronoun *zhī* 之 after *yǐ* 以 .

> **149.** Yì jiāng yǒu yǐ lì wú guó hū 亦 將 有 以 利 吾 國 乎
> Surely you are going to have whereby to benefit my country.
> (*Mèng* 1A/1)

An important use of *yǐ* 以 is to introduce what is semantically the direct object of verbs of 'giving, telling, teaching, etc.' (see Section IV.8, examples **71-73**).

With *wéi* 為 'be,' *yǐ* 以 forms a special idiom: *yǐ* 以 X *wéi* 為 Y 'take X to be Y,' 'regard X as Y.'

> **150.** Bǎixìng jiē yǐ wáng wéi ài yě 百 姓 皆 以 王 為 愛 也
> The common people all took Your Majesty to be stingy. (*Mèng* 1A/7)

When the object pronoun is omitted after *yǐ* 以 , *yǐ* 以 and *wéi* 為 come together, giving rise to what eventually became a compound word, *yǐwéi* 以 為 'think.' In the classical language, however, the two words must still be construed separately.

> **151.** Mín yóu yǐ wéi xiǎo yě 民 猶 以 為 小 也
> The people still considered it to be small. (*Mèng* 1B/2)

The phrase *suǒ yǐ* 所 以 'that by which' must always be given its full value in Classical Chinese. It does not have the meaning 'therefore' which it has acquired in the modern language.

The expression *shì yǐ* 是 以 'because of that, therefore,' used as a sentence connective, in contrast to *yǐ shì* 以 是 'with this, etc.,' used as part of a predicate phrase, gets its word order from contrastive exposure (see Section VIII, below).

When followed by a clause nominalized by *zhī* 之 or *qí* 其 and closed by *yě* 也 , *yǐ* 以 acts as a subordinating conjunction meaning 'because' (see Section XV.5).

(ii) *Yòng* 用 'use; with'

In the preclassical language, *yòng* 用 is used as an instrumental coverb, like *yǐ* 以 . In the classical language, however, it is only found as a full verb, 'to use.'

(iii) *Yǔ* 與 'accompany; give; with; and'

As a full verb, *yǔ* 與 has the primary meaning of 'accompany, be with.'

152. Zhèng zhí shì yǔ 正 直 是 與
Associate with the correct and straight (*Shī* 207/4, Karlgren 1950a
For 是 recapitulating a preposed object, see Section VIII.1 below.)

153. Wú zhòng ér hòu fá zhī, yù yù wǒ shuí yǔ 無 眾 而 後 伐 之 ， 欲 禦 我 誰 與
If we attack him after he has lost the masses, though he should wish to resist us, who will be with him? (*Zuǒ* Zhuāng 27/*fù* 1)

The meaning 'give,' which is more common than 'accompany' for *yǔ* 與 as a full verb in the classical language, is probably to be understood as a causative usage. There is also a derivative, *yù* 與 , written with the same character, meaning 'participate in, be present at.' (The character is also used for the question particle *yú* 與 — see Section III.1a.)

The coverbal use of *yǔ* 與 in the sense of 'accompanying, with' is found already in the preclassical language and remains common throughout the classical period.

154. Gǔ zhī rén yǔ mín xié lè 古 之 人 與 民 偕 樂
The men of old shared their pleasures with the people. (*Mèng* 1A/2)

155. Bù yǔ è rén yán 不與惡人言

He would not speak with an evil man. (*Mèng* 2A/9)

Yǔ 與 is common in comparisons.

156. Huò wèn hū Zēng Xī yuē, wú zǐ yǔ Zǐlù shú xián 或 問 乎 曾 西 曰 ，吾 子 與 子 路 孰 賢

Some one asked Zēng Xī, 'You and Zǐlù, which is superior?' (*Mèng* 2A/1)

157. Wáng zì yǐ wéi yǔ Zhōu Gōng shú rén qiě zhì 王 自 以 為 與 周 公 孰 仁 且 智

Which does Your Majesty consider more virtuous and wise, yourself or the Duke of Zhōu? (*Mèng* 2B/9)

By a further extension of meaning, yǔ 與 is used as a coordinating conjunction, 'and,' between nouns. Though the derivation from the subordinating coverb 'with' is clear, it is equally clear that when the conjoined nouns are on the same syntactic level and can be interchanged without altering the meaning, the role of yǔ 與 has become one of marking coordination (see Section VII.1).

158. Huì bǐ xiǎo xīng, wéi shēn yǔ mǎo 嘒 彼 小 星 ， 維 參 與 昴

Tiny are those little stars, they are Shēn and Mǎo. (*Shī* 21/2)

159. Gǔ yǔ yú biē bù kě shēng shí ... 穀 與 魚 鱉 不 可 勝 食

If the grain and the fish and turtles are more than can be eaten ... (*Mèng* 1A/3)

(iv) Wèi 為 'for, on behalf of, for the sake of'

Wèi 為 is no doubt a derivative of wéi 為 'make; be,' although the semantic relation is not entirely clear. As a full verb, it means 'be on the side of, support.'

160. Fūzǐ wèi Wèi jūn hū 夫 子 為 衛 君 乎

Is the master for the Lord of Wèi? (*LY* 7/15)

More commonly it is a coverb.

161. Wèi zhǎng zhě zhé zhī ... 為 長 者 折 枝

If it is a matter of breaking a branch [or: rubbing the knuckles] for an older person ... (*Mèng* 1A/7)

Most cases in which wèi 為 appears to occupy the position of the main verb are, in fact, best interpreted as coverbal, with another main verb understood.

162. ... ér wáng qǐ wèi shì zāi 而王豈為是哉

... yet can it be that Your Majesty [goes to war] for this? (*Mèng* 1A/7)

With a nominalized verbal expression as its object and followed by yě 也, *wèi* 為 is used to introduce an explanatory noun predicate.

163. Wèi qí xiàng rén ér yòng zhī yě 為其象人而用之也

It was because he made representations of human beings and sacrificed them. (*Mèng* 1A/4)

(v) Zì 自, Yóu 由, Cóng 從 'follow; from'

These three words, all of which mean 'go along, follow' as full verbs, are used as coverbs in the sense of 'from.' Zì 自 (to be distinguished from the homophonous reflexive pronominal adverb zì 自 'self,' written with the same graph, is seldom found as a full verb, but occasional examples can be found.

164. Wèi gǎi lǐ ér yóu qiān zhī, qún chén jù sǐ ,bù gǎn zì yě 未改禮而猶遷之，群臣懼死，不敢自也

If, without changing the code of ritual, you still alter the practice, your many subjects, in fear of death, dare not follow. (*Zuǒ* Zhāo 5/1)

Examples of zì 自 as a coverb 'from' in a temporal sense are found in **116** and **147** above. It is also common in a spatial sense.

165. ... zì Chǔ zhī Téng ... 自楚之滕

... went to Téng from Chǔ ... (*Mèng* 3A/4)

As a full verb yóu 由 means 'to follow along (a road),' often in a metaphorical sense.

166. ... shě zhèng lù ér bù yóu ... 舍正路而不由

... to abandon the correct path and not follow it ... (*Mèng* 4A/11)

As a coverb, 'from,' it is used in spatial, temporal, and logical senses.

167. Tuō rì, yóu Zōu zhī Rén, jiàn Jìzǐ 他日，由鄒之任，見季子

On another day, going from Zōu to Rén, he visited Jĭzĭ. (*Mèng* 6B/5)

168. Yóu Tāng zhì yú Wŭ Dīng 由 湯 至 於 武 丁
From Tang down to Wŭ Dīng ... (*Mèng* 2A/1)

169. Hé yóu zhī wú kě 何 由 知 吾 可
From what do you know I can? (*Mèng* 1A/7)

    Cóng 從 is common as a main verb meaning 'to follow; pursue' and less frequent than *zì* 自 and *yóu* 由 in the sense of 'from,' but it does occur.

170. Liáng rén ... shīshī cóng wài lái 良 人 ⋯ 施 施 從 外 來
The husband ... jauntily came in from outside. (*Mèng* 4B/33)

(b) *Coverbs of Place:* Yú 于, Yú 於, and Hū 乎 — *Locative Complements*

(i) *Yú* 于 'go; to, at'
Yú 于 (EMC wuă) is etymologically related to *wăng* 往, EMC wuaŋ', 'go.' It is common in the preclassical language, both as a coverb, which always follows the main verb, and as a verbal auxiliary before other verbs of motion, indicating inceptive or continuative aspect, as in: *huáng niăo yú fēi* 黃 鳥 于 飛 'The yellow birds go-flying' (*Shī* 2). As a coverb in the *Shījīng*, it is mainly used to indicate destination after verbs of motion or, less commonly, location where motion is not involved. It is occasionally found in time expressions, such as *yú jīn* 于 今 'till now,' or to indicate the recipient of an action. In this text it is clearly distinct from *yú* 於 'in, at, from, than' (see (ii) below). It survives in the *Zuŏzhuàn* and *Guóyŭ* but already there is a tendency for *yú* 於 to take over its functions. In Mencius and other texts of the Warring States period it is rare, except in quotations from earlier works (see **175** below). It is ironic that it has now been revived as the standard abbreviated form of *yú* 於, with which it did not become homophonous before modern times.[14]

(ii) *Yú* 於 'in, at, to, from, than, etc.'
This word, EMC ʔɨă, was quite distinct from *yú* 于, EMC wuă, with a different initial and an unrounded main vowel. Even in Early Mandarin of the Yuán period, as recorded in the *Zhōngyuán yīnyùn* the two words were

distinct, the former being in upper level tone and the latter in lower level tone. The primary verbal meaning of *yú* 於 is 'to be in, at' without any implication of motion. Although it is seldom used as an independent verb, occasional examples can be found.

171. Biān bǐ cán, guó gù shǒu, gǔ duó zhī shēng yú ěr, ér nǎi yòng chén Sī zhī jì, wǎn yǐ 邊 鄙 殘 ， 國 固 守 ， 鼓 鐸 之 聲 於 耳 ， 而 乃 用 臣 斯 之 計 ， 晚 矣
When the borders and outlying regions are in ruins, the capital is closely invested, the sound of drums and clappers is in your ears, then it will be too late to use the plans of your servant Sī. (*HF* 2 p. 13)[15]

Its verbal character is also clearly shown by the fact that it can take a subject and be nominalized by the insertion of *zhī* 之 (on this idiom see (vii) below).

(iii) *Hū* 乎

As a coverb, *hū* 乎, EMC ɣɔ, is found as a variant of *yú* 於 'in at' from the *Shījīng* onwards (example **174** below). It never occurs in phrase initial position and is probably an unstressed form which lost its glottal stop initial through being attached enclitically to the preceding word.[16] The fusion word *zhū* 諸 (see Section I.4 above) is equivalent to *zhī hū* 之 乎 in both senses of *hū* 乎, as a final question particle and as a variant of *yú* 於.

(iv) Locative complements

In the classical language, coverbal phrases introduced by *yú* 於 mostly follow the main verb, providing a locative complement that defines the destination or locus of an action. The coverb is thus equivalent to an English preposition such as 'in, at, to' or even 'from,' depending on the main verb which it follows.

172. Wáng lì yú zhǎo shàng 王 立 於 沼 上
The king was standing above his pond. (*Mèng* 1A/2)

173. Hénèi xiōng, zé yí qí mín yú Hédōng, yí qí sù yú Hénèi 河 內 凶 ， 則 移 其 民 於 河 東 ， 移 其 粟 於 河 內
If there is a crop failure in Hénèi, I move the people to Hédōng and move the grain to Hénèi. (*Mèng* 1A/3)

174. Chū hū ěr zhě fǎn hū ěr zhě yě 出 乎 爾 者 反 乎 爾 者
也

What goes out from you will be what returns to you. (*Mèng*
1B/12)

175. Wú wén chū yú yōu gǔ, qiān yú qiáo mù zhě 吾 聞 出 於
幽 谷 遷 于 喬 木 者

I have heard of [birds] that 'came out of dark valleys and moved to
lofty trees.' (*Mèng* 3A/4; quoting *Shī* 165/1, which, however, has
zì 自 instead of *yú* 於)

Note that a locative phrase after *chū* 出 can also mean '(go out) to,'
depending on the context.

176. ... jiē yù chū yú wáng zhī tú 皆 欲 出 於 王 之 塗

... will all wish to go out on Your Majesty's roads. (*Mèng* 1A/7)

Locative phrases introduced by *yú* 於 or *hū* 乎 are used to express
comparison after adjectives (examples **35** and **104** above) and agency after
passive verbs (examples **53** and **92** above).

Apparent exceptions to the rule that locative complements follow the
verb occur when such phrases are moved to the front of the sentence for
topicalization, contrast or emphasis.

177. Yú wǒ xīn yǒu qīqī yān 於 我 心 有 戚 戚 焉

In *my* heart there was a responsive feeling. (*Mèng* 1A/7. Here the
pronominal substitute *yān* 焉 'in it' recapitulates the exposed
phrase in its normal position after the verb.)

The common introductory phrase *yú shì* 於 是 'thereupon' may be
regarded as a special case of this exposure of a locative phrase.

(v) Omission of the coverb in locative complements

It is possible to omit the coverb in locative complements.

178. Zhèng rén yǒu yù mǎi lǚ zhě. Xiān zì duó qí zú ér zhì zhī qí
zuò 鄭 人 有 欲 買 履 者。先 自 度 其 足 而 置 之
其 坐

There was a man of Zhèng who wished to buy shoes. He first
measured his feet himself and placed it (the measure) on his seat.
(*HF* 32, p. 209)

See **78** above for another example. In such cases two bare nouns following a verb have the order (1) direct (accusative) object, (2) locative complement, rather than (1) indirect (dative) object, (2) direct (accusative) object (see Section IV.8a above). Conditions under which this construction is possible need to be worked out in detail.

(vi) The pronominal substitutes *yúan* 爰 and *yān* 焉
Neither *yú* 于 nor *yú* 於 can be followed by the object pronoun *zhī* 之. Instead we find the particles *yúan* 爰, EMC wuan, from *yú* 于 and *yān* 焉, EMC ian, from *yú* 於. The former is found mostly in the *Shījīng*, where it may be glossed as 'there; then, thereupon.' The latter is normal in classical texts from the *Shījīng* onward and can have all the possible meanings of *yú* 於 + *zhī* 之: 'in it, to it, from it, by it, than it, etc.' For examples, see **54, 56, 59, 90, 103**.

(vii) X *zhī yú* 之 於 Y
Phrases in which *yú* 於 has its own subject and is nominalized by inserting *zhī* 之 are commonly used to introduce a topic.

> **179.** Guǎ rén zhī yú guó yě, jìn xīn yān ěr yǐ 寡人之於國也，盡心焉耳矣
> As for my [behaviour] towards my country, I exhaust my mind in it and that's all. (*Mèng* 1A/3. *Yú guó* in the topic phrase is recapitulated by *yān* in the predicate.)

Note that some such word as 'behaviour' has to be introduced into the English translation because English cannot nominalize a preposition. In such cases *hū* 乎 is never substituted for *yú* 於 and *zhī yú* 之 於 is never contracted to *zhū* 諸. In the following example from the *Lúnyǔ*, *wú* 吾 'I, my' precedes *yú* 於 directly without *zhī* 之 but this is normal for personal pronouns used in the genitive, whether before nouns or as the subjects of nominalized verbs.

> **180.** Shǐ wú yú rén yě, tīng qí yán ér xìn qí xìng. jīn wú yú rén yě, tīng qí yán ér guān qí xìng 始吾於人也，聽其言而信其行。今吾於人也，聽其言而觀其行
> Formerly my [attitude] towards men was to listen to their words and trust in their conduct. Now my [attitude] towards men is to listen to their words and observe their conduct. (*LY* 5/10)

For additional examples of this construction see **41** and **94** above.

(c) *Descriptive Complements with* Rú 如 *and'* Yóu 猶

Phrases introduced by *rú* 如 'like' may be placed after a verb to add a descriptive complement in much the same way that phrases introduced by *yú* 於 add locative complements.[17]

> **181.** Shèng rén chí tiānxià, shǐ yǒu shū sù rú shuǐ huǒ 聖人治天下，使有菽粟如水火
>
> When a sage rules the world, he causes it to have beans and grain like water and fire. (*Mèng* 7A/23)

> **182.** Liáng jūn jiāng shǎng shàn ér xíng yín, yǎng mín rú zǐ, gài zhī rú tiān, róng zhī rú dì 良君將賞善而刑淫，養民如子，蓋之如天，容之如地
>
> A good ruler will reward good and punish licentiousness, nurture the people like children, cover them like Heaven, make space for them like the Earth. (*Zuǒ* Xiāng 14/*fù* 3)

Though *yóu* 猶 in the sense of 'like' (for which the graph 由 is sometimes substituted) is not a verb at all and has quite a different origin from *rú* 如, it can also be used to introduce descriptive complements.

> **183.** ... mín guī zhī yóu shuǐ zhī jiù xià 民歸之由水之就下
>
> ... the people will turn to him like water going downwards. (*Mèng* 1A/6)

Note the omission of final *yě* 也, which is required when *yóu* 猶 introduces an independent predicate.

(d) *Coverbs as Subordinating Conjunctions*

Certain transitive verbs are used impersonally to introduce what correspond to subordinate clauses of time, supposition, cause, etc.

> **184.** Jí qí shǐ rén yě, qì zhī 及其使人也，器之
>
> When he (the superior man) employs others, he uses them according to their capacities. (*LY* 13/25)

As a full verb *jí* 及 means 'reach.' It is used here impersonally in a temporal sense with a nominalized clause object, marked as embedded by *yě* 也, literally, 'Coming to his employing men.' Other coverbs used in this way include *zhì yú* 至於 'arrive at; coming to, when'; *bì* 比 'beside; by the time that' (example **215**); *shǐ* 使 'make, cause; supposing'; *yǐ* 以 'use; using, by means of; because,' etc. See Section XV below.

VI. Numerical Expressions

1. As Predicates
Like adjectives, numbers and expressions of quantity form predicates without any copula or final particle.

185. Miè guó zhě wǔ shí 滅 國 者 五 十
His extinctions of countries were fifty. (*Mèng* 3B/9)

186. Wén Wáng zhī yòu fāng qī shí lǐ
文 王 之 囿 方 七 十 里
Wén Wáng's park was 70 *li* square. (*Mèng* 1B/2)

The particle of verbal negation *bù* 不 is used, and other adjuncts of verbal predicates, such as the adverb *yǐ* 已 'already' and the marker of perfect aspect *yǐ* 矣, are also found.

187. Zhí bù bǎi bù ěr 直 不 百 步 耳
It was only not 100 paces. (*Mèng* 1A/3)

188. Nián yǐ qī shí yǐ 年 已 七 十 矣
His years were already 70. (*Mèng* 5A/9)

Note the use of *jiāng* 將 with numerical expressions in the sense of 'approximately.'

189. Jīn Téng jué cháng bǔ duǎn, jiāng wǔ shí jǐ yě 今 滕 絕
長 補 短 , 將 五 十 里 也
Now if you cut off the long to supplement the short, Téng would be roughly 50 *li* [square]. (*Mèng* 3A/1)

2. As Complements
An expression of quantity may be added after another predicate as a complement.

190. Xī sàng dì yú Qín qī shí bǎi lǐ 西 喪 地 於 秦 七 百 里
On the west we lost land to Qín, 700 *li* [= we lost 700 *li* of land to Qín]. (*Mèng* 1A/5)

The syntax may be compared to that of a locative complement (see Section V.6b.v above).

3. As Modifiers of Nouns

Most commonly numerals are placed directly in front of nouns in Classical Chinese without the need for a classifier.

191. Wú hé ài yī niú 吾何愛一牛

Why should I begrudge one ox? (*Mèng* 1A/7)

Measure words, with or without a preceding numeral, may similarly modify nouns directly.

192. Yú xīn zhī bù jiàn, wèi bù yòng míng yān 輿薪之不見，為不用明焉

That a cartload of firewood is not seen, is because of not using one's eyesight on it. (*Mèng* 1A/7)

193. Dé bǎi lǐ zhī dì ér jūn zhī, jiē néng yǐ cháo zhūhóu, yǒu tiānxià 得百里之地而君之，皆能以朝諸侯，有天下

If they had got 100 *li* of territory and ruled over it, they [the ancient sages] could all have thereby brought the feudal lords to their courts and obtained the rulership of All-under-Heaven. (*Mèng* 2A/2)

Less commonly, numerals and measures follow a noun in apposition.

194. Qí wèi Wèi gù, fá Jìn Guān Shì, sàng chē wǔ bǎi 齊為衛故，伐晉冠氏，喪車五百

On behalf of Wèi, Qí attacked the Guān Clan of Jìn and lost 500 chariots. (*Zuǒ* Āi 15/7)

195. Jiē cì yù wǔ jué, mǎ sān pǐ 皆賜玉五玨，馬三匹

He gave them each five pairs of jades and three horses. (*Zuǒ* Zhuāng 18/fù 1)

As in the last case, apart from measure words, special numeral adjuncts are used for counting certain nouns in this construction. These include *pǐ* 匹 for 'horses,' *shèng* 乘 and *liàng* 輛 for 'carriages,' and *gè* 个 for 'arrows.' This is no doubt the forerunner of the more general use of classifiers, which begins to appear in Hàn times.[18] It is noteworthy that the nouns in question are all ones that are frequent in a military context. In most cases the noun so quantified is the object of a verb, and the expression

of quantity can be regarded as a complement, as in Section VI.2 above.
Note, however:

> **196.** Dāng Qín zhī lóng, huáng jīn wàn yì wéi yòng 當秦之
> 隆，黃金萬鎰為用
> At the time of Qín's prosperity, ten thousand *yì* of yellow gold
> were used. (*ZGC*, Qín cè 40/14/13)

4. *Yòu* 有 '**and**'

Note the use of *yòu* 有 (departing tone) in the sense of 'and' in numerical
expressions.

> **197.** Yóu Yáo Shùn zhì yú Tāng, wǔ bǎi yòu yú suì 由堯舜
> 至於湯，五百有餘歲
> From Yáo and Shùn to Tāng was five hundred and more years.
> (*Mèng* 7B/38)

VII. Noun Phrases and Nominalization

1. Coordination and Subordination of Nouns

(a) *Coordination*

Simple juxtaposition is sufficient to indicate coordination: *fùmǔ* 父母 'father and mother.' 'And' between nouns may be expressed by the coverb *yǔ* 與 (see V.6a.iii).

> **198.** Zǐ hǎn yán lì yǔ mìng yǔ rén 子罕言利與命與仁
> The master seldom spoke of profit, fate, and goodness. (*LY* 9/1)

Another coverb used for 'and' in the preclassical language and also in the *Zuǒzhuàn* is *jí* 及 'reach, arrive at.'

> **199.** Yǔ jí rǔ jiē wáng 予及汝皆亡
> I and you will perish together. (*Mèng* 1A/2, quoting *Shū* 10.97 Tāngshì)

> **200.** Sòng jí Zhèng píng 宋及鄭平
> Sòng and Zhèng made peace. (*Zuǒ* Yǐn 7/5)

This usage re-emerges in postclassical texts like the *Shǐjì* 史記.

(b) *Subordination*

Subordination between nouns is expressed by the formula: N_2 *zhī* 之 N_1, in which N_1 is the head of the phrase, N_2 is the modifier and *zhī* 之, which is etymologically the same word as modern *de* 的, is the marker of subordination.

> **201.** Wáng zhī zhū chén 王之諸臣
> Your Majesty's various ministers. (*Mèng* 1A/7)

Zhī 之 may be omitted, especially between monosyllables.

> **202.** Láo yú wáng shì 勞於王事
> They labour in the king's business ... (*Mèng* 5A/4)

The relation between the two nouns need not be that of possession. Thus in 梁惠王 'King Huì of Liáng,' Liáng, the name of the country, is a modifier specifying which King Huì is meant.

Qí 其 is the general pronoun substitute for N + 之 : *qí shǒu* 其手 'his hand.' After personal pronouns *zhī* 之 is normally omitted: *wú shǒu* 吾手 'my hand.'

Nouns may also be modified by verb phrases or adjectives (which in Chinese are like verbs in their syntax).

203. Bù rěn rén zhī xīn 不忍人之心
… the heart that cannot bear the afflictions of others. (*Mèng* 2A/6)

204. Wǔ dúo rén zhī jūn 侮奪人之君
A ruler who insults and robs people … (*Mèng* 4A/17)

Since adjectives are a kind of verb, modification of nouns by adjectives is a special case of this more general construction. It is, of course, a very frequent type. *Zhī* 之 is usually omitted after a monosyllabic adjective, but inserted in other cases:

205. … xián shèng zhī jūn 賢聖之君
… worthy and sage rulers. (*Mèng* 2A/1)

Compare the following example where *zhī* 之 is omitted after one of these adjectives used by itself:

206. Téng jūn zé chéng xián jūn yě 滕君則誠賢君也
The ruler of Téng is truly a worthy ruler. (*Mèng* 3A/4)

The use of a verbal phrase to modify a noun can be considered a special case of the more general construction, called nominalization, that is discussed in the next section. Thus, the modifying phrases in **203**, **204**, and **205** are derived from the sentences: *xīn bù rěn rén* 心不忍人 'the heart cannot bear the afflictions of others'; *jūn wǔ dúo rén* 君侮奪人 'the ruler insults and robs people'; *jūn xián shèng* 君賢聖 'rulers are worthy and sage.' The subjects are omitted in the modifying phrases since they are identical with the head nouns that the phrases modify. An alternative construction in which the head noun is replaced by the pronominal substitute *zhě* 者 and the subject of the modifying sentence is retained is discussed in Section VII.2c below.

2. Nominalization

(a) *Unmarked Nominalization*
Verbal phrases may be treated as nouns simply by being placed in the noun predicate construction. This is used mainly:

(i) in order to contrast two predicates

207. Shì bù wéi yě, fēi bù néng yě 是不為也，非不能也

This is not-doing, it is not not-being-able. (*Mèng* 1A/7)

(ii) to add an explanation or conclusion after another predicate

208. ... shì yì zǒu yě 是亦走也

... this is also running away. (*Mèng* 1A/3)

In this construction the subject, if expressed, is not separated from the verb by *zhī* 之, as it would be in the case of marked nominalization (see (b) below).

209. Shǐ zhī zhǔ shì ér shì zhì, bǎi xìng ān zhī, shì mín shòu zhī yě 使之主事而事治，百姓安之，是民受之也

He put him in charge of affairs and the affairs were well administered and the people were peaceful under him. This was the people's accepting him (i.e., this showed that the people accepted him). (*Mèng* 5A/5)

210. Yúyuè Yí Mò zhī zǐ shēng ér tóng shēng, zhǎng ér yì sú, jiào shǐ zhī rán yě 于越夷貉之子生而同聲，長而異俗，教使之然也

That the children of Yùyuè and the Yí and Mò make the same sounds when they are born but have different customs when they grow up is because teaching makes them so. (*Xún* 1/4-5)

It should also be distinguished from the case of nouns derived from verbs, which cannot take verbal adjuncts like objects or adverbial modifiers. Thus, in the following example *shǐ* 始, which is primarily an intransitive verb, 'begin,' (with, of course, the inherent capability of being used transitively in a causative sense [IV.4]), is equivalent to the derived noun 'beginning' in English, not the homophonous verbal noun (gerund) 'beginning.'

211. Wàng dào zhī shǐ yě 王道之始也

It is the beginning of the kingly way. (*Mèng* 1A/3)

If instead we had: *wàng dào shǐ yě* 王道始也, one may suppose that the meaning would be: 'it is that the kingly way is beginning.' That is, it would have a more active, dynamic meaning instead of merely equating a certain state of affairs with the potentiality of achieving true kingship. On

the other hand, as we shall see below, *wàng dào zhī shǐ yě* 王 道 之 始
也, used as a topic phrase rather than as a predicate, would have this active,
dynamic meaning: 'when the kingly way was beginning.' This is one of the
subtleties of Classical Chinese syntax that needs more study. A further
point that needs investigation is whether any verb can give rise to a derived
noun like *shǐ* 始 'beginning' in the same way that any verb can appear in a
nominalized verbal phrase or whether, as one suspects, such derived verbs
are separate lexical items, with their individual eccentricities.

Modification of a noun by a verb or verb phrase as in **203**, **204**, and
205 above appears to be a form of unmarked nominalization but, as we
shall see below, there is an alternative construction with the same meaning
in which the head noun is replaced by *zhě* 者 and the subject of the
modifying phrase appears on the surface linked to the verb by *zhī* 之. Both
constructions can be derived from the same base form which requires marked
nominalization, with deletion of either one of the two occurrences of N_1.

(b) *Marked Nominalization by Inserting* Zhī 之 [19]
A verb phrase is formally nominalized by inserting *zhī* 之 between the
subject, if present, and the verb: *wáng lái* 王 來 'king comes' → *wáng zhī
lái* 王 之 來 'king's coming.' This may be compared to the English
gerund construction, except, of course, that there is no morphological
change in the verb itself in Chinese. *Qí* 其 is used as a substitute for N +
之 before verbs, just as before nouns: *qí lái* 其 來 'his coming' and after
personal pronouns *zhī* 之 is normally omitted: *wú lái* 吾 來 'my
coming.' (In addition, the particles *zhě* 者 and *suǒ* 所 can serve as marks
of nominalization — see (c) and (d) below.)

This kind of nominalization can be used in a variety of constructions,
e.g.,

(i) As subject of a sentence:

212. Gù wáng zhī bù wàng, bù wéi yě, fēi bù néng yě 故 王 之
不 王 , 不 為 也 , 非 不 能 也
Therefore Your Majesty's not becoming a true king is [a matter of]
not-doing, it is not not-being-able. (*Mèng* 1A/7. The predicate in
this sentence consists of two coordinate unmarked nominalized
verbal phrases embedded in the noun predicate construction.)

(ii) As object of a verb:

213. Wáng ruò yǐn qí wú zuì ér jiù sǐ dì, zé niú yáng hé zé yān
王若隱其無罪而就死地，則牛羊何擇焉

If Your Majesty was pained by its going without guilt to the place
of execution, then what was there to choose between an ox and a
sheep? (*Mèng* 1A/7)

Note especially the usage after verbs of 'knowing, fearing, hoping, etc.' to
express what is 'known, feared, hoped for, etc.'

214. Hé yóu zhī wú kě yě 何由知吾可也

From what do you know that I can? (*Mèng* 1A/7. Literally: know
my being possible)

In such cases, as here, one frequently finds the particle *yě* 也 at the end of
the nominalized phrase.

(iii) As object of a coverb:

215. Bì qí fǎn yě ... 比其反也

(By his returning =) When he returned ... (*Mèng* 1B/7)

Note that here too, where the phrase is translatable as a clause, we find final
yě 也.

(iv) Absolutely, at the beginning of a sentence, as a topic phrase or one
that sets the time or occasion for what follows; usually followed by *yě* 也
(see XV.4e):

216. Chéng Jì zhī jiāng shēng yě, Huán Gōng shǐ bǔ 成季之
將生也，桓公使卜

When Chéng Jì was going to be born, Duke Huán had divination
made [about it]. (*Zuǒ* Mǐn 2/*fù* 1)

The circumstances under which *yě* 也 is inserted to mark the end of a
subordinate noun clause require further investigation. In the case of **213** and
214 the difference seems to be between a preceding if-clause, without *yě*
也, and the main predicate, with *yě* 也. In cases like **215** and **216** where
the initial modifying clauses have final *yě* 也, the modifying clause is
temporal rather than conditional.[20]

Unlike the English gerund construction, a noun linked to a following
verb by nominalizing *zhī* 之 in Chinese can only be the subject or another
preverbal element. There is no 'objective genitive' in Chinese. On the other
hand, in the absence of an overt subject, nominalizing *zhī* 之 may be
inserted after another preverbal element such as a time word.

217. Gǔ zhī wéi guān yě, jiāng yǐ yù bào 古 之 為 關 也 ，
將 以 禦 暴

The establishment of frontier barriers in ancient times was to
prevent violence. (*Mèng* 7B/8)

218. Wú cháng qǐ ér wàng yǐ, bù rú dēng gāo zhī bó jiàn yě 吾
嘗 跂 而 望 矣 ， 不 如 登 高 之 博 見 也

I once stood on tip toe and looked into the distance. It was (not
like the seeing all around of climbing up high =) not as good as
climbing up high and seeing all around. (*Xún* 1/7)

In this example, the noun clause 登 高 之 博 見 can be derived from the
sentence (吾) 登 高 而 博 見 '(I) climb up high and see all around.' The
fact that, in the absence of an explicit subject (II.2), the particle *ér* 而 is
replaced by *zhī* 之 in order to mark the clause as nominalized, shows that
the first of two verbs in series functions grammatically, as well as
semantically, as a modifier of the following, main, verb.

219. Bǐ jiàn lái zhī bìng qín 彼 見 來 之 并 禽

When he sees that, if they come, they will both be seized … (*Shǐjì*
66.2172)

Here *lái* 來 'come' is functioning as an if-clause: *lái, bìng qín* 來 ， 并
禽 'If we come, we will both be seized.' Yet for the sake of nominalization
it is treated as an adjunct of the verb *qín* 禽 'be seized.'

A verbless noun predicate can also be 'nominalized' by *qí* 其 when it
is embedded as an object clause.

220. Yǐ shì zhī qí tiān yě 以 是 知 其 天 也

By this I know that it was Heaven [that did it]. (*Zhuāng* 3/13)

It should be noted that the nominalization by insertion of 之 *zhī*,
which is quite foreign to Modern Chinese, was already becoming
obsolescent in the Hàn period and clause objects often omit this marker in
texts such as the *Shǐjì*.

(c) Zhě 者

The particle *zhě* 者 is the pronoun substitute for the head, N₁, in the noun
phrase construction N_2 *zhī* 之 N_1. It is etymologically related to *zhī* 之
and to colloquial *de* 的, which has a parallel function in the modern
language. Though N_2 modifying *zhě* 者 is most commonly a nominalized
verb phrase, this is not necessarily the case, as in the following:

221. Sān jiā zhě yǐ Yōng chè 三 家 者 以 雍 徹
Those of the Three Families use the Yōng ode while clearing away the sacrificial vessels. (*LY* 3/2; equivalent to *sān jiā zhī rén* 三 家 之 人)

When, as is more commonly the case, N_2 is a verb or verb phrase, *zhě* 者 also serves as a mark of nominalization: *gēng zhě* 耕 者 'a plowing one, a ploughman,' *shā rén zhě* 殺 人 者 'one who kills people.' Note that *zhě* 者 in these cases stands for the subject of the verb, which is to be understood as either indefinite (as in the translations supplied) or anaphoric if a definite subject can be supplied from the preceding context, 'the one who was ploughing,' 'the one who killed people,' etc. If a noun subject is expressed, then N_2 is derived from a sentence in which the subject if N_1 and the formula can be expanded to: $[N_1 + VP]_N$ 之 N_1, where VP stands for 'verb phrase' and subscript $_N$ after the bracket stands for the operation of nominalization. Thus, [*wáng shā rén*]$_N$ *zhī wáng* → *wáng zhī shā rén zhī wáng* → *wáng zhī shā rén zhě* 王 之 殺 人 者 : [[king kills people]$_N$]'s king → [king's killing people]'s king → king's killing people one = a king who kills people.

222. Niǎo shòu zhī hài rén zhě xiāo 鳥 獸 之 害 人 者 消
The birds and beasts that had injured people disappeared. (*Mèng* 3B/9)

If, instead of deleting the second occurrence of N_1 in the formula and replacing *zhī* 之 by *zhě* 者, we delete the first occurrence, within the modifying clause, we derive the construction found in examples **203** and **204** above, in which a verb phrase appears as the modifier of a noun: [*wáng shā rén*]$_N$ *zhī wáng* → *shā rén zhī wáng* 'a king who kills people.' As shown by the translations, these two constructions are equivalent in meaning and both correspond to relative clauses in English.

Zhě 者 may also stand for the verb phrase as a whole: 'the doing X, the thing of doing X' rather than 'the one who does X,' e.g., *gēng zhě* 耕 者 'ploughing,' *shā rén zhě* 殺 人 者 'the killing of people.'

223. Bù wéi zhě yǔ bù néng zhě zhī xíng, hé yǐ yì 不 為 者 與 不 能 者 之 形 ， 何 以 異
How do the forms of not-doing and not-being-able differ? (*Mèng* 1A/7)

Only context can distinguish between these interpretations.

(d) Suǒ 所

Suǒ 所, as a full word, means 'place,' as in *wáng suǒ* 王 所 'the king's place,' *dé qí suǒ* 得 其 所 'get his (proper) place.' When placed in front of a verb it nominalizes it and most commonly stands for the direct object: *suǒ shā* 所 殺 'those whom he killed,' *suǒ yǒu* 所 有 'what he has, what exists.' For examples see **8, 20, 31, 32, 56.** It can also stand for the destination after a transitive verb of motion (IV.6):

> **224.** Tuō rì jūn chū, zé bì mìng yǒu sī suǒ zhī 他 日 君 出 ，
> 則 必 命 有 司 所 之
>
> On other days when you have gone out, you have always given
> orders to your officers as to where you were going. (*Mèng* 1B/16)

Or it can act as a locative complement:

> **225.** Yáo Shùn zhī chí tiān xià, qǐ wú suǒ yòng qí xīn zāi 堯 舜
> 之 治 天 下 ，豈 無 所 用 其 心 哉
>
> When Yáo and Shùn ruled the world, could it be that they had
> nothing on which they exercised their minds? (*Mèng* 3A.4)

Such phrases may also be followed by *zhě* 者 , which then stands for the object or complement referred to by *suǒ* 所 rather than the subject.

> **226.** Suǒ wèi gù guó zhě 所 謂 故 國 者
> What one calls 'an ancient kingdom' ... (*Mèng* 1B/7)

The subject may be expressed by Noun + *zhī* 之 or *qí* 其 : *wáng zhī suǒ shā zhě* 王 之 所 殺 者 'those whom the king killed.' Note the use of *suǒ* 所 with coverbs: *suǒ yǐ* 所 以 'that by which' (*not* 'therefore' in Classical Chinese), *suǒ yǔ* 所 與 'those with whom.' For the passive construction with *wéi* 為 ... *suǒ* 所 ..., see Section IV.9b.

In the preclassical language, *yōu* 攸 is equivalent to later *suǒ* 所 .

> **227.** Wáng zài líng yòu, yōu lù yōu fú 王 在 靈 囿 ，麀 鹿
> 攸 伏
>
> The King was in his Spirit Park, where the deer and stags lay
> resting. (*Shī* 242/2, quoted in *Mèng* 1A/2)

VIII. Topicalization and Exposure

An element in a sentence may be given special prominence by being taken out of its normal position and placed in front. One common situation in which this occurs is when some element which is not grammatically the subject is announced as 'topic.' Exposure also occurs, however, when an element, such as the object of the verb, is given contrastive emphasis without becoming the topic, and since the grammatical devices involved are similar it is convenient to deal with the two matters together. The subject, which normally occupies a position at the head of a sentence, can also be exposed to give it contrastive emphasis or to announce it as not merely the grammatical subject, but also the topic of discourse. (For word order inversion in exclamatory sentences see XIV.3.)

1. Exposure of an Element That Is Not the Subject

228. Rán ér bù wàng zhě, wèi zhī yǒu yě 然 而 不 王 者 ，未 之 有 也

It has never happened that in such circumstances true kingship was not obtained. (*Mèng* 1A/3)

This is equivalent to *wèi yǒu rán ér bù wàng zhě yě* 未 有 然 而 不 王 者 也 (cf. *wèi yǒu rén ér yí qí qīn zhě yě* 未 有 仁 而 遺 其 親 者 也 *Mèng* 1A/1). When the object is exposed, it is repeated by *zhī* 之, which in turn is shifted to the position between the negative particle and the verb by regular rule.

229. Wàn qǔ qiān yān, qiān qǔ bǎi yān, bù wéi bù dūo yǐ 萬 取 千 焉 ，千 取 百 焉 ，不 為 不 多 矣

To take 1000 from ten thousand, or 100 from 1000, is already a large amount (not not-many). (*Mèng* 1A/1)

Here the base forms are *qǔ qiān yú wàn* 取 千 於 萬 and *qǔ bǎi yú qiān* 取 百 於 千. When the noun objects of the coverb *yú* 於 are exposed, they are repeated by *yān* 焉, substituting for *yú zhī* 於 之. Compare also example **65** in Section IV.7 above.

230. Wàn shèng zhī guó, shì qí jūn zhě, bì qiān shèng zhī jiā 萬 乘 之 國 ，弒 其 君 者 ，必 千 乘 之 家

The one who murders the ruler of a country of ten thousand

chariots will certainly be [head of] a house of 1000 chariots. (*Mèng* 1A/1)

Here the base form would be *shì wàn shèng zhī guó zhī jūn zhě* 弑 萬 乘 之 國 之 君 者. The repeating pronoun is the possessive *qí* 其. As in the previous example, the exposed element is rhetorically repeated and contrasted by *qiān shèng zhī guó* 千 乘 之 國 in the next sentence.

231. wǔ mǔ zhī zhái, shù zhī yǐ sāng 五 畝 之 宅， 樹 之 以 桑

Let them plant the household plots of five *mǔ* with mulberries. (= shù wǔ mǔ zhī zhái yǐ sāng 樹 五 畝 之 宅 以 桑 ; *Mèng* 1A/3)

In late Preclassical Chinese of the *Shījīng* and the early Classical Chinese of the *Zuǒzhuàn* and *Guóyǔ*, the exposure construction differed in an important way. A preposed object was repeated by a pronoun, usually *zhī* 之 or *shì* 是, placed *in front of* the verb instead of after it. This is no doubt a survival of a more widespread placing of pronoun objects in front of the verb in the preclassical language.

232. Róng Dí shì yīng 戎 狄 是 膺
The Róng and Dí, them he repressed. (*Shī* 300/4)

233. Guǎ rén zhī cóng jūn ér xī yě, yì Jìn zhī yāo mèng shì jiàn 寡 人 之 從 君 而 西 也， 亦 晉 之 妖 夢 是 踐
That I am following your ruler and going west surely fulfills the strange dream in Jìn. (*Zuǒ* Xī 15/14 = jiàn Jìn zhī yāo mèng 踐 晉 之 妖 夢)

234. Bìng ér hòu zhì yān, hé chí zhī yǒu 病 而 後 質 焉， 何 遲 之 有
If we run into difficulties and then offer them hostages, will it be too late? (*Zuǒ* Dìng 8/10 = yǒu hé chí 有 何 遲)

Note that in the following example the repeating pronoun is placed in front of a particle of negation instead of between the negative and the verb.

235. Shì zhī bù wù, ér yòu yān cóng shì 是 之 不 務 而 又 焉 從 事
If we do not devote our efforts to this, to what else should we apply ourselves? (*Zuǒ* Zhāo 32/5)

In the case of the coverb *yǐ* 以 , which regularly omits *zhī* 之 as its object, a preposed noun object is not repeated by a pronoun.

236. Ruò Jìn jūn zhāo yǐ rù, zé bì zǐ xī yǐ sǐ. xī yǐ rù, zé zhāo yǐ sǐ 若 晉 君 朝 以 入 ， 則 婢 子 夕 以 死 ， 夕 以 入 ， 則 朝 以 死

If the Lord of Jìn enters in the morning, then we women and children die in the evening; if he enters in the evening, we die in the morning. (*Zuǒ* Xī 15/14 — zhāo 朝 'morning' and xī 夕 'evening' are placed in front of the coverb yǐ 以 for the sake of rhetorical contrast but are not followed by a recapitulating pronoun as they would be in the case of an ordinary verb.)

One stereotyped survival of this construction both in standard Classical Chinese and later Literary Chinese is with the verb *wèi* 謂 .

237. Fūzǐ zhī wèi yě 夫 子 之 謂 也

It (the poem) refers to you, sir. (*Mèng* 1A/7. This is derived from: wèi fū zǐ 謂 夫 子 by moving the object fū zǐ 夫 子 in front and repeating with zhī 之 — more literally: Your honour, him it refers to.)

238. Fēi cǐ zhī wèi yě 非 此 之 謂 也

I did not mean this. (*Mèng* 2B/2 = bù wèi cǐ 不 謂 此)

The use of *fēi* 非 as the negative particle in the above example is a carry-over from the earlier construction, in which the exposed element was often introduced by *wéi* 唯 (惟, 維), its negative *fēi* 非, or adnominal particles such as *jiāng* 將 or *bì* 必 .

239. Shì fū yě, jiāng bù wéi Wèi gúo zhī bài 是 夫 也 ， 將 不 唯 衛 國 之 敗

This fellow will ruin not only the country of Wèi. (*Zuǒ* Chéng 14/6)

Note that here the exposed object, though clearly contrastive, is not placed before the subject and can hardly be called the 'topic.'

240. Yú bì chén shì zhù 余 必 臣 是 助

I certainly subjects them help = I will certainly help my subjects. (*Zuǒ* Zhāo 22/2)

2. Exposure of the Subject

If the subject is the element to which special emphasis or contrast is given, it is not displaced since its normal position is in front of the verb, but it can nevertheless be marked as exposed.

In the *Shījīng* and *Zuǒzhuàn*, this is done by inserting the resumptive pronoun *shí* 實 or *shí* 寔 'this' between the subject and the verb. The exposed subject, like an exposed object, is often introduced by one of the adnominal articles *wéi* 唯, *fēi* 非, *jiāng* 將, *bì* 必, etc.

241. Cǐ èr rén zhě shí shì guǎ jūn 此 二 人 者 實 弒 寡 君
It was these two men who murdered our ruler. (*Zuǒ* Yǐn 4/6)

242. Fēi zhī zhī shí nán 非 知 之 實 難
It is not knowing it that is difficult. (*Zuǒ* Zhāo 10/5)

In other forms of Classical Chinese the demonstrative *shì* 是 may be used for the resumption of an exposed subject, e.g.,

243. Wáng zhī bù wàng shì zhé zhī zhī lèi yě 王 之 不 王 是 折 枝 之 類 也
Your Majesty's not achieving true Kingship is in the category of breaking a branch. (*Mèng* 1A/7)

244. Tiān yě, fēi rén yě, tiān zhī shēng shì shǐ dú yě 天 也 ， 非 人 也 。 天 之 生 是 使 獨 也
It was Heaven. It was not man. Heaven's giving me life it was that made me one-footed. (*Zhuāng* 3/13)

3. *Zé* 則 Marking Exposure

Besides its common function as a particle meaning 'then' introducing the apodosis of a condition, *zé* 則, which is no doubt deictic in origin, related to the demonstrative stem in *zī* 茲 'this, here,' *cǐ* 此 'this,' etc., is used to mark an exposed noun phrase as contrastive. Most commonly, but not exclusively, the exposed element is the subject.

245. Shì zé zī bù yuè 士 則 茲 不 悅
I, Shì, am not pleased at this. (*Mèng* 2B/12)

246. Shì zé kě yōu yě 是 則 可 憂 也
This is a thing to be concerned about. (*Mèng* 4B/28)

247. Kǒngzǐ yuē, shèng zé wú bù néng 孔 子 曰 ， 聖 則 吾 不 能
Confucius said, 'To be a sage I am not capable.' (*Mèng* 2A/2)

248. Niǎo zé zé mù, mù qǐ néng zé niǎo 鳥 則 擇 木 ， 木 豈 能 擇 鳥

The bird chooses its tree; how can a tree choose its bird? (*Zuǒ* Ai 11/6)

4. X *zhī yú* 之 於 Y

Both the subject and a postverbal element may be topicalized in a locative phrase with *yú* 於 nominalized by *zhī* 之. (See also Section V.6b.vii.)

> **249.** Jūnzǐ zhī yú qín shòu yě, jiàn qí shēng bù rěn jiàn qí sǐ
>
> 君子之於禽獸也，見其生不忍見其死
>
> A gentleman's attitude to birds and animals is that if he sees them alive he cannot bear to see them die. (*Mèng* 1A/7. Derived from *jūnzǐ jiàn qín shòu zhī shēng* ... 君子見禽獸之生 …)

Such nominalized phrases with *yú* 於 as the verb are not confined to topicalization. They occur in other situations where a main verb has been deleted.

> **250.** Zhōu Gōng zhī bù yǒu tiān xià, yóu Yì zhī yú Xià, Yī Yǐn zhī yú Yīn yě.
>
> 周公之不有天下，猶益之於夏，伊尹之於殷也
>
> The Duke of Zhōu's not possessing the empire was like Yì's situation in Xià, and Yī Yǐn's in Yīn. (*Mèng* 5A/6)

5. Other Particles Marking Topicalization or Contrastive Exposure

(a) Yě 也

The use of *yě* 也 in these constructions is illustrated in such examples as **249** above. It is found especially, as there, when the topic phrase is a nominalized verbal phrase. Compare the use of *yě* 也 after nominalized phrases that are objects of a verb. A further example is:

> **251.** Zhàng fū zhī guàn yě, fù mìng zhī, nǔ zǐ zhī jià yě, mǔ mìng zhī
>
> 丈夫之冠也，父命之，女子之嫁也，母命之
>
> The father orders the capping of a young man, the mother orders the marriage of a daughter. (*Mèng* 3B/2)

Topic marker use of *yě* 也 is also often found with proper names. This is particularly common in the *Lúnyǔ*, e.g.,

252. Lǐ yě sǐ, yǒu guān ér wú guǒ 鯉也死 ， 有棺而無椁

When Lǐ died, he had a coffin but no coffin case. (*LY* 11/8)

Note also *jīn yě* 今 也 'now,' placed contrastively at the head of a sentence, a usage similar to topicalization (see example **382** and XII.3a).

(b) Wéi 唯 (隹 ， 惟 ， 維)

The preclassical copula, *wéi* 唯, performs a similar role to *yě* 也 in the classical language in marking introductory noun phrases as topics, e.g.,

253. Wéi tiān yǒu hàn 維天有漢

In the sky there is the Milky Way. (*Shī* 203/5)

(c) Zhě 者

In addition to its role in nominalization (VII.2c), *zhě* 者 occurs after nouns in exposed position as a marker of contrastive emphasis.

254. Fú míng táng zhě, wáng zhě zhī táng yě 夫明堂者 ， 王者之堂也

The Hall of Light is a hall belonging to a King. (*Mèng* 1B/5)

Like *yě* 也 , *zhě* 者 is used after proper names. *Míng táng* 明堂 in the above example is really a proper noun. In the following example *zhě* 者 is used after a proper noun which is not in exposed position within its own clause but is effectively the exposed subject of the following clause.

255. Yǒu Yán Huí zhě, hào xué 有顏回者 ， 好學

There was Yán Huí. He loved learning. (*LY* 6/3)

In time expressions like *gǔ zhě* 古者 'in ancient times,' or *xī zhě* 昔者 'formerly' *zhě* 者 also has a similar function to *yě* 也 .

(d) Fú 夫

Fú 夫 (EMC buǎ) as a demonstrative pronoun is discussed in the next section. Its more common use is as an introductory particle announcing a topic as in example **254** above and the following. It often seems to have a generalizing force and is probably related to *fán* 凡 (EMC buam) 'all' (see XIII.1b).

256. Fú fū jiàn jí shì yuē, bǐ wū gǎn dāng wǒ zāi, cǐ pǐ fū zhī yǒng, dí yī rén zhě yě 夫撫劍疾視曰 ， 彼惡敢當我哉 ， 此匹夫之勇 ， 敵一人者也

To put one's hand on one's sword, look fierce and say 'How dare he face me,' is the courage of a common fellow, which is suitable only for confronting a single foe. (*Mèng* 1B/A)

257. Fú wǒ nǎi xíng zhī 夫 我 乃 行 之

As for me, I *did* it. (*Mèng* 1A/7)

Note that there is a double focus in the sentence: *I* (the king), in contrast to *you* (Mencius) and *did*, as opposed to *understood*. *Fú* 夫 emphasizes the subject while at the same time the effect of the particle *nǎi* 乃 is to throw emphasis forward on to the verb.

An important use of *fú* 夫 is with interrogative pronouns. The effect seems to be like adding 'ever' or the like in English. That is, it emphasizes the interrogative by widening its scope.

258. Fú shuí yǔ wáng dí 夫 誰 與 王 敵

Who in the world will oppose Your Majesty? (*Mèng* 1A/5)

(e) Rùo Fú 若 夫

Rùo fú 若 夫 'but as for...' introduces a topic contrasted with something immediately preceding.

259. Dài Wén Wáng ér hòu xīng zhě, fán mín yě. ruò fú háo jié zhī shì, suī wú Wén Wáng, yóu xīng 待 文 王 而 後 興 者 ，凡 民 也 。若 夫 豪 傑 之 士 ，雖 無 文 王 ， 猶 興

Those who wait for a King Wén to bestir themselves are ordinary men. As for real heroes, even without a King Wén they still bestir themselves. (*Mèng* 7A/10)

The first topic of such a correlative pair may be introduced by *nǎi ruò* 乃 若. This seems to be a locution peculiar to Mencius.

260. Nǎi ruò qí qíng zé kě yǐ wéi shàn yǐ, nǎi suǒ wèi shàn yě. Ruò fú wéi bù shàn, fēi cái zhī zuì yě 乃 若 其 情 則 可 以 為 善 矣 ，乃 所 謂 善 也 。若 夫 為 不 善 ，非 才 之 罪 也

As far as one's inner nature is concerned, one can be good. This is what I mean by [nature's being] good. As for becoming bad, it is not the fault of one's basic capacity. (*Mèng* 6A/6)

IX. Pronouns and Related Words[21]

1. Personal Pronouns

(a) *First Person*

There are two series of first person pronouns in Classical Chinese: (1) those with initial j- in Middle Chinese including *yú* 余 (EMC jiǎ), *yǔ* 予 (EMC jiǎ') and preclassical *yí* 台 (EMC jɨ), together with *zhèn* 朕 (EMC drim') which probably also had the same Old Chinese initial originally;[22] and (2) those with initial ŋ- in Middle Chinese, including *wú* 吾 (EMC ŋɔ) and *wǒ* 我 (EMC ŋaʼ) and preclassical *áng* 卬 (EMC ŋaŋ).[23] Judging by the use on the oracle bones in which *yú* 余 and *zhèn* 朕 refer (almost) exclusively to the king himself while *wǒ* 我 refers to Shang collectively, the original distinction was between singular (set 1) and plural (set 2).[24] By the time of the early Zhōu bronze inscriptions, the distinction was breaking down and it was becoming possible to use *wǒ* 我 as singular 'I', but the older usage continues in such expressions as *yú yī rén* 余 一 人 'I, one man,' the formula used by the Zhōu king, on the one hand, and *wǒ guó* 我 國 'our country' on the other. By classical times *yú* 余 and *yǔ* 予 were obsolescent and the ŋ- forms were normal in a singular as well as a plural sense. When *yú* 余 and *yǔ* 予 survive, they are still confined to the singular. In traditional reading pronunciation 予 is considered to be just a graphic alternative to 余 and is read *yú* (lower level tone) in the sense of 'I' in contrast to its reading *yǔ* (rising tone) in the sense of 'give.' In the *Shījīng*, however, it rhymes in rising tone in both senses. This is also true of the rhymes in the *Chǔcí*, which makes a clear distinction in usage between 余 and 予, resembling that between *wú* 吾 and *wǒ* 我, that is, reserving 予 to object position (mostly, but not exclusively postverbal).[25]

> **261.** Yǔ zhù miáo zhǎng yǐ 予 助 苗 長 矣
> I have been helping the sprouts to grow. (*Mèng* 2A/2)

Wú 吾 and *wǒ* 我 were differentiated in grammatical usage. *Wú* 吾 occurs only in front of the word on which it depends. It is most commonly possessive — *wú shǒu* 吾 手 'my hand' — or subjective — *wú lái* 吾 來 'I come' or 'my coming,' but it can also appear as an object standing between a negative particle and the verb: *bù wú zhī* 不 吾 知 'does not know me.' *Wǒ* 我 can occur both in front of a noun, as possessive, or a verb, as subject, and after a verb as object. It seems to be more emphatic and contrastive than *wú* 吾 and might be compared to the disjunctive form *moi* in French versus *me* or *je*.

> **262.** Zēngzǐ yuē, 'Jìn Chǔ zhī fù bù kě jí yě. Bǐ yǐ qí fù, wǒ yǐ wú rén, bǐ yǐ qí jué, wǒ yǐ wú yì, wú hé qiàn hū zāi'. 晉 楚 之 富 不 可 及 也 ，彼 以 其 富 ，我 以 吾 仁 ，彼 以 其 爵 ，我 以 吾 義 ，吾 何 慊 乎 哉
>
> Zēngzǐ said, 'The wealth of Jìn and Chǔ cannot be attained to. They with their wealth, I with my benevolence, they with their honours, I with my righteousness, why should I be dissatisfied?' (*Mèng* 2B/2)

In this passage where there is strong contrast — *I* as opposed to *they* — *wǒ* 我 is used; otherwise *wú* 吾.[26]

    Preclassical *yí* 台 (with various alternative graphic forms on inscriptions) and *zhèn* 朕 are mostly possessive, occasionally nominative. They are very rare in texts of the classical period. The First Emperor of Qín chose *zhèn* 朕 as a special first person pronoun for his own use and thereafter it survived through imperial times as a way for the emperor to refer to himself. Preclassical *áng* 卬 occurs in a handful of examples in the *Shījīng* and *Shūjīng*, mostly but not exclusively as a singular.

    Various expressions of a self-deprecatory nature were commonly used in place of first person pronouns, e.g., *guǎrén* 寡人 'bereft person,' *gū* 孤 'orphan,' *bùgǔ* 不榖 'unworthy' — terms used by rulers; *chén* 臣 'your subject' — used by a minister to his ruler; *pú* 僕 'your slave' — used between equals (Japanese *boku*); *qiè* 妾 'your slave' — used by women; *qiè* 竊 'private' — used in documentary style (compare Japanese *watakushi*). Another humble way of referring to oneself was by use of one's personal name (*míng* 名).

(b) *Second Person*

The various forms of the second person pronoun originally all had initial *n-, like cognate forms in Tibeto-Burman. The ancestral form of modern *nǐ* 你 was *ěr* 爾 (EMC ɲiă'), perhaps originally pronounced something like *nəjʔ. By regular phonetic change, the reading form became *ěr* but in the colloquial language it became *nǐ*, now written 你. Other forms were *rǔ* 汝 (EMC ɲiă') often written 女, *ér* 而 (EMC ɲi), *ruò* 若 (EMC ɲiak) and, in the preclassical language, *nǎi* 乃 (EMC nəj') and *róng* 戎 (EMC ɲuwŋ). In classical texts, both *ěr* 爾 and *rǔ* 汝 are used both as subject and object. There are differences in usage in different texts but what these are has not been clearly established. *Ér* 而, like *wú* 吾, is used only as subject or possessive. It is comparatively uncommon.

263. Yú ér zǔ yě 余 而 祖 也
I am your grandfather. (*Zuǒ* Xuān 3/9)

264. Ér nǎi jīn zhī zhī hū 而 乃 今 知 之 乎
Do you know it now? (*Zhuāng* 7.1)

Ruò 若 is common in the *Zhuāngzǐ* and some later texts, but is not found in the *Mencius* or earlier texts. It occurs as both subject and object.

Several of the words meaning 'you' are homophonous with words meaning 'like,' 'thus,' etc. and are written with the same characters: *ěr* 爾 'thus, so,' *ruò* 若 'like,' *ér* 而 'so, then,' *nǎi* 乃 'then.' Compare also *rú* 如 'like,' which differs only in tone from *rǔ* 汝 'you.' In preclassical texts, *nǎi* 'then' was written with a different character, 廼, distinct from *nǎi* 乃 'you, your,' which suggests that it may also have been pronounced differently. The roots for 'you' and 'like' may have originally differed in some way in their initial consonants.

Corresponding to the humble forms used for the first person are numerous honorific forms used as terms of address. One mode of honorific address is to use the appropriate title, e.g., *wáng* 王 'your majesty.' More general terms are *jūn* 君 'lord,' *gōng* 公 'lord,' *qīng* 卿 'minister' (used by a ruler to his minister), *zǐ* 子 'master' or 'sir' (also *fū zǐ* 夫 子, *wú zǐ* 吾 子). Note the expression *bì xià* 陛 下 'your majesty,' literally 'beneath the steps (of the throne).' The subject, not daring to address the ruler directly, addresses instead the servant seated below. Similar expressions, graded by the rank of the person addressed, were *diàn xià* 殿 下 'your highness,' *gé xià* 閣 下 'your excellency.' *Zú xià* 足 下 'beneath the feet' was originally an expression of the same kind which came to be used as a respectful address between men of more or less equal rank. *Xiān shēng* 先 生 'elder born' appears as early as the Warring States, used especially to teachers.

Such honorifics could in many cases also be used when referring to others in the third person.

(c) *Third Person*

There is no general third person pronoun equivalent to modern *tā* 他, which has the reading pronunciation *tuō* and means 'other' in Classical Chinese.

(i) *Zhī* 之 comes closest to being a general third person pronoun. It is, however, almost exclusively confined to being object of a verb or coverb; *shā zhī* 殺 之 'kills him,' *yóu zhī* 由 之 'from it.' One must, of course, distinguish the object pronoun *zhī* 之 from the verb *zhī* 之 'go to,' written with the same character. The mark of noun subordination *zhī* 之, on the other hand, is no doubt etymologically related to the pronoun.

In rare instances in a few texts, notably the *Shījīng* and *Zhuāngzǐ*, *zhī* 之 occurs as an attributive demonstrative 'this':

265. Zhī èr chóng yòu hé zhī 之 二 蟲 又 何 知
And what do these two worms know? (*Zhuāng* 1.10)

As noted above, *zhī* 之 is always omitted after *yǐ* 以 in pre-Han texts, and *yǐ* 以 alone is then equivalent to *yǐ zhī* 以 之. The omission of *zhī* 之 with the negative particles *bù* 不, *fú* 弗, etc., is discussed below.

Zhī 之 forms part of a number of contractions:

- *zhū* 諸 = 之 + 乎 : *yǒu zhū* 有 諸 'is it so?' = 有 之 乎
- *zhū* 諸 = 之 + 於 (or perhaps better 之 + 乎, where 乎 is a variant of 於 (V.6b(iii)): *jiā zhū bǐ* 加 諸 彼 'apply it to those' = 加 之 於 彼
- *zhān* 旃 = 之 + 焉 (comparatively uncommon, there are a few examples in *Zuǒzhuàn*)
- *nài hé* 奈 何 = *ruò zhī hé* 若 之 何 (see IV.8g).

On *yān* 焉 as a substitute for *yú* 於 + *zhī* 之, which is not a contraction, see (e) below. So also *rán* 然 and *yún* 云 as equivalents to *rú* 如 + *zhī* 之 (f) and *yuē* 曰 + *zhī* 之 (g). On *fú* 弗 and *wù* 勿 which did not originate as contractions but were apparently interpreted as equivalent to *bù* 不 + *zhī* 之 and *wú* 毋 + *zhī* 之 in Warring States times, see XI.1c and XI.2b.

For the use of *zhī* 之 to repeat an exposed object placed in front of the verb, see Section VIII.1.

(ii) There is no third personal subject pronoun as such. When one is required for contrast or emphasis one of the demonstrative pronouns is used.

266. Shì Lǔ Kǒng Chiū yú 是 魯 孔 丘 與
Is he Kǒng Chiū of Lǔ? (*LY* 18.6)

267. Bǐ zhàng fū yě, wǒ zhàng fū yě, wú hé wèi bǐ zāi 彼 丈 夫 也，我 丈 夫 也，吾 何 畏 彼 哉
He is a man, I am a man. Why should I be in awe of him? (*Mèng* 3A/1)

Otherwise a third person subject is expressed by its noun or omitted altogether, sometimes even when the subject changes.

(iii) *qí* 其 as a pronoun serves as a substitute for Noun + 之, either in front of another noun (possessive) or in front of a verb (nominalization): *qí qī* 其 妻 'his wife,' *qí lái* 其 來 'his coming.'

Qí 其 as a possessive pronoun must be distinguished from the modal particle *qí* written with the same character (XII.3a). Attempts have been made to derive one from the other but they have not proved convincing so far. The modal particle, which is found already on the oracle bones, is the older form. The possessive pronoun *qí* is not found on the oracle bones, early bronze inscriptions, or the genuine parts of the *Shūjīng*, where one has instead *jué* 厥. The *Shījīng* uses both, *jué* being confined almost exclusively to the *Dàyǎ* and *Sòng* sections which are thought to be earlier. *Jué* does not occur except in quotations in texts of the classical period.[27]

In the Warring States period, *qí* 其 is sometimes found as a demonstrative, more or less equivalent to a definite article, rather than a possessive, e.g.,

268. Qí rén fú néng yìng yě 其 人 弗 能 應 也
The man could not answer. (*HF* 36, p. 265)

(iv) Postclassical third person pronouns include *yī* 伊, *qú* 渠, and *tā* 他. *Tā* 他 begins to occur in the modern sense in colloquial passages in post-Hàn texts.

(v) *Yān* 焉 behaves like a combination **yú zhī* 於 之, which is never found. Though equivalent to **yú zhī* 於 之 in meaning, *yán* 焉 . is clearly not derived phonologically from a fusion of these two elements. It is probably derived from *yú* 於 by the addition of a suffix *-n inherited from Sino-Tibetan that may originally have been been a mark of non-perfective or durative aspect, the anaphoric pronominal meaning being a secondary development. [28]

269. Wàn qǔ qiān yān ... 萬 取 千 焉
10,000, to take 1,000 *from it* ... (*Mèng* 1A/1. Topicalized form of *qǔ qiān yú wàn* 取 千 於 萬 'to take 1,000 from 10,000').

270. Sī tiān xià zhī mín zhì yān 斯 天 下 之 民 至 焉
Then the people of the world will come *to him*. (*Mèng* 1A/3)

271. Dài yǒu shèn yān 殆 有 甚 焉
It may be even worse *than that*. (*Mèng* 1A/7)

In some texts (though not in the *Mencius* or *Lúnyǔ*) *yān* 焉 can occur before the verb in the sense of 於 是 *yú shì* 'then.'

272. Bì zhī luàn zhī suǒ zì qǐ, yān néng chí zhī 必 知 亂 之 所 自 起 ， 焉 能 治 之

One must know where disorder arises from, then one can control it. (*Mò* 14/1)

In Middle Chinese the postverbal particle, *yān* 焉 'in it, there,' had a voiced onset (EMC ian) which should have given a modern pronunciation *yán* in second tone, while the interrogative *yān* 焉 'where, how' had a glottal stop (EMC ʔian) corresponding to the modern pronunciation in the first tone. This distinction is still maintained in reading pronunciation in some dialects such as Cantonese. Nevertheless, the two words no doubt have a common origin. The initial glottal stop would have been lost in the postverbal particle because it was always enclitic, that is, an unaccented word pronounced in close association with the preceding word.[29] *An* 安 (EMC ʔan) which is a variant of *yān* 焉 as an interrogative particle, also occurs occasionally in preverbal position in the sense of 'then.'

273. ... ér bào guó ān zì huà yǐ ··· 而 暴 國 安 自 化 矣

... and rebellious countries will *then* transform themselves. (*Xún* 7/14)

In this sense *àn* 案 is sometimes written instead of *ān* 安 . This seems to imply the addition of a formative suffix *-s but examples are so few that one suspects it may be simply an arbitrary graphic distinction.

(vi) *Rán* 然 '(it is) so' bears the same relationship to *rú* 如 'like' that *yān* 焉 does to *yú* 於 . Thus, it can be a complete sentence: *Rán* 然 'It is so'; or an initial clause: *rán zé* 然 則 'if it is so, then ...'; *suī rán* 雖 然 'though it is so ...'; or an imbedded sentence as in *shǐ zhī rán* 使 之 然 'make it so,' etc. For examples see **11, 36, 210, 228**, etc. For use of *rán* to form adverbs of manner, see X.5. For the conjunction *ránhòu* 然 後 'afterwards' see XV.4f.

(vii) *Yún* 云 , EMC wun, 'say (so)' bears a similar relation to *yuē* 曰 , EMC wuat, 'say,' which like *yú* 於 and *rú* 如 (in the sense of 'be like') is never followed by the object pronoun *zhī* 之 .

274. Yuē, cóng yú yán, bì wéi Mèng sūn. Zài sàn yún. Jié cóng zhī. 曰 ， 從 余 言 ， 必 為 孟 孫 。 再 三 云 。 羯 從 之

He said, 'If you follow my advice, you will certainly be the heir of the Mèngs.' He said it two or three times. Jié followed his advice. (*Zuǒ* Xiāng 23/11)

275. Jìn Píng Gōng zhī yú Hài Táng yě, rù yún zé rù, zuò yún zé zuò, shí yún zé shí 晉平公之於亥唐也，入云則入，坐云則坐，食云則食

Duke Píng of Jìn's behaviour towards Hài Táng was that when he (Táng) said 'enter' he entered, when he said 'sit' he sat, when he said 'eat' he ate. (*Mèng* 5B/3)

In normal word order the quoted phrases 'enter,' 'sit,' and 'eat' would follow the verb of saying, *yuē* 曰, in object position. Here they are placed in front of the verb because they are rhetorically in contrast, a construction that requires recapitulation by a pronoun after the verb (VIII.1). Therefore *yún* 云 is used instead of *yuē* 曰.

The contrast between *yún* 云 and *yuē* 曰 was probably originally aspectual, that is, 'say' as an indefinite act without any time reference (*yún*) versus 'say' as a definite act on a particular occasion (*yuē*). Thus, *yún* 云 is often used to introduce quotations from books, as in: *Shī yún* 詩 云 'The Book of Odes says' in contrast to *yuē* 曰, which introduces words spoken on a particular occasion. It can also be used as an intransitive verb 'to speak,' as in the phrase *mò yún* 墨 云 'be silent or speak' (*Xún* 21/46), or in an example like the following:

276. Zhòngfù zhī bìng bìng yǐ, kě bù huì yún 仲父之病病矣，可不諱（謂）云

Your illness is critical, you may speak without avoidance. (*Zhuāng* 24/51)[30]

Yún 云 may close a quotation introduced by *yuē* 曰. In many such cases, the quotation is not a main predicate but forms part of a subordinate clause. *Yuē* 曰 is never nominalized by insertion of *zhī* 之 after the subject or by *qí* 其 standing for N + *zhī* 之. Instead the clause introduced by *yuē* 曰 is placed in apposition to *yún* 云 'say so,' as here:

277. Zǐ yūē, rǔ ān zhī yú lè yún zhě 子曰，汝安知魚樂云者

When you said, 'How do you know the fishes' pleasure?' (*Zhuāng* 17/90. Literally: You say, 'You how know fishes' pleasure' say-so thing.')

Compare the use of *rán* 然 to close an expression introduced by *rú* 如 or *ruò* 若.

278. Jīn yán wàng ruò yì rán, zé Wén Wáng bù zú fǎ yú 今言
王 若 易 然 ， 則 文 王 不 足 法 與

Now when you speak of kingship as being easy, [does it mean
that] King Wén (who did not achieve kingship in his lifetime) was
not worthy of being taken as a model? (*Mèng* 2A/1)

   Yún ěr 云 爾 'say thus' after a quotation introduced by *yuē* 曰
indicates imagined speech.[31] (For *ěr* 爾 'thus' see IX.2i below.)

279. Qí xīn yuē, shì hé zú yǔ yán rén yì yě yún ěr 其 心 曰 ，
是 何 足 與 言 仁 義 也 云 爾

In their hearts they say, 'How is he worthy to be spoken to about
benevolence or righteousness?' (*Mèng* 2B/2)

(d) *Reflexive Personal Pronoun*

The reflexive personal pronoun *jǐ* 己 'self' is used as a pronoun in all
positions — subject or object of a verb and attributive to a noun. It thus
differs syntactically from the reflexive pronominal adverb *zì* 自 (XIII.4)
which always occurs immediately in front of the verb.

280. Shè zhě zhèng jǐ ér hòu fā 射 者 正 己 而 後 發

An archer sets himself correctly before he shoots. (*Mèng* 2A/7)

281. Fú rén zhě, jǐ yù lì ér lì rén, jǐ yù dá ér dá rén 夫 仁 者 ，
己 欲 立 而 立 人 ， 己 欲 達 而 達 人

The man of virtue, himself wishing to be established, establishes
others, himself wishing to advance, advances others. (*LY* 6/30)

282. Rén yǐ wéi jǐ rèn 仁 以 為 己 任

Virtue he takes to be his own responsibility. (*LY* 8/7)

Jǐ 己, unlike *zì* 自, can be an indirect reflexive, referring not to the subject
of its own verb but to that of a clause in which its clause is embedded.

283. Wú yǒu bù rú jǐ zhě 無 友 不 如 己 者

Do not make friends of those who are your inferiors. (*LY* 1/8; *bù
zì rú* 不 自 如 would mean 'not equal to themselves.')

284. Bù huàn rén zhī bú jǐ zhī 不 患 人 之 不 己 知

I do not worry that people do not know me. (*LY* 1/16. Not: *bù zì
zhī* 不 自 知 'do not know themselves.')

Note that *shēn* 身 'body, person' can also be used as equivalent to a
reflexive pronoun.

285. Shēn wéi tiānzǐ, dì wéi pǐfū, kě wèi qīn ài zhī hū 身為天
子，弟為匹夫，可謂親愛之乎

Being himself Son of Heaven and his younger brother being a
commoner, could he have been said to have treated his brother with
the love due to a close relative? (*Mèng* 5A/3)

(e) *Personal Pronouns with Negative Particles*

One of the special rules of word order in Classical Chinese is that personal
pronoun objects are placed between the negative particle and the verb
(II.3c.ii). In addition to the following examples, see **284** above.

286. Fù mǔ zhī bù wǒ ài 父母之不我愛

That my parents do not love me … (*Mèng* 5A/1)

287. Gù bù wú yuàn yě 故不吾遠也

Therefore he did not keep me at a distance. (*Zuǒ* Zhāo 20/3)

288. Lóugōu bù yú qī yě 僂句不余欺也

The Lóugōu [tortoise-shell] did not deceive me. (*Zuǒ* Zhāo 25/*fù* 3)

289. Méng yuē, wǒ wú ěr zhà, ěr wú wǒ yú 盟曰，我無
爾詐，爾無我虞

Their covenant was: Let us not deceive you, let you not be
concerned about us. (*Zuǒ* Xuān 15/2)

The third person pronoun *zhī* 之 is normally omitted when its verb is
governed by the particle of simple negation *bù* 不 'not' or the negative
imperative (or subjunctive) *wú* 毋 (無) 'do not.'

290. Shú néng yǔ zhī? Tiān xià mò bù yǔ 孰能與之。天
下莫不與

'Who can give it *to him*?'… 'No one in the world will not give it
(to him).' (*Mèng* 1A/6)

291. Qí qǔ zhū mín zhī bù yì yě, ér yǐ tuō cí wú shòu bù kě hū
其取諸民之不義也，而以他辭無受不可乎

Is it not possible to refuse to accept it (無受) because his taking
it from the people was unrighteous but giving another reason?
(*Mèng* 5B/4)

For *zhī* 之 placed in front of *bù* 不 when it recapitulates an object
preposed for contrast or emphasis in the language of the *Zuǒzhuàn*, see
VIII.1 above.

Exceptionally, especially when the perfect particle yǐ 矣 is added, zhī 之 may follow the verb even after a negative. This seems to make the statement more emphatic.

292. Shèng rén wú bù dé ér jiàn zhī yǐ 聖人吾不得而見之矣

A sage I shall not get to see. (*LY* 7/26)

This is especially common with the negative particles *fú* 弗, *wù* 勿 and *miè* 蔑 which originally ended in *-t. See XI.1c, XI.2b, XI.2h. Occasional examples in which other personal pronouns follow a negated verb also occur.

293. Yǒu shì ér bù gào wǒ, bì bù jié yǐ 有事而不告我，必不捷矣

If you have some business and don't tell me, it will certainly not succeed. (*Zuǒ* Xiāng 28/6)

294. Fú bù wù rǔ hū 夫不惡女乎

Does he not hate you? (*Zuǒ* Xiāng 26/6)

With the negative particles *wèi* 未 and *mò* 莫, zhī 之 is normally retained but placed between the negative and the verb.

295. Chén wèi zhī wén yě 臣未之聞也

Your servant has never heard about them. (*Mèng* 1A/7)

296. Mò zhī néng yù yě 莫之能禦也

No one can prevent it. (*Mèng* 1A/7)

2. Demonstratives

The three main demonstrative pronouns in Classical Chinese are *shì* 是, *cǐ* 此, and *bǐ* 彼. *Shì* 是 is usually anaphoric (referring back to something), with no particular implication of closeness or remoteness. It may be translated by either 'this' or 'that'; *Cǐ* 此 and *bǐ* 彼, on the other hand, make a contrast between 'this (here)' and 'that (over there).'

(a) Shì 是

Shì 是 may be used pronominally or adjectivally to refer to persons or things and as a pronoun may be subject or object of a verb. On its function to recapitulate a phrase or series of phrases which is the subject of a noun predication, out of which its later use as a copula developed, see III.4 above.

Probably because of the frequent collocation: *shì* 是 X *yě* 也, *fēi* 非 Y *yě* 也 'It is X, it is not Y,' *shì* 是 and *fēi* 非 came to be regarded as opposites and were used in the senses 'right' and 'wrong,' 'to call right,' and 'to call wrong.' This usage is not found (or is very rare) in *Zuǒzhuàn*, *Lúnyǔ,* and earlier texts but is common in *Mencius* and other texts of the Warring States period.[32]

297. Yǎn zhī chéng shì yě ... 掩 之 誠 是 也
If [merely] covering them (i.e., the bodies of dead parents) were really right ... (*Mèng* 3A/5)

298. Wú shì fēi zhī xīn, fēi rén yě 無 是 非 之 心，非 人 也
Not to have a mind which calls things right or wrong is not human. (*Mèng* 2A/6)

Shì 是 forms part of the common sentence connectives *shì gù* 是 故 'for this reason, therefore,' *yú shì* 於 是 'thereupon,' and *shì yǐ* 是 以 'therefore.' The word order in the last of these can be explained as preposing for the sake of topicalization, the expected repetition of the object by *zhī* 之 being omitted, as always, after *yǐ* 以. *Yǐ shì* 以 是 also occurs in the full sense 'because of this.' Note also *yú shì hū* 於 是 乎 for *yú shì* 於 是 in the *Zuǒzhuàn*.

For the use of *shì* 是 (like *zhī* 之) to resume a preposed object, see Section VIII on Topicalization.

(b) Cǐ 此

Cǐ 此 'this (here),' like *shì* 是, occurs freely as subject, object, or attributive. It can also be used to resume a phrase which is the subject of a noun predication.

299. Cǐ shuài shòu ér shí rén yě 此 率 獸 而 食 人 也
This is leading animals to eat men. (*Mèng* 1A/4)
It did not, however, become a copula.

(c) Bǐ 彼

Like *shì* 是 and *cǐ* 此, *bǐ* 彼 can be used either attributively or as an independent pronoun, but it is most frequent as the latter. In the latter usage it frequently has a personal reference, taking the place of a third personal pronoun. In this respect it differs from *shì* 是 and *cǐ* 此, which are occasionally found with personal reference but are mostly not so used.

300. Bǐ yī shí, cǐ yī shí yě 彼 一 時 ， 此 一 時 也
That was one time, this is another time. (Impersonal reference; *Mèng* 2B/13)

301. Bǐ duó qí mín shí 彼 奪 其 民 時
Those (other rulers) rob their people of their proper seasons. (Personal reference; *Mèng* 1A/5)

302. Bǐ wū zhī zhī 彼 惡 知 之
How were they (i.e., *those* people who criticized the king) to know it? (Personal reference; *Mèng* 1A/7)

We find it used attributively in:

303. Xiàng bù dé yǒu wéi yú qí guó. Tiānzǐ shǐ lì chí qí guó ér nà qí gòng shuì yān. gù wèi zhī fàng, qǐ bào bǐ mín zāi. 象 不 得 有 為 於 其 國 。 天 子 使 吏 治 其 國 而 納 其 貢 稅 焉 。 故 謂 之 放 ， 豈 暴 彼 民 哉
Xiàng was not able to play an active role in his kingdom. The Son of Heaven sent an official to govern his kingdom and to pay its tribute and taxes to him (i.e., to Xiang). Hence one refers to him as 'banished.' How could he have been allowed to oppress those people [of his kingdom]? (*Mèng* 5A/3)

In the following example, note the attributive use of *bǐ* 彼 with a general rather than a particular reference.

304. Bǐ qiè gōu zhě zhū, qiè guó zhě wéi zhū hóu 彼 竊 鉤 者 誅 ， 竊 國 者 為 諸 侯
The (literally: that) stealer of a clasp is executed; one who steals a country becomes a feudal lord. (*Zhuāng* 10/19)

As is apparent from the translation, this shift from a particularizing to a generalizing meaning may be compared to one use of the definite article in English ('the tiger is a tawny beast' — not one particular tiger but any tiger).

Bǐ 彼 sometimes forms a possessive by adding *zhī* 之 , as in:

305. Bēi fú. Shì rén yǐ xíng sè míng shēng wéi zú yǐ dé bǐ zhī qíng 悲 夫 ， 世 人 以 形 色 名 聲 為 足 以 得 彼 之 情
Is it not sad? The people of the world think that the form, color, name, and sound (of something) are sufficient to get the nature of that (thing)? (*Zhuāng* 13/67)

An alternative construction in which *qí* 其 is inserted between the demonstrative and the noun is also found.

306. Bǐ qí dào yuǎn ér xiǎn 彼其道遠而險
The road to that place is long and perilous. (*Zhuāng* 20/17)

The same thing is also found occasionally with other demonstratives.

307. Cǐ qí gù hé yě 此其故何也
What is the reason for this? (*Mò* 9/38)

The following are less common demonstratives.

(d) Sī 斯

Sī 斯 'this,' is used in place of *cǐ* 此 in the *Lúnyǔ* and the 'Tán Gōng' 檀弓 section of the *Lǐjì*, which is closely akin to the *Lúnyǔ*.

308. Qí sī zhī wèi yú 其斯之謂與
Surely it means this. (*LY* 1/15)

309. Lǐ zhī yòng, hé wéi guì, xiān wáng zhī dào, sī wéi měi 禮之用，和為貴，先王之道，斯為美
In the carrying out of ritual, harmony is the most important; in the way of the ancient kings, this was the greatest excellence. (*LY* 1/12)

310. Jūnzǐ zhī zhì yú sī yě, wú wèi cháng bù dé jiàn yān 君子之至於斯也，吾未嘗不得見焉
When superior men have come here, I have never failed to meet them. (*LY* 3/24)

It also occurs a few times in this sense in the *Odes* and in *Mencius* (only attributively, see example **475**) but seldom elsewhere.[33] In other texts it is only a connective, 'then.'

(e) Zī 茲

Zī 茲 (EMC tsɨ) 'this' is normal as a near demonstrative in the oracle bones and bronze inscriptions, the *Shūjīng,* and in the Zhōu Sòng 周頌 and Dà Yǎ 大雅 *Odes*. It survives to a limited extent in classical texts. We find it used adverbially in the following two passages in *Mencius*:

311. Jīn zī wèi néng 今茲未能
For the present I am not yet able. (*Mèng* 3B/8)

312. Shì, zé zī bù yuè 士 ， 則 茲 不 悅
I, Shì, am displeased at this. (*Mèng* 2B/12)

(f) Shí 實 *and* Shí 寔

Shí 實 (EMC ʑit, for *dʑit ?) and the variant *shí* 寔 (EMC dʑik) represent
a pronoun related to *shì* 是 (EMC dʑiă') that is found in the *Shūjīng*,
Zuǒzhuàn, and *Guóyǔ*. It is used to recapitulate the subject and mark it as
contrastive (see VIII.2 above).[34]

313. Rén shí yǒu guó 人 實 有 國
It is others who possess the country. (*Zuǒ* Xī 9 *fù* 2)

(g) Shí 時

Shí 時 (EMC dʑi) 'this,' also related to *shì* 是, is found only in the
preclassical language. At that period it seems to be a relatively unemphatic
form as opposed to both *shì* 是 and *shí* 實.

314. Yǒng xí ěr jí, shí wàn shí yì 永 錫 爾 極 ， 時 萬 時
億
Forever they will give you the utmost blessings; they will be in
myriads, in myriads of myriads. (*Shī* 209/4 Cf. Karlgren 1950a)

(h) Fú 夫

Fú 夫 'that' (EMC buă, to be distinguished from *fū* 夫 EMC puă 'man,
male person' written with the same character) is probably related to *bǐ* 彼
'that' (EMC piă'), though the voiced initial is a problem.[35] Though fairly
common in the *Zuǒzhuàn*, it is less so in later Warring States texts.

315. Suī Chǔ yǒu cái, Jìn shí yòng zhī. Zǐmù yuē, fú dú wú zú
yīn hū? Duì yuē, suī yǒu ér yòng Chǔ cái shí duō. 雖 楚 有
財 ， 晉 實 用 之 。 子 木 曰 ， 夫 獨 無 族 姻 乎 。
對 曰 。 雖 有 而 用 楚 財 實 多
'Though Chǔ has the talent, it is Jìn that makes use of it.' Zǐmù
said, 'Are *they* (i.e., the Jìn rulers) alone without clansmen and
relatives by marriage?' He replied, 'Though they have, their use of
talent from Chǔ, *that* is greater.' (*Zuǒ* Xiāng 26 *fù* 6)

316. Fú Yǐn Shì wū zhī yǔ zāi 夫 尹 士 惡 知 予 哉
How should *that* Yǐn Shì know me? (*Mèng* 2B/12. Though this is

the standard interpretation, it seems possible to interpret *fú* here is the generalizing particle: '*any* Yīn Shì ... ')

(i) Ěr 爾

Besides *rán* 然, discussed above, *ěr* 爾 and *ruò* 若 (next section), among the words derived from the family of words beginning in *n- meaning 'like, so, etc.' are used as demonstrative pronouns. In this sense *ěr* 爾 is sometimes said to be a fusion of *rú cǐ* 如 此 but, though *cǐ* 此 and *ěr* 爾 rhymed in Middle Chinese, they are usually considered the rhyme to come from different Old Chinese rhyme groups. In the classical period, *ěr* 爾 is more like an independent pronoun than a combination of verb and pronoun. While *bù rán* 不 然 is common, *bù ěr* 不 爾 only occurs in post-Hàn texts and only with the meaning, 'if it is not so.'

> **317.** Dé qí xīn yǒu dào. Suǒ yù yǔ zhī jù zhī, suǒ wù wù shī ěr yě 得其心有道。所欲與之聚之，所惡勿施爾也
>
> There is a way to gain their hearts. It is thus — what they desire, gather for them, what they hate, do not impose. (*Mèng* 4A/10)

As here, and in the expression *yún ěr* 云 爾 (see example **279** above), *ěr* 爾 is most frequently found at the end of a sentence, but it can also occur attributively as in:

> **318.** Fēi tiān zhī jiàng cái ěr shū yě 非天之降才爾殊也
> It is not that Heaven's bestowing of talent is so different. (*Mèng* 6A/7)

(j) Ruò 若

In the preclassical language, *ruò* 若 was a verb meaning 'agree, accord with, conform to, etc.' and could also be used adverbially in the sense of 'thus,' for example, in the frequent formula *wáng ruò yuē* 王 若 曰 'The king thus said ...' at the beginning of bronze inscriptions. Besides its other uses in the classical language as a verb meaning 'like,' a conjunction 'if,' etc., we sometimes find what appears to be a survival of its earlier usage when it is found attributively to an embedded clause in the sense of 'that kind of, such.'

> **319.** Yǐ ruò suǒ wéi qiú ruò suǒ yù 以若所為求若所欲

To seek for that sort of wish with that sort of action (*Mèng* 1A/7)

3. Interrogatives

Interrogative pronouns fall into two main groups: (a) those referring primarily to persons, which begin with dʑ- in Middle Chinese pronunciation — *shuí* 誰 and *shú* 孰; (b) those referring primarily to things, which begin with ɣ- in Middle Chinese pronunciation — *hé* 何, *xī* 奚, *hé* 曷, *hú* 胡, *hé* 盍, etc. A third group, (c) with initial glottal stop in Middle Chinese appear to be derived from the coverb *yú* 於 with the addition of various elements — *ān* 安, *yān* 焉, *wū* 惡, *wū hū* 惡乎, etc.

(a)(i) *Shuí* 誰

Shuí 誰 (EMC dʑwi) 'who' can be either subject or object. Note that it precedes the verb even when it is the object. It can also appear as the complement in a noun predication.

320. ... yóu shuǐ zhī jiù xià, pèirán shuí néng yù zhī 由水之就下，沛然誰能禦之

... like water going downward in a torrent, who can stop it? (*Mèng* 1A/6)

321. Xiàng rén zhǎng yú bó xiōng yì suì, zé shuí jìng 鄉人長於伯兄一歲，則誰敬

[Suppose that] a man of the village is a year older than your elder brother, then which do you respect? (*Mèng* 6A/5)

322. Zhuī wǒ zhě shuí yě 追我者誰也

Who is it that is pursuing me? (*Mèng* 4B/24)

With the copula verb *wéi* 為, *shuí* 誰 follows.

323. Zǐ wéi shuí 子為誰

Who are you? (*LY* 18/6)

As object of most coverbs *shuí* 誰 precedes in the normal way.

324. Wáng shuí yǔ wéi shàn 王誰與為善

With whom (i.e., with whose help) will the king do good? (*Mèng* 3B/6)

With *yú* 於, which has the syntax of a copula, it follows.

325. Dào qiè zhī xíng, yú shuí zé ér kě hū 盜竊之行，於誰責而可乎

For the thefts and robberies, on whom is it right to lay the blame? (*Zhuāng* 25/50)

When used possessively, *shuí* 誰 is mostly followed by *zhī* 之.

326. Shì shuí zhī guò yǔ 是 誰 之 過 與

Whose fault is this? (*LY* 16/1)

In Hàn and later texts *zhī* 之 may be omitted: *shuí zǐ* 誰 子 'whose son.'

Shuí 誰 may also occur attributively, without *zhī* 之, before nouns referring to human beings, where it must be translated into English as 'what' or 'which' — *shuí shì* 誰 氏 'what clan?,' *shuí rén* 誰 人 'what man?'

(ii) *Shú* 孰 'which'

Shú 孰 (EMC dʑuwk) is one of a group of words in *-k including *gè* 各 (EMC kak) 'each,' *huò* 或 (EMC ɣwək) 'some,' and *mò* 莫 (EMC mak) 'none,' which are confined to preverbal position referring to the subject, and which usually select the subject from a larger group.

327. Zōu rén yǔ Chǔ rén zhàn, zé wáng yǐ wéi shú shèng 鄒 人 與 楚 人 戰 ， 則 王 以 為 孰 勝

If the men of Zōu fought with the men of Chǔ, which does Your Majesty think would win? (*Mèng* 1A/7)

It is often found in comparisons.

328. wú zǐ yǔ Zǐ Lù shú xián 吾 子 與 子 路 孰 賢

As between you, sir, and Zǐ Lù , which is superior? (*Mèng* 2A/1)

Sometimes the group from which *shú* 孰 selects is indefinite and the meaning is hardly different from *shuí* 誰 referring to the subject.

329. Shú néng yī zhī ... Shú néng yǔ zhī 孰 能 一 之 。 ··· 孰 能 與 之

Who can unite it? ... Who can give it to him? (*Mèng* 1A/6)

In the first case the set of possible subjects is, no doubt, a limited one, the rulers of states, and *shú* 孰 might be rendered 'which (ruler),' but in the second case it is not obvious how one could define such a limited set.

Shú 孰 sometimes refers to things, replacing *hé* 何 which cannot normally be used for the subject.

330. Dú lè yuè, yǔ rén lè yuè, shú lè 獨 樂 樂 ， 與 人 樂 樂 ， 孰 樂

Which is better, to enjoy music alone or to enjoy music with other people? (*Mèng* 1B/1)

In the previous examples which involve comparisons between two things, A and B, the pattern is A (與) B 孰 + Adj. This is the normal word order with such words that define the scope of the subject (see Section XI). The order A 孰 與 B + Adj. is also found. This is a possible word order at surface level because of the verbal nature of the coverb *yǔ* 與. It preserves the order Subj. + *shú* 孰 + V.

331. Zǎo jiù zhī, shú yǔ wǎn jiù zhī biàn 早救之，孰與晚救之便

Would it be more convenient to go to their aid earlier rather than later? (*ZGC*, Qí cè 50/103/30)

Sometimes A 孰 與 B is used by itself to make a comparison without an adjective expressed.

332. Cóng tiān ér sòng zhī, shú yǔ zhì tiān mìng ér yòng zhī 從天而頌之，孰與制天命而用之

Is it better to follow Heaven and sing praises to it or to institute its mandate and use it? (*Xún* 17/44)

Shú 孰 is rarely found as object, but there are occasional examples.

333. shèng rén yǒu bǎi, wú shú fǎ yān 聖人有百，吾孰法焉

There are a hundred sages. Which among them shall I take as my model? (*Xún* 5/28. The role of *yān* 焉 in this sentence seems to be to refer back to the preposed topic *shèng rén* 聖人, the group of people out of whom *shú* 孰 selects, hence 'among them.')

(iii) *Chóu* 疇

Chóu 疇 (EMC druw) 'who,' found in the *Shūjīng*, is an etymologically related word.

(b)(i) *Hé* 何

Hé 何 'what; why, etc.' is the ordinary interrogative pronoun for things. It is used: (1) to form a noun predicate, *hé yě* 何也 or *hé yú* 何與, *hé yé* 何邪 'is what' (sometimes meaning 'is for what reason, why?'); (2) as object of a verb or coverb, *hé yù* 何欲 'what do you want?,' *hé yǐ* 何以 'by means of what,' as well as the destination of a verb of motion, *hé zhī* 何之 'where is he going?'; and (3) adverbially 'how, why' — *wáng hé bì yuē lì* 王何必日利 'Why must Your Majesty say "profit"?' Whether as (2) or (3) it precedes the verb. Like *shuí* 誰, it follows a copula or the coverbs *yú* 于 and *yú* 於.

334. Qí diào wéi hé 其釣維何

What is your fishing line? (*Shī* 24/3)

335. Cǐ rì yǒu shí, yú hé bù zāng 此日有食，于何不臧

That this sun is eclipsed, wherein lies its evil? (*Shī* 193/2; Karlgren 1950a)

336. Yǒu běn zhī zhě … yú hé běn zhī, shàng běn zhī yú gǔ zhě shèng wáng zhī shì 有本之者 … 於何本之，上本之於古者聖王之事

There is the matter of giving it a foundation … In what does one give it a foundation? One gives it a foundation above in the precedents of the ancients, the sage kings. (*Mò* 35/6)

In the preclassical language *rú* 如 'like' had the syntax of a copula and *rú hé* 如何 is the regular word order for 'is like what?' Later this was regularized to *hé rú* 何如.[36]

337. Yè rú hé jī 夜如何其

How is the night? (*Shī* 182/1; jī 其 is here a preclassical question particle.)

Yuē 曰 is replaced by *yún* 云 both as the copula 'is called' (III.3) and as the verb 'to say.'

338. Qí míng yún hé 其名云何

What is its name? (*Guǎn* 56, p. 302)

339. Zǐzhāng yuē, Zǐxià yún hé? 子張曰，子夏云何

Zǐzhāng said, 'What does Zǐxià say?' (*LY* 19/3)

Hé 何 also follows when it is the second object of a verb that takes two objects: *wèi zhī hé* 謂之何 'call it what?' (as opposed to *hé wèi* 何謂 'refer to what'), *rú zhī hé*, 如之何 'what about it?' (sometimes abbreviated to *rú hé* 如何. See IV.8g).

Hé 何 may also be used attributively to nouns, as in *hé rén* 何人 'what (sort of) man?' A common locution is *hé gù* 何故 'what reason, why.' Note the use of *hé* 何 in front of a preposed object in front of the verb, resumed by *zhī* 之 (see VIII.1). This construction is even found in *Mencius*:

340. Kòu chóu hé fú zhī yǒu 寇 讎 何 服 之 有

What mourning clothing should be worn for an enemy? (*Mèng* IVB/3. More literally: (For) an enemy what [mourning] clothing there is it?)

Hé 何 is not normally used as the subject of a verb. Where it would be required one finds *shú* 孰 instead. A rare exception is the use of *hé shí* 何 實 in *Zuǒzhuàn*, where *shí* 實 has its normal function in that text of recapitulating a subject which is given contrastive emphasis.

341. Jīn zī zhū hóu hé shí jí, hé shí xiōng 今 茲 諸 侯 何 實 吉 , 何 實 凶

At this time which of the feudal lords will be lucky and which unlucky? (*Zuǒ* Zhāo 11/4)

(ii) *Xī* 奚

Xī 奚 is found as a less frequent alternative to *hé* 何 in preverbal or prenominal constructions but not as an independent noun predicate. See examples **424** and **576**.

(iii) *Hú* 胡

Hú 胡 is found already in the preclassical language and is mostly confined to adverbial usage meaning 'why, how.' Note also *hú wèi* 胡 為 'why' in which *hú* 胡 'why' replaces *hé* 何 'what' as the object of the coverb *wèi* 為. Compare English 'why for?' *Hú* 胡 is not very common in texts of the classical period.

(iv) *Hé* 曷

Hé 曷 (EMC ɣat) is found in the preclassical language in adverbal usage, mostly as 'when' but also sometimes as 'why,' 'how,' 'what.' It is not found in *Mencius* except in quotations but is fairly common in some other texts such as *Xúnzǐ* and the *Gōngyáng zhuàn*. The difference between *hé* 曷 and *hé* 何 in these texts has not been made clear. *Hài* 害 (EMC ɣàjʰ < *-ats) is sometimes used for *hé* 曷 in preclassical texts, where it should probably be read *hé*.

(v) *Hé* 盍

Hé 盍 (EMC ɣap) = *hé bù* 何 不 'why not?' Phological ly it makes better sense to regard it as a contraction of *hú bù* 胡 不 rather than *hé bù* 何 不.

342. Hé gè yán ěr zhì 盍各言爾志
Why don't you each tell your wishes? (*LY* 5/26)

(c)(i) *Yān* 焉, *Ān* 安
The interrogative pronoun *yān* 焉 'how? where?' which always appears in front of the verb is a positional variant of the third person pronoun substitute *yān* 焉 'in it, there, etc.' which appears in postverbal position.

343. Tiānxià zhī fù kuī zhī, qí zǐ yān wǎng 天下之父歸之，其子焉往
When the fathers of the world turned to him (King Wén), where [else] could the sons go? (*Mèng* 4A/13)

344. Ěr yān néng měi wǒ zāi 爾焉能浼我哉
How can you defile me? (*Mèng* 2A/9)

As with postverbal *yān* 焉, the meaning of preverbal *yān* 焉 corresponds to the locative coverb *yú* 於 + a pronominal element, in this case interpreted as interrogative rather than anaphoric.[37]

Ān 安 is identical in syntax and meaning with interrogative *yān* 焉. See example **277** above. It is much less common than *yān* 焉 in relatively early texts such as the *Zuǒzhuàn* and the *Lúnyǔ* and even in *Mencius*, but becomes more frequent in later texts of the Warring States.

(ii) *Wū hú* 惡乎, *wū* 惡, *wū* 烏
Wū hú 惡乎 'how, where,' sometimes shortened to *wū* 惡, is equivalent in meaning to *yú hé* 於何.

345. Yǒu kǎo zhī zhě … Wū hū kǎo zhī? Kǎo xiān shèng dà wáng zhī shì 有考之者⋯惡乎考之，考先聖大王之事
There is the matter of searching it out … In what does one search it out? One searches it out in the precedents of the former sages, the great kings. (*Mò* 37/3)

346. Wū zài qí wéi mín fù mǔ yě 惡在其為民父母也
Wherein lies his being father and mother to the people? (*Mèng* 1A/4; equivalent to qí wéi mín fù mǔ yě, zài yú hé 其為民父母也在於何 with exclamatory inversion of subject and predicate.)

Though there are problems about explaining the phonology, it seems quite likely that *wū hú* 惡 乎 is in fact derived from *yú hé* 於 何 , which is quite rare in texts of any period.[38]

In late Warring States and Hàn texts *wū* 烏 is sometimes found instead of *wū* 惡 .

4. Indefinite Pronouns

Some of the notions conveyed in English by indefinite pronouns, 'one, someone, any, another, etc.,' are expressed in Chinese by adnominal or adverbial particles of inclusion and restriction (see Section XI). There are, however, also a few words with such meanings that behave syntactically like nouns.

(a) Tuō 他

Tuō 他 'other,' is used either substantively or adjectivally.

> **347.** Wáng gù zuǒ yòu ér yán tuō 王 顧 左 右 而 言 他
> The king looked to left and right and spoke of other things. (*Mèng* 1B/6)

> **348.** Tuō rì xiàn yú wáng yuē ... 他 日 見 於 王 曰
> On another day he appeared before the king and said ... (*Mèng* 1B/1)

(b) Mǒu 某

Mǒu 某 'some one, a certain one' is used either to refer to a specific person without using the name, or more vaguely to some one unspecified.

> **349.** Zǐ gào zhī yuē, mǒu zài sī, mǒu zài sī 子 告 之 曰 ，某 在 斯 ， 某 在 斯
> The master said, 'So-and-so is here, so-and-so is here' (making introductions for a blind visitor). (*LY* 15/42)

> **350.** Mǒu kòu jiāng zhì 某 寇 將 至
> Such and such marauders are going to arrive. (*Zuǒ* Xī 19/7)

Mǒu 某 is sometimes used to refer to oneself instead of using one's own name.

(c) Rén 人

Rén 人 'person' may be used as an indefinite pronoun meaning 'some one else, other people.'

351. Zǐ yuē, bù huàn rén zhī bù jǐ zhī, huàn bù zhī rén yě 子
曰，不患人之不己知，患不知人也

The master said, 'I do not worry about others' not knowing one. I
worry about not knowing others.' (*LY* 1/16)

It can also mean 'each.'

352. Bù ruò rén yǒu suǒ bǎo 不若人有其寶

It would be better for each to keep what he values. (*Zuǒ* Xiāng
15/fu3)

The use of the reduplicated form *rénrén* 人人 to mean 'everyone' is
found in both Classical and Modern Chinese.

353. Rén rén qīn qí qīn, zhǎng qí zhǎng, ér tiān xiá píng 人人
親其親，長其長，而天下平

If everyone loved their parents and respected their elders as they
should, the whole world would be peaceful. (*Mèng* 4A/12)

X. Adverbs

The term 'adverb' is used broadly to refer to words which stand in front of verbs (including adjectives) and modify their meaning or application. It is even extended somewhat illogically to the small group of words which can similarly stand in front of verbless noun predicates — *yì* 亦 'also,' *yòu* 又 'also, moreover,' *bì* 必 'necessarily,' *chéng* 成 'really,' *xìn* 信 'really,' *gù* 固 'definitely,' *zhí* 直 'only,' etc. (III.1b). It is a heterogenous category grouped together for convenience, including both full words (nouns and verbs) used adverbially and empty words which are used primarily in this function. This section is concerned only with the former. Adverbial particles of negation, time, aspect, etc., are dealt with in other sections.

1. Adverbial Use of Nouns

As well as taking nouns as subjects, objects, or other types of complements, verbs may have nouns as adverbial modifiers. In the following examples, the noun describes the manner of action of the verb.

> **354.** Shǐ rén lì ér tí 豕 人 立 而 啼
> The pig stood up like a man (literally, 'man-stood') and cried. (*Zuǒ Zhuāng* 8/5)

> **355.** Yù qí zǐ zhī Qí yǔ yě 欲 其 子 之 齊 語 也
> If he wants his son to speak in the manner of Qí ... (literally, 'Qí-speak'). (*Mèng* 3B/6)

This construction can be derived by a transformation from a complement phrase introduced by *rú* 如 or *ruò* 若 : *lì rù rén* 立 如 人 , *yǔ rú Qí [rén]* 語 如 齊 [人] (see V.6c).

A similar transformation is possible with a locative complement.

> **356.** Shùn qín mín shì ér yě sǐ, ... Míng qín qí guān ér shuǐ sǐ, ... Jì qín bǎi gǔ ér shān sǐ 舜 勤 民 事 而 野 死 ··· 冥 勤 其 官 而 水 死 ··· 稷 勤 百 穀 而 山 死
> Shun was diligent about the people's affairs yet he died in the wilderness ... Ming was diligent in his office yet he died in the river ... Ji was diligent in the cultivation of the hundred cereals yet he died in the mountain. (*GY* 4, p. 166)

The nouns in adverbial position here are equivalent to locative phrases placed after the verb: *sǐ yú yě ... yú shuǐ ... yú shān* 死 於 野 ... 於 水 ... 於 山 .

Another case in which a noun may appear in adverbial position is when a part of the body is the instrument, e.g.,

357. Zǐ yù shǒu yuán tiān xià hū 子 欲 手 援 天 下 乎

Do you want (me) to save the world with my hand? (*Mèng* 4A/18)

This can be transformationally derived from a coverbal phrase introduced by *yǐ* 以 . Compare with *yuán zhī yǐ shǒu* 援 之 以 手 earlier in the same passage.

2. Adjectives as Adverbs

Adjectives placed in front of a verb form adverbs of manner or degree, e.g.,

358. Tiān xià yòu dà luàn 天 下 又 大 亂

The world again became greatly disordered. (*Mèng* 3B/9)

359. Bó xué ér xiáng shuō zhī, jiāng yǐ fǎn shuō yuē yě 博 學 而 詳 說 之 ，將 以 反 說 約 也

In studying extensively and expounding it (what one has studied) minutely, one aims to go back and expound what is essential. (*Mèng* 4B/15)

Adjectives can themselves be modified adverbially to indicate degree.

360. ... shèn xǐ 甚 喜

... was very pleased. (*Mèng* 2B/10)

361. Ruò shì zé dì zǐ zhī huò zī shèn 若 是 則 弟 子 之 惑 滋 甚

If that is so, then your disciple's perplexity is even (literally: increasingly) greater. (*Mèng* 2A/1)

As the last example shows, an adjective used as an adverb of manner can only be turned into a predicate if the verb it modifies is nominalized: *dì zǐ shèn huò* 弟 子 甚 惑 'I am very perplexed' → *dì zǐ zhī huò shèn* 弟 子 之 惑 甚 'Your disciple's perplexity is very great.' This shows that the functioning as an adverb is a basic property of adjectives in contrast to the adverbial function of nouns which is comparatively rare and is transformationally related to more normal constructions in which the noun is linked to the main verb by a coverb.

3. Verbs as Adverbs

As already discussed above (V.5), verbal phrases linked to a main verb by *ér* 而 (which can also be omitted) can have a quasi-adverbial force, rather than simply expressing consecutive action or components of a single action. Such usage must, however, be distinguished from true adverbial use of certain verbs with restricted, grammaticalized meanings e.g., *lì* 立 'stand,' adverb 'on the spot, immediately.'

> **362.** Gù wǒ yǒu shàn, zé lì yù wǒ, wǒ yǒu guò, zé lì huǐ wǒ 故 我 有 善 ，則 立 譽 我 ，我 有 過 ，則 立 毀 我
> Therefore, when I have good points, they immediately praise me; when I have errors, they immediately blame me. (*Guǎn* 32 'Xiǎo chēng,' p. 179)

Other examples include *jìn* 盡 'exhaust,' adverb 'completely' (XIII.1g); *yǐ* 已 'stop,' adverb 'already' and, with adjectives, 'very' (XII.1c); etc.

4. Numerical Expressions as Adverbs

Numerical expressions, like adjectives, can be used as adverbs.

> **363.** Wǔ jiù Tāng, wǔ jiù Jié zhě, Yī Yǐn yě 五 就 湯 ， 五 就 桀 者 ，伊 尹 也
> He who five times went to Tāng and five times went to Jié was Yī Yǐn. (*Mèng* 6B/6)

For 'twice' and 'thrice' there are special adverbial forms, *zài* 再 and *sàn* 三:

> **364.** Jì Wénzǐ sàn sī ér hòu xíng. Zǐ wén zhī yuē, zài zé kě yǐ 季 文 子 三 思 而 後 行 。子 聞 之 曰 ，再 則 可 矣
> Jì Wén thought thrice before acting; when the master heard this, he said, 'Twice would be all right.' (*LY* 5/20)

Yī 一 'one,' used adverbially, may simply mean 'once' but may also have extended implications such as 'once and for all' or 'completely.' In an initial clause it can have a conjunctive force like 'once' in English. That is, it not only modifies the verb of its own clause, but it also marks its clause as a temporal modifier of the following clause.

> **365.** Yī zhèng jūn, ér guó dìng yǐ. 一 正 君 而 國 定 矣
> Once rectify the ruler and the country will be settled. (*Mèng* 4A/21)

Other quantitative expressions besides numerals can be used as adverbs, as in:

366. Bù rì chéng zhī. 不 日 成 之

In less than a day they completed it. (*Shī* 242/1, quoted in *Mèng* 1A/2)

Rì 日 is here a quantity of time, not the noun 'day.' Hence it can be negated by *bú* 不 .

5. Expressive Adverbs in *Rán* 然 , *Rú* 如 , etc.

Rán 然 , which occurs in a variety of ways by itself as an equivalent for *rú zhī 如 之 'is like this,' also occurs as a suffix forming expressives which describe the manner of an action, e.g.,

367. Cù rán wèn ... 卒 然 問

He abruptly asked ... (*Mèng* 1A/6)

368. Tiān yóu rán zuò yún ...天 油 然 作 雲

Heaven copiously forms clouds. (*Mèng* 1A/6)

Such expressives are often formed by reduplicated syllables.

369. Máng máng rán guī ... 芒 芒 然 歸

He wearily returned home ... (*Mèng* 2A/2)

370. Wàng wàng rán qù zhī 望 望 然 去 之

He would haughtily leave him. (*Mèng* 2A/9)

Or reduplication may be used alone, without *rán* 然 , as in:

371. Shī shī cóng wài lái 施 施 從 外 來

He jauntily came in from outside. (*Mèng* 4B/33)

Less commonly, other particles such as *rú* 如 or *yān* 焉 are used in place of *rán* 然 , as suffixes for expressive adverbs.

XI. Negation

Negative particles fall into two groups, distinguished by the type of initial: (a) p/f, (b) m/w. Forms with initial f- and w- resulted from a process of regular phonetic change that affected labial consonants in LMC. P/f negatives imply simple negation; m/w negatives imply non-existence.

1. P/f Negatives

(a) Bù 不

Bù 不 is the particle of simple verbal negation, of which many examples have been given above. The expected reading pronunciation for the Old Chinese morpheme written with this graph is *fōu*, corresponding to the reading EMC puw found in the *Qièyùn* rhyme dictionary. It is preserved in a few proper names. The colloquial reading, which preserves the Old Chinese initial *p- unchanged *bù*, strictly speaking belongs to another word, EMC put, properly represented by the graph 弗 (see below) which had replaced EMC puw in colloquial usage between Hàn and Táng. EMC put, or rather, an enclitic variant of it, EMC pə t, also lies behind Modern Cantonese pɐt 不 and corresponding forms in other southern dialects.[39]

(b) Fǒu 否

Fǒu 否, originally written simply as 不 and not infrequently found so written in early texts, was the form taken by *bù* 不 (i.e., *fōu*) when the verb which it negated was omitted and the particle stood on its own in phrase final position. In *Mencius*, *fǒu* 否 is most frequently found as an answer to a question: 'No.'

> **372.** ... zé wáng xǔ zhī hū ? Yuē, fǒu 則 王 許 之 乎 。曰 , 否
> '... then would Your Majesty allow it?' He replied, 'No.' (*Mèng* 1A/7)

It also occurs in a form of alternative question:

> **373.** Rú cǐ zé dòng xīn fǒu hū 如 此 則 動 心 否 乎
> If it were like this, would it stir your mind or not? (*Mèng* 2A/2)

In other texts, we find a variety of other uses, e.g., *fǒu* 否 standing for *bù* 不 + deleted verb in the main clause of a declarative sentence or in an 'if' clause.

374. Gào zé shū, bù rán, zé fǒu 告 則 書 ， 不 然 ， 則 否

If it was announced, it was recorded; otherwise not (*Zuǒ* Yǐn 11/*fù* 4)

375. Yì zé jìn, fǒu zé fèng shēn ér tuì 義 則 進 ， 否 則 奉 身 而 退

If it is right, he comes forward; if not, he takes his person and withdraws. (*Zuǒ* Xiāng 26/3)

A rather common usage is in indirect (embedded) questions, e.g.,

376. Zhī kě fǒu, zhī yě 知 可 否 ， 知 也

To know what is possible and what is not is to know. (*Zhuāng* 10/12)

The character 否 originally stood for another word, *pǐ* 否 'bad, evil,' found especially in the expression *zāngpǐ* 臧 否 'good and evil.' In this sense and reading it is the name of one of the hexagrams in the *Book of Changes.*

On the final particle *fú* 夫 'is it not?,' which may be a contraction of unaccented *bù* 不 + *hū* 乎, see XIV.2f.vii.

(c) Fú 弗

There has been much discussion of the meaning of this particle, EMC put, which has been traditionally regarded as just a less common variant of *bù* 不, EMC puw. One popular idea has been that *fú* 弗 is a fusion of *bù* 不 + the object pronoun *zhī* 之, which is plausible phonologically and can be supported by examples like the following:

377. Dé zhī zé shēng, fú dé zé sǐ 得 之 則 生 ， 弗 得 則 死

If he gets it he will live, if he does not get it he will die. (*Mèng* 6A/10)

in which *dé zhī* 得 之 in the affirmative is matched by *fú dé* 弗 得 in the negative. Against this is the fact that the object pronoun *zhī* 之 is regularly omitted even with *bù* 不, as in:

378. Kǒngzǐ jìn yǐ lǐ, tuì yǐ yì. dé zhī bù dé, yuē, yǒu mìng. 孔 子 進 以 禮 ， 退 以 義 。 得 之 不 得 ， 曰 ， 有 命

Confucius entered office according to propriety and retired from it according to righteousness. Whether he obtained it or did not obtain (it), he said, 'It was ordained.' (*Mèng* 5A/8)

Moreover, when it first appears on the oracle bones, and also in preclassical texts such as the *Shūjīng*, *fú* 弗 appears freely in front of both intransitive verbs and verbs with noun objects. There is reason to think that at that period it was one of a set of particles ending in *-t associated with an aspectual distinction between a continuing state or an action going on (*bù* 不) and realization of a potentiality or a change of state (*fú* 弗)[40]. Even in texts of the classical period there are certain recurrent patterns in which it collocates with the final particle *yǐ* 矣, often with an intransitive verb or with a verb followed by an expressed object, that suggest an aspectual meaning.

379. zì jīn Zhèng guó bù sì wǔ nián fú dé níng yǐ 自 今 鄭 國 不 四 五 年 弗 得 寧 矣

Within four or five years from now the country of Zhèng will have no peace. (*Zuǒ* Xiāng 8/3)

380. Suī yǔ zhī jū xué, fú ruò zhī yǐ 雖 與 之 俱 學 ， 弗 若 之 矣

Though he studies along with him, he will not come up to him. (*Mèng* 6A/9)

In this and similar examples, the pronoun object follows the verb instead of preceding it. If we assume that the normal position of a pronoun between the negative particle and the verb is that of an unstressed clitic, when we find it following the verb as here, it presumably gives a greater degree of emphasis to the statement, something that also often seems to be implicit in the use of the perfect particle at the end of the sentence.

It is, nevertheless, true that in the Warring States period *fú* 弗 does mostly occur where a pronoun *zhī* 之 can be understood between it and the following verb which suggests that the final -t was reinterpreted as the initial consonant of the pronoun fused with the negative particle. It seems clear that in the end, sometime between Hàn and Táng, both the aspectual force of *put and any association it may have acquired with the object pronoun became attenuated and it survived simply as a stronger form of *pə-. Compare the replacement of *ne* by *not* < *nought* in English or the simple *ne* by *ne … pas* and then by *pas* alone in French. The history of *bù* 不 and *fú* 弗 is complicated by the fact that the character *fú* 弗 was tabooed for a time during the Hàn dynasty because it was part of the personal name of Liú Fúlíng 劉 弗 陵 who reigned as the Emperor Zhāo 昭 from -86 to -74. We know from manuscript evidence that this resulted in the replacement of 弗 by 不 in the transmitted text of the *Dao de jing* 道 德 經 . The extent to which the taboo has influenced the transmission of other pre-Hàn texts is uncertain. What seems clear is that in post-Hàn Chinese, 不 took over as a normal way of writing both *pùt and *pâ and that eventually the pronunciation with *-t prevailed in common usage. As mentioned above, modern readings of 不 in all dialects are derived from *put or *pə t, with irregular retention of bilabial [p] instead of labiodental [f].

(d) Fēi 非

Fēi 非 , the negative particle used with nouns, is an early contraction of *bù wéi* 不 唯 , not in the classical sense of 'only' but in the preclassical sense of a copula and noun marker.[41] Its use in noun predication is described above. It is also found with nouns and verb phrases treated as nouns which do not form main predicates. The translation 'if not' or 'unless' is often appropriate when an expression negated by *fēi* 非 occurs as a conditional clause (XV.2b.vi), before the main predicate, e.g.,

381. Fēi qí dào, zé yī dān shí bù kě shòu yú rén 非 其 道 ，
則 一 簞 食 不 可 受 於 人
If it is not in accordance with the proper way, even one basket of food should not be accepted from another person. (*Mèng* 3B/4.
Literally: if it is not its way)

Other derived uses of *fēi* 非 that must be noted are: (1) as an adjective 'wrong,' opposite of *shì* 是 'right' (IX.2a); (2) as a verb 'to deny, call wrong.'

382. Jīn yě, nán mán jué shé zhī rén fēi xiān wáng zhī dào 今
也 ，南 蠻 鴃 舌 之 人 非 先 王 之 道
Now the shrike-tongued southern barbarian denies the doctrines of the former kings. (*Mèng* 3A/4)

In preclassical language we sometimes find *fēi* 匪 or *fēi* 棐 instead of *fēi* 非 .

(e) Pǒ 叵

Pǒ 叵 is a (not very common) contraction of *bù kě* 不 可 'is not possible.'

(f) Hé 盍

Hé 盍 , EMC ɣap, is a contraction of *hé bú* 何 不 or *hú bú* 胡 不 'why not' (see IX.3b(v) below).

2. M/w Negatives

(a) *Wú* 毋 , *wú* 無 and *wú* 无

These characters originally represented two distinct morphemes: (1) a prohibitive particle, properly written 毋 ; and (2) a verb meaning 'not have' (opposite of *yǒu* 有 'have'), properly written 無 (or 无 in some texts, e.g., *Zhuāngzǐ*). The morphemes were already homophonous in late Zhōu times and are confused in many texts such as *Mencius*, but were very likely pronounced differently at an early period. Thus, 毋 appears to have *mǔ* 母 as phonetic, which would put it into the *-ə (ɣ) rhyme category, while 無 belongs in the *-a(ɣ) category.

(i) *Wú* 毋 (無) as prohibitive particle

383. Zé wú wàng mín zhī duō yú lín guó yě. 則 無 望 民 之 多 於 鄰 國 也
Then don't hope that your people will be more numerous than in neighbouring countries. (*Mèng* 1A/3)

384. Wáng wú zuì suì. 王 無 罪 歲
Let Your Majesty not blame the harvest. (*Mèng* 1A/3)

385. Jī tún gǒu zhì zhī xù wú shī qí shí 雞 豚 狗 彘 之 畜 無 失 其 時
In the raising of chickens, pigs, dogs, and swine do not lose their time [of breeding]. (*Mèng* 1A/3)

Note that in the second example, the subject of the second person imperative is expressed.

Prohibitive *wú* 無 can also be used in subordinate clauses where one cannot use an imperative in English, suggesting that it should be interpreted as a kind of subjunctive particle rather than simply prohibitive,[42] e.g.,

386. Wú yǐ zé wàng hū? 無 以 (= 已) 則 王 乎
If I am not to stop, then [shall I speak about] kingship? (*Mèng* 1A/7)

387. Suī yù wú wàng, bù kě dé yǐ. 雖 欲 無 王 , 不 可 得 已

Even if he wished that he should not become king, it could not be
managed. (*Mèng* 4A/10)

(ii) *Wú* 無 'not have.'

See Section IV.7 above.

(b) Wù 勿 *'do not'*

Wù 勿 (EMC mut) 'do not,' bears the same relation to prohibitive *wú* 毋
(無) as *fú* 弗 (EMC put) does to *bú* 不 . That is, the ancestral forms of
the two graphs on the oracle bones appear to have an aspectual distinction,
while in the Warring States period there is reason to think that the final -t
of *wù* 勿 may have been interpreted as the incorporated object pronoun *zhī*
之 . The surviving aspectual meaning is illustrated in example **382**, while
the apparent incorporation of the pronoun object is illustrated in **383**.

> **388.** Wáng yù xíng wáng zhèng, zé wù huǐ zhī yǐ. 王 欲 行 王
> 政 ，則 勿 毀 之 矣
>
> If Your Majesty wishes to practice kingly government, then don't
> destroy it. (*Mèng* 1B/5. The question of whether or not to destroy
> the Hall of Light has been posed to Mencius by the king. The
> implication of the final perfect particle, presumably strengthened
> by the use of *wù* 勿 instead of *wú* 無 , seems to be that that
> settles the matter and leaves no room for further argument.)

> **389.** Bǎi mǔ zhī tián, wù duó qí shí 百 畝 之 田 ，勿 奪 其
> 時
>
> Do not deprive the hundred *mǔ* fields of their times (of
> cultivation). (*Mèng* 1A/3)

In this sentence we should expect the preposed indirect object of *duó* 奪
'deprive' (see IV.8b above.), *bǎi mǔ zhī tián* 百 畝 之 田 'hundred *mǔ*
fields,' to be repeated by the pronoun *zhī* in its normal position between the
negative and the verb and this could be represented by the final *-t of *wù*
勿 . Contrast *wú shī* 無 失 'let them not lose' in the immediately
preceding sentence, (example **379**) in which the preposed element is the
subject of the verb rather than its object and so would exclude the object
pronoun between the negative and the verb.

　　Like prohibitive *wú* 無 , *wù* 勿 can be used in embedded sentences:

> **390.** Rén jiē yǒu zhī, xián zhě néng wù sàng ěr. 人 皆 有
> 之 ，賢 者 能 勿 喪 耳

All men have it; it is just that the wise are able to keep from
losing it. (*Mèng* 6A/10)

(c) Wáng 亡

Wáng 亡, which, in texts of the classical period, is most commonly a verb
meaning 'lose' (trans.) or 'disappear, abscond, die' (intrans.), is sometimes
found in the sense of *wú* 無 'not have' but without an expressed object.
Traditionally it is then read *wú*, but this is not supported by a rhyme in the
Shījīng and seems to be merely a late explanation by commentators for
which there is no good ancient authority.[43] The two words are no doubt
etymologically closely related. *Wáng* 亡 is in fact the graphic form found
on the oracle bones where *wú* 無 would appear in later texts. This usage is
especially common in the *Lúnyǔ* but is not confined to that text.

> **391.** Rén jiē yǒu xiōng dì, wǒ dú wáng 人 皆 有 兄 弟 ， 我
> 獨 亡
> Every one has brothers, I alone have not. (*LY* 12/5)

> **392.** Wèn yǒu yú, yuē, wáng yǐ 問 有 餘 ， 曰 ， 亡 矣
> If (his father) asked whether there was anything left, he would say,
> 'there is not.' (*Mèng* 4A/20)

(d) Wǎng 罔

Wǎng 罔 is sometimes used in the sense of *wú* 無 in the preclassical
language. It is not, however, like *wáng* 亡 in the *Lúnyǔ*, an equivalent to
wú zhī 無 之 with the object pronoun omitted.

(e) Mò 莫

Mò 莫 (EMC mak) is used adverbially to define the scope of the subject in
the sense of 'no one, nothing, none' (XIII.3b). In postclassical times *mò*
莫 is found as a prohibitive particle, 'do not.'

(f) Wèi 未

Wèi 未 is an aspectual negative. It is probably derived from the existential
negative root *m- + the perfective particle *jì* 既 'already,'[44] and thus means
'not already' = 'not yet' or 'never.' It is incompatible with the final particle
yǐ 矣, which implies change of state, that is, the close of one situation and
the beginning of another. On the other hand, *yě* 也, which seems to imply

a continuing state when it occurs after verbal predicates, is very common with *wèi* 未.

393. Jiàn niú wèi jiàn yáng yě. 見 牛 未 見 羊 也

You saw the ox but you had not seen the sheep. (*Mèng* 1A/7)
For further discussion see XII.1b below.

Four less common m/w negatives are described below.

(g) Wéi 微

Wéi 微, also used for a full word meaning 'small, minute; secret,' is the *m- negative formed from the preclassical copula *wéi* 唯, corresponding to *fēi* 非 from *bù* 不 + *wéi* 唯.[45] Like *fēi* 非 it is used to negate nouns and occurs in various patterns in the *Shījīng*. In the classical period it is not very common but does occur occasionally in the first clause of a conditional sentence meaning 'if it had not been for ...'

394. Wéi Yǔ wú qí yú hū 微 禹 吾 其 魚 乎

If it had not been for Yǔ, would we not, surely, have been fish?
(*Zuǒ* Zhāo 1/*fù* 3. Note the absence of a copula. A textual variant has *qí wéi yú hū* 其 為 魚 乎.)

(h) Mǐ 靡

Mǐ 靡 is a particle glossed as *wú* 無 'not have' in the *Shījīng*:

395. Tiān mìng mǐ cháng 天 命 靡 常

Heaven's Mandate has no constancy. (*Shī* 235/5)

(i) Miè 蔑

Miè 蔑 (EMC mɛt), otherwise 'destroy,' is a negative particle, found mostly in the *Zuǒzhuàn* and *Guóyǔ*. It is a *-t form corresponding to *wú* 無 'not have' in the same way that *fú* 弗 and *wù* 勿 corresponds to *wú* 毋 'do not.' Thus, it is frequently accompanied by final *yǐ* 矣.[46]

396. Chén chū Jìn jūn, jūn nà Chóng'ěr, miè bú jì yǐ 臣 出 晉 君 ，君 納 重 耳 ，蔑 不 濟 矣

If I expel the ruler of Jìn and you bring in Chóng'ěr, everything will be successful. (*Zuǒ* Xī 10/*fù*. Literally: 'there will be no not succeeding')

(j) Mò 末

Mò 末 (EMC mat) is similar to *miè* 蔑, mostly in the *Lúnyǔ*.

> **397.** Bù yuē rú zhī hé, rú zhī hé zhě, wú mò rú zhī hé yě yǐ yǐ
> 不 曰 如 之 何 ， 如 之 何 者 ， 吾 末 如 之 何 也 已 矣
>
> If a man does not continually ask himself, 'What am I to do about it, what am I to do about it,' there is no possibility for my doing anything about him. (*LY* 15/16, Waley 1938)

XII. Aspect, Time, and Mood

In inflected languages verbs very often have formal distinctions to show the tense (in English, past, present, or future), the aspect (primarily whether and in what sense the situation described is looked on as complete or incomplete), or the mood/modality (terms that can cover various things including the nature of the speech-act involved — statement, question, command — and the attitude of the speaker towards the necessity or possibility of what is being said). Though Chinese in general is regarded as an uninflected language, Modern Mandarin does have verbal suffixes marking aspectual distinctions (*-le* 了 , *-zhe* 著 , *-guo* 過 , etc.) and other dialects have comparable formations. Classical Chinese does not have such suffixes but, as we have noted at various points above, there seem to be traces in certain sets of grammatical particles of an earlier system of dental suffixes marking aspectual distinctions — *-n for imperfective/durative and *-t for perfective/punctual — that had at one time been a more general feature of word formation.[47] In the classical language one cannot set up morphological paradigms of this kind, but distinctions of an aspectual kind are important both in the syntax of verbs as such and in distinctions between sentence types expressed by final particles.

1. Verbal Aspect — Preverbal Particles
In Modern Mandarin the verbal suffix *-le* 了 is used to indicate perfectivity, that is, that an event is looked upon as complete or a bounded whole.[48] In the classical language an equivalent role is played by the preverbal particles *jì* 既 and *yǐ* 已 . Modern *-le* 了 is derived from the verb *liǎo* 了 'to finish, dispose of' and classical perfective adverbs have a similar etymology. The earliest is *jì* 既 which is frequent in both the *Shījīng* and the *Shūjīng*. In the classical period it survived but its functions were partly taken over by *yǐ* 已 , the morpheme found in modern *yǐjīng* 已經 'already.' The negative particle corresponding to *jì* 既 was *wèi* 未 'not yet, never.' (Sentence final *le* 了 in Modern Chinese, as a mark of change of state, corresponds quite closely to the sentence final particle *yǐ* 矣 , treated in 2a below. By contrast, final *yě* 也 after verbal predicates can serve as a mark of unchanged, continuing state.)

(a) Jì 既

As a full verb *jì* 既 means 'use up, finish, complete' as in:

398. Rì yǒu shí zhī, jì 日有食之，既

There was an eclipse of the sun; it was complete. (*Chūnqiū* Huán 3/4)

More commonly *jì* 既 precedes the main verb adverbially to show that the action is complete. In the main clause of a sentence *jì* 既 is commonly followed by the final particle *yǐ* 矣 marking the fact that the completion of the action results in a new situation.

399. Wén shǒu Biàn zhě jiāng pàn; chén shuài tú yǐ tǎo zhī, jì dé zhī yǐ 聞守卞者將叛，臣帥徒以討之，既得之矣

I heard that the guardian of Biàn was going to revolt. I led my followers to punish him and have taken it (Biàn). (*Zuǒ* Xiāng 19/2)

400. Rán zé fū zǐ jì shèng yǐ hū 然則夫子既聖矣乎

If so, then, have you, master, attained sagehood? (*Mèng* 2A/2)

The omission of final *yǐ* in an introductory clause sets up an expectation of a conclusion to follow and *jì* 既 may then be translated as a perfect participle 'having done so-and-so' or as a conjunction 'when, after, since.'

401. Bīng rèn jì jiē ... 兵刃既接

When the weapons have crossed ... (*Mèng* 1A/3)

Jì ér 既而, with the verb that should come immediately after *jì* 既 omitted, has an anaphoric meaning, 'after (this), afterwards.'

402. Jì ér fān rán gǎi yuē ... 既而幡然改曰 ···

After this, he abruptly changed and said ... (*Mèng* 5A/7)

Note the combination *jì* ... *yòu* ... 既 ... 又 ... 'both ... and ...' in which *jì* 既 is more like a coordinating than a subordinating conjunction. The first action modified by *jì* 既 is still looked upon as a bounded whole that logically precedes the second introduced by *yòu* 又.

403. Jì yù qí shēng, yòu yù qí sǐ, shì huò yě 既欲其生，又欲其死，是惑也

Having wished it to live, also to wish it to die, this is confusion.
(*LY* 12/10)

(b) Wèi 未

Wèi 未, EMC mujʰ, 'not yet, never,' is an aspectual negative particle that has the opposite meaning to *jì* 既 in the affirmative. That is, it looks upon an action as not completed. Etymologically it seems to be formed from the existential negative root *m- in *wú* 毋 plus *jì* 既, EMC kɨjʰ, hence 'not already' → 'not yet' (see XI.2f above). Note the contrast between *wèi* 未 and *jì* 既 in successive passages in a case like:

404. Wèi jiàn jūn zǐ, nì rú zhōu jī … Jì jiàn jūn zǐ, bù wǒ xiá qì 未 見 君 子 , 惄 如 調 飢 … 既 見 君 子 , 不 我 遐 棄

While I have not yet seen the lord, I am desirous as if morning-hungry … When I have seen the lord, he will not remove and reject me. (*Shī* 10/1, 2, Karlgren 1950a)

Since 'not yet' implies a continuing situation, *wèi* 未 is inconsistent with final *yǐ* 矣 and this combination is never found. Instead one regularly finds final *yě* 也, which contrasts with *yǐ* 矣 as a mark of a continuing situation after verbal predicates, following *wèi* 未 in the main clause of a sentence.

405. Wèi yǒu rén ér yí qí qīn zhě yě 未 有 仁 而 遺 其 親 者 也

There has never yet been a case of one who, being benevolent, abandoned his parents. (*Mèng* 1A/1)

406. Jīn jì shù yuè yǐ. wèi kě yǐ yán yú 今 既 數 月 矣 。 未 可 以 言 與

Now you have been (in this office) several months. Have you yet had no occasion to speak? (*Mèng* 2B/5; *yú* 與 is equivalent to *yě hū* 也 乎)

Just as *jì* 既 in an introductory clause can have the force of a subordinating conjunction 'after,' *wèi* 未 in the same situation means 'before.'

407. Wèi chéng, yī rén zhī shé chéng 未 成 , 一 人 之 蛇 成
Before he had finished, another man's snake was finished. (*ZGC*,

Qí cé 2, 117/57/16)

(c) *Preverbal* Yĭ 已
As a verb, *yĭ* 已 means 'stop, finish.'

408. Rén jiē wèi wǒ huǐ Míng Táng. Huǐ zhū, yǐ hū? 人 皆 謂
我 毀 明 堂 。 毀 諸 ， 已 乎
People all tell me to destroy the Hall of Light. Should I destroy it,
or should I stop? (*Mèng* 1B/5)

It also has various uses as a grammatical particle. Its earliest use as a
preverbal particle seems to be as an intensive adverb before adjectives in the
sense of 'very,' 'excessively,' 'too,' a usage that is already found in the
preclassical language. Compare the later use of *jué* 絕 'cut off' in the sense
of 'extremely.'

409. Jūnzĭ yĭ Qí rén shā Āi Jiāng yĕ wéi yĭ shèn yĭ 君 子 以
齊 人 殺 哀 姜 為 已 甚 矣
The superior man will judge the putting to death of Āi Jiāng by
the people of Qí as excessive. (*Zuǒ* Xī 2/10)

In the classical period it was used like *jì* 既 as a preverbal particle
'already' to indicate completed action. This is rare or nonexistent in the
preclassical language, but in the classical period it gradually takes over from
jì 既 especially in the main predicate of a sentence, where it is usually
accompanied by final *yĭ* 矣.

410. Nián yĭ qī shí yĭ 年 已 七 十 矣
He was already 70 years old. (*Mèng* 5A/9)
Yĭ 已 can also occur, like *jì* 既, in an initial clause.

411. Shèng rén yĭ sĭ, zé dà dào bù qĭ, tiānxià píng ér wú gù yĭ 聖
人 已 死 ， 則 大 盜 不 起 ， 天 下 平 而 無 故 矣
When the sages have died, the great robbers will not arise and the
world will be at peace and without troubles. (*Zhuāng* 10/16)
Jì 既 and *yĭ* 已 can occur together, as in:

412. Yǔ jì yĭ zhī zhī yĭ 予 既 已 知 之 矣
I already know it. (*Mèng* 6B/13)
Yĭ 已 can occur, especially in somewhat later texts, like *jì* 既 in an
initial clause. So also can *yĭ ér* 已 而 instead of *jì ér* 既 而.

413. Yǐ ér dà yú shí zhī 已 而 大 魚 食 之
Afterwards a great fish ate it. (*Zhuāng* 26/12)

2. Sentential Aspect — Sentence Final Particles

(a) Yǐ 矣

The correlation between the preverbal markers of perfective aspect, *jì* 既 and *yǐ* 已, and sentence final *yǐ* 矣, and between the negative *wèi* 未 and sentence final *yě* 也, has been illustrated above. Although aspect is generally looked on as a characteristic of verbs while sentence final particles in Chinese are traditionally classified as 'modal particles' (*yǔqìcí* 語 氣 詞), this seems to provide prima facie evidence to suggest that at least part of the meaning of *yǐ* 矣 and *yě* 也 must be involved with the same basic semantic contrasts that are expressed by the perfective/nonperfective contrast that applies to verbs.

It has long been recognized that the final particle *yǐ* 矣 of Classical Chinese closely resembles sentence final *le* 了 in Modern Chinese in its meaning and syntactic behaviour. If, as has often been assumed, sentence final *le* 了 is etymologically the same as the perfective suffix *-le* 了 , and, furthermore, if one could connect the classical final particle *yǐ* 矣 etymologically with the verb *yǐ* 已 'stop' and the derived preverbal particle *yǐ* 已 'already,' the case for regarding both *yǐ* 矣 and sentence final *le* 了 as aspect markers would seem overwhelming. There are, however, serious difficulties in the way of such a conclusion. Other modern dialects often use etymologically quite separate morphemes for the two functions performed by *le* 了 in Mandarin, and doubts have been raised as to whether sentential *le* 了 is etymologically the same word as suffix *-le* 了 in Mandarin itself.[49] There are also good reasons for doubting that there is any etymological connection between *yǐ* 矣 and *yǐ* 已. Nevertheless, I think there is good reason to think that both sentential *le* 了 in Mandarin and final *yǐ* 矣 in Classical Chinese are basically aspectual in function.

Li and Thompson (1981) adhere to the traditional practice of Chinese grammarians in classifying sentential *le* 了 as a member of an undivided class of *yǔqìcí* 語 氣 詞. For *le* 了 they propose the general meaning 'currently relevant state.' Nevertheless they elsewhere (Li, Thompson, and Thompson 1982) recognize that *le* 了 has aspect as at least part of its meaning, which they propose to characterize as perfect in contrast to the perfective force of the verb suffix *-le* 了 . This is confusing in terms of the ordinary nontechnical use of 'perfective' as an adjective derived from 'perfect,' but corresponds to a technical use of the terms by linguists. The Slavic languages provide the definition of perfective as meaning simply an action viewed as a bounded whole. In contrast to this, perfect in languages like Greek and English relates the completion of the action to the time of utterance (in the case of the present perfect) or to some definite past or future time in the case of the past perfect (or pluperfect) and future perfect. Whereas 'it rained' simply means that a period of rain occurred at some time in the past, 'it has rained' has the additional implication that the period of rain in question has some particular relevance at the time of utterance, perhaps by confirming or disconfirming an expectation or by ending a period of drought, or something else that the speaker and auditor are aware of in the situation.

'Perfect,' in this sense, seems particularly appropriate in cases like **399** and **400** where *yĭ* 矣 completes the main clause of a sentence in which the verb is preceded by perfective *jì* 既 or *yĭ* 已 . What the addition of *yĭ* 矣 seems to do is to assert that as a result of the completed action that is referred to, a new situation has arisen (or had arisen or will arise in the future if the time of reference in the utterance is in the past or future). 'Change of state' is a meaning that is commonly assigned to sentence final *le* 了 and is also one that fits very well with the concept of referring the situation described in the sentence to its reference time. Another term that has been used to cover at least part of the functions of *le* 了 is 'inchoative,' that is, applying to a situation that is new or only new to the speaker (Chao 1968:798). This is also a concept that is aspectual in nature and that applies equally well to many occurrences of *yĭ* 矣 . Whether, in the end, 'perfect' will turn out to be the most appropriate designation for Mandarin *le* 了 and Classical *yĭ* 矣 must await further study, but I adopt it provisionally in order to emphasize its aspectual character, even though it applies to sentences as a whole and not simply to verbs.[50]

Many examples of *yĭ* 矣 have been given above. Here are a few more. As in the second example below, it often makes a vivid future.

414. Miáo zé gǎo yĭ 苗 則 槁 矣
The sprouts had dried up. (*Mèng* 2A/2)

415. Shàng xià jiāo zhēng lì ér guó wéi yĭ 上 下 交 征 利 而 國 危 矣

Those above and those below will contend with each other for profit and the country will be in danger. (*Mèng* 1A/1, i.e., 'the country will have reached the state of being in danger.')

(b) Yě 也

As noted in XI.2f, the negative particle *wèi* 未, which has the aspectual meaning of a continuing state, excludes the perfective particle *yǐ* 矣 and is frequently accompanied by final *yě* 也. This suggests that *yě* 也, besides its use as mark of noun predication, can have an aspectual meaning after verbs, that is, the opposite of that of *yǐ* 矣. The two uses can be related through the fact that noun predication is normally aspectless, i.e., has no implication of completion or change of state. This interpretation is also possible in cases in which *yě* 也 follows a verbal predicate without *wèi* 未. Compare *yě* 也 and *yǐ* 矣 in:

> **416.** Qí rén yuē, suǒ yǐ wèi Chí Wā, zé hǎo yǐ. Suǒ yǐ zì wèi, zé wú bú zhī yě. 齊人曰，所以為蚔蠅，則好矣，所以自為，則吾不知也
> The people of Qí said, 'As for what he did for Chí Wā, that was good. As for what he did for himself, we don't know.' (*Mèng* 2B/5)

The contrast is between a closed situation about which a judgement has been made and no more needs to be said and an open situation that still awaits a conclusion.

(c) Yǐ 已 (yě yǐ 也 已, yě yǐ yǐ 也 已 矣)

The use of *yǐ* 已, which may in turn be followed by perfective *yǐ* 矣, after noun predicates to express a new realization on the part of the speaker has been discussed in III.1e. *Yě yǐ* 也 已 or *yǐ* 已 alone are also sometimes found after the types of verbal predicates that can take *yě* 也.

> **417.** rán zé wáng zhī suǒ dà yù, kě zhī yǐ 然 則 王 之 所 大 欲 ，可 知 已
> If that is so, what your majesty greatly desires may be known. (*Mèng* IA/7)

As in the noun predicates with *yǐ* 已 and *yě yǐ yǐ* 也 已 矣 in examples **23** and **24**, the final particle indicates a new realization on the part of the speaker rather than an objectively new situation. See also example **397**.

3. Time Words

(a) *Time Expressions in Topic Position*
Some time expressions such as *jīn yě* 今 也 'now,' *xī* 昔 or *xī zhě* 昔 者 'formerly,' *gǔ* 古 or *gǔ zhě* 古 者 'in ancient times,' *chū* 初 'previously' and *rán hòu* 然 後 'afterwards' are commonly placed at the head of the sentence in topic position instead of in adverbial position between the subject and the verb. (Note that *jīn* 今 alone, like English 'now,' is often a weak introductory particle without a specific time reference.)

(b) Cháng 嘗
Cháng 嘗 'once' (also written 甞) as a full verb means 'to taste, try.' As a preverbal particle it indicates past tense.

> **418.** Rán ér Kē yě, cháng wén qí lüè 然 而 軻 也 ，嘗 聞 其 略
>
> Still I, Kē (i.e., Mencius), once heard the general outline of them. (*Mèng* 5B/2)

Cháng 嘗 is frequently found with *yǐ* 矣, in the affirmative, or in the combination *wèi cháng ... yě* 未 嘗 ... 也, in the negative.

> **419.** Wú cháng wén dà yǒng yú fū zǐ yǐ 吾 嘗 聞 大 勇 於 夫 子 矣
>
> I once heard about supreme courage from the Master. (*Mèng* 2A/2)

> **420.** Wèi cháng yǔ zhī yán xíng shì yě. 未 嘗 與 之 言 行 事 也
>
> You never spoke with him about the business of the mission. (*Mèng* 2B/6)

(c) Céng 曾
Céng 曾 has the same meaning as *cháng* 嘗 but is later in appearing in the language:

> **421.** Liáng Wáng yǐ cǐ yuàn Àng, céng shǐ rén cì Àng. 梁 王 以 此 怨 盎 ，曾 使 人 刺 盎
>
> The Prince of Liáng because of this bore a grudge against Àng and once sent a man to stab him. (*Shǐjì* 101.2744)

Céng 曾 'once' is to be distinguished from the particle *zēng* 曾, written with the same character, which is commonly glossed as *nǎi* 乃 or *zé* 則 'then,' but which seems to be an adverb meaning something like 'just' or 'even.'

422. Er hé zēng bǐ yǔ yú Guǎn Zhòng? 爾 何 曾 比 予 於 管 仲

Why do you even compare me with Guǎn Zhòng? (*Mèng* 2A/1)

(d) Jiāng 將

Jiāng 將 indicates futurity. There is usually an implication of intention involved.

423. Jiāng yǐ xìn zhōng. 將 以 釁 鍾

We are going to consecrate a bell with it. (*Mèng* 1A/7)

In preclassical language, *jiāng* 將 is a full verb, 'to bring, take, use, etc.,' and it survives in the sense of 'lead (an army)' into later Chinese. In early colloquial Chinese it is a co-verbal particle, like modern *bǎ* 把, used to antepose the object of a verb. It is therefore sometimes said that the classical particle of futurity is also derived from the verb 'to take,' but it is clear that syntactically the future particle *jiāng* 將 is not a verb. It comes before a negative particle and cannot itself be negated: *jiāng bù lái* 將 不 來 'will not come,' <u>not</u> *不 將 來. It also comes in front of interrogative pronouns:

424. Zǐ jiāng xī zhī? 子 將 奚 之

Where will you go? (*Zhuāng* 12/70)

Another peculiarity of the syntax of *jiāng* 將 is that in early Classical Chinese is that it can occur, like *wéi* 唯 'only' and *bì* 必 'necessarily,' in front of the subject or an anteposed object:

425. Jiāng Zhèng shì xùn dìng. 將 鄭 是 訓 定

It is Zhèng that we are going to tame and settle. (*Zuǒ* Xuān 12/3)

426. Jiāng tiān xià shí hè. 將 天 下 實 賀

The whole world will bring congratulations. (*Zuǒ* Zhào 8/3)

This is only superficially like the later colloquial *jiāng* 將 = *bǎ* 把.

For *jiāng* 將 with numerical expressions in the sense of 'approximately,' see VI.1.

(e) Qiě 且

Qiě 且 may also be used like *jiāng* 將 to indicate futurity.

427. Bìng yù, wǒ qiě wǎng jiàn. 病愈，我且往見

When my illness is better, I shall go to see him. (*Mèng* 3A/5)

Compare also example **101**. For *qiě* 且 in other meanings see examples **103, 116, 157, 488, 524, 531**. The meaning 'temporarily,' as in Modern Chinese *gūqiě* 姑且, is rare in pre-Hàn texts but becomes common in Hàn times.

(f) Fāng 方

Fāng 方 as an adverbial particle expresses simultaneity, 'just then.'

428. Jí qí zhuàng yě, xuè qì fāng gāng, jiè zhī zài dòu 及其壯也，血氣方剛，戒之在鬭

When he reaches maturity, his physical powers are just then strong and one warns him against strife. (*LY* 16/7)

When a sentence containing *fāng* 方 is used as an initial time clause in another sentence, *fāng* 方 may be placed in front as if it were a coverb and the clause is nominalized by inserting *zhī* 之 between the subject and the verb.

429. Fāng tiān zhī xiū, fú jìng fú xiū. Huǐ qí kě zhuī? 方天之休，弗敬弗休。悔其可追

Just now when Heaven is favourable, if you are not reverent it will not be favourable. How can later repentance recover the lost opportunity? (*Zuǒ* Ai 16/*fù* 1)

(g) Shǐ 始

Shǐ 始 'begin' is used as an adverb meaning 'for the first time, first.'

430. Chén shǐ zhì yú jìng, wèn guó zhī dà jìn, rán hòu gǎn rù. 臣始至於境，問國之大禁，然後敢入

When I first reached the frontier, I inquired about the great prohibitions before I dared enter. (*Mèng* 1B/2)

In *Zhuāngzǐ* we find *wèi shǐ* 未始 used like *wèi cháng* 未嘗 in the sense of 'not yet.'

431. Fú dào wèi shǐ yǒu fēng, yán wèi shǐ yǒu cháng 夫道未始有封，言未始有常

The Way has never had borders, saying has never had norms.
(*Zhuāng* 2/55; Graham 1981:57)

(h) Chū 初

Chū 初 'begin, first' can also be used adverbially like *shǐ* 始 meaning 'for the first time.' More frequently, however, it is an introductory time word meaning 'previously,' used to make a break in a narrative and take the time back to an earlier occasion.

> **432.** Chū, Jí qù yú Sòng Zǐcháo 初 ，疾娶于宋子朝
> Previously, Jí had taken [a daughter] of Zǐcháo of Sòng to wife.
> (*Zuǒ* Āi 11/6)

4. Modality

In Indo-European languages the expression of modality, that is of subjective attitudes such as wishing, intending, imagined possibility, etc., like that of aspect and tense, is included in the system of verbal inflection. In English there are still some vestiges of the old subjunctive mood — 'I wish I were rich …' 'If he were prime minister …' etc. — and there is a system of modal auxiliaries — 'can, may, shall, will, ought, must, dare, etc.' The same ideas can also be expressed by full verbs such as 'wish, intend, hope, etc.' or by adjectives and adverbs such as 'possible, possibly, perhaps.'

In Chinese there is no subjunctive mood, since verbs are uninflected. There are, however, analogues to modal auxiliaries in (a) verbs like *néng* 能 'can, be capable of,' *gǎn* 敢 'dare,' *kěn* 肯 'be willing to,' *yù* 欲 'wish' (also 'intend, will') which take clause objects; (b) the verb *dé* 得 'get' which does not take a clause object but is used in series with a following verb in the sense of 'get to do, can' (*huò* 獲 'catch' is used in a similar way in later texts); (c) the adjectives *kě* 可 'possible,' *zú* 足 'sufficient, worthy,' *nán* 難 'difficult,' *yì* 易 'easy' which take passive verbs as complements; (d) other adjectives like *yí* 宜 'fitting, suitable,' *kě* 可 in the sense of 'ought, should,' which take active verbs as complements.

Other modal notions are expressed by adverbial or adnominal particles. *Jiāng* 將 , discussed above as a particle denoting futurity, often implies intentionality rather than simply future time. *Bì* 必 'necessarily' which can occur adverbially in front of noun predicates (**18, 22**) as well as verbs (**148, 224**, etc.), and as an adnominal particle introducing an exposed noun phrase (**240**), takes the place of an auxiliary verb equivalent to English 'must.' There remain a few special particles that are primarily modal in implication.

(a) Qí 其

Qí 其 qualifies a statement as possible or probable rather than a matter of known fact. It is very common in the preclassical language, tending to die out in classical times except in certain stereotyped formulas.[51] Most commonly it is found in the rhetorical question formula *qí ... hū* 其 ... 乎 which expects the agreement of the listener, like 'is it not ...' in English.

> **433.** Qí wú hòu hū? 其 無 後 乎
>
> Surely he must have no descendants. (*Mèng* 1A/4)

We also find *qí* 其 having the same kind of implication in sentences without final *hū,* e.g.,

> **434.** Dāng jīn zhī shì, shě wǒ qí shuí yě 當 今 之 世 , 舍 我 其 誰 也
>
> In the present day world, who is there except me? (Implying that there is no one; *Mèng* 2B/13)

> **435.** Zǐ qí yǒu yǐ yù wǒ lái. 子 其 有 以 語 我 來
>
> You must surely have some advice to give me. (*Zhuāng* 4/39. *Lái* 來 is here a final exclamatory particle.)

> **436.** Shùn qí zhì xiào yǐ. 舜 其 至 孝 矣
>
> Shun was surely most filial. (*Mèng* 6B/3)

A related usage in somewhat earlier texts is the use of *qí* 其 in the conclusion of a contrary to fact conditional sentence.

> **437.** Rú yǒu zhèng, suī bù wú yǐ, wú qí yù wén zhī.
> 如 有 政 , 雖 不 吾 以 , 吾 其 與 聞 之
>
> If there had been government business, though they do not employ me, I would surely have been present and heard of it. (*LY* 13/14. *Yù* 與, in departing tone, is 'to be present, participate in.')

> **438.** Wéi Guǎn Zhòng, wú qí pī fà zuǒ rèn yǐ 微 管 仲 , 吾 其 被 髮 左 衽 矣
>
> If it had not been for Gǔan Zhòng, we would surely have our hair hanging loose and our lapels buttoned on the left. (*LY* 14/17)

A frequent usage is in imperative sentences in which *qí* 其 apparently has the effect of softening the command into a wish or exhortation.

439. Wú zǐ qí wú fèi xiān jūn zhī gōng. 吾 子 其 無 廢 先 君 之 功

You should not destroy the former ruler's achievement. (*Zuǒ Yǐn* 3/5)

A fully satisfying analysis of the functions of *qí* 其 in the preclassical and early classical language has yet to be made.

(b) Dài 殆, Shūjī 庶 幾

Adverbs of more explicit meaning than *qí* 其 which have a similar effect in lessening the certainty of an assertion include: *dài* 殆 'dangerous; is in danger of; maybe' (example **271**), *shūjī* 庶 幾 'almost' (literally, 'many-few' = 'more or less'). The latter, like *qí* 其, can be used to express a wish.

440. Wáng shū jī gǎi zhī. 王 庶 幾 改 之

The king might, I hoped, change his mind. (*Mèng* 2B/12)

(c) Gài 蓋

Gài 蓋 is an introductory particle whose primary meaning may originally have been to affirm the truth of a statement but which, in context, can have the effect of opening a possibility of doubt.[52]

441. Gài yǒu zhī yǐ, wǒ wèi zhī jiàn yě 蓋 有 之 矣 ， 我 未 之 見 也

There may well have been such cases, but I have never seen them. (*LY* 4/6)

A frequent usage is to introduce a final explanatory clause ending in *yě* 也 (see VII.2a.ii above). Here *gài* is commonly translated by the conjunction 'for,' though this meaning really belongs to the construction as a whole rather than to the introductory particle.

442. Suī shū sì cài gēng, wèi cháng bù bǎo, gài bù gǎn bù bǎo. 雖 疏 食 菜 羹 ， 未 嘗 不 飽 ， 蓋 不 敢 不 飽 也

Even if it was coarse rice and vegetable soup, he never failed to eat his fill, for he dared not do otherwise. (*Mèng* 5B/3)

(d) Wú 毋 (無) and Wù 勿

The prohibitory particles *wú* 毋 or 無, and *wù* 勿 (XI.2a and b) have modality as part of their meaning. As noted above they can occur in subordinate sentences where one cannot translate them simply as imperative. Such constructions need to be more thoroughly analyzed.

(e) Níng 寧

Níng 寧 'rather,' to be distinguished from the full word *níng* 寧 'quiet, peaceful,' expresses a preference for one course of action over another.

443. Bì bào chóu. Níng shì Róng Dí. 必 報 讎 ， 寧 事 戎 狄

We must have vengeance on our foes. We would rather serve the Róng and Dí barbarians (than not do so). (*Zuǒ* Xī 15/14)

The comparison is often made explicit with *yǔ* 與 :

444. Lǐ, yǔ qí shē yě, níng jiǎn 禮 ， 與 其 奢 也 ， 寧 儉

In ceremonies it is better to be sparing than extravagant. (*LY* 3/4)

On the rhetorical question formula *wú níng* 毋 寧 , see XIV.2.

XIII. Adnominal and Adverbial Words of Inclusion and Restriction

Notions such as 'all,' 'some,' 'any,' 'none,' and 'only' are expressed partly by adnominal particles, i.e., particles which precede nouns or noun phrases and partly by pronominal adverbs, i.e., particles which although affecting the one or other of the nouns dependent on a verb (its subject or object) are placed in adverbial position in front of the verb. Restriction and inclusion ('only,' 'completely') may also apply properly to the verb itself or to the whole predicate and be indicated by adverbs and/or final particles. For convenience the adnominals and adverbials in question are treated together.

1. Words of Inclusion

(a) Zhū 諸 *'all; members of the class of'*
Zhū 諸 (EMC tɕia) is a derivative of the same pronominal root as *zhī* 之 (EMC tɕɨ) and *zhě* 者 (EMC tɕia').[53] Though usually given the translation 'all,' it indicates the membership of a class rather than a numerical totality.

> **445.** Wáng zhī zhū chén jiē zú yǐ gòng zhī. 王之諸臣皆足以供之
> Your various ministers are sufficient to provide them. (*Mèng* 1A/7. That is, your ministers, severally or collectively, as a class, not all of them together as would be implied if one translated: 'All your ministers.')

The common expression *zhū hóu* 諸侯 'the feudal lords' means members of that class of people, not necessarily every single one of them. It can even be used as a singular 'a feudal lord.'

A peculiar usage of *zhū* 諸 which shows its pronominal origin is in the rhetorical question formula *qí zhū ... yú* 其諸 ... 與 found in the *Lúnyǔ* and the *Gōngyáng zhuàn*. It corresponds to the more common formula *qí ... hū* 其 ... 乎 but, as the use of the question particle *yú* 與 instead of *hū* 乎 would indicate, the predicate is nominal rather than verbal:

> **446.** Fū zǐ zhī qiú zhī yě, qí zhū yì hū rén zhī qiú zhī yú 夫子之求之也，其諸異乎人之求之與
> Is it not that our master's way of seeking for information is

different from that of other people? (*LY* 1/10. Nominal predication
with final *yě* 也 (here combined with the final question particle as
yú 與) making an explanatory comment.)

447. Qí wú Zhòngsūn. Qí zhū wú Zhòngsūn yú?
齊 無 仲 孫 。 其 諸 吾 仲 孫 與

There was no Zhòngsūn in Qí. Surely it must have been our (Lǔ's)
Zhòngsūn. (*Gōng* Mǐn 1/6)

The function of *zhū* 諸 in this construction seems clearly to be connected
with nominalization and to be comparable to that of *zhě* 者 at the end of a
phrase.

Dū 都 (EMC tɔ, colloquial Mandarin *dōu*) is used adverbially in its
modern sense of 'all' in some Hàn texts, but was not usual in Literary
Chinese. It is probably etymologically a variant form of *zhū* 諸 .

(b) Fán 凡 'all'

In the sense of 'all,' *fán* 凡 (EMC buam) normally introduces a noun
phrase in exposed position at the head of a sentence.

448. ... zé fán kě yǐ dé shēng zhě, hé bú yòng yě 則 凡 可 以
得 生 者 ，何 不 用 也

... then why should he not use every means that can preserve life?
(*Mèng* 6A/10)

As an adjunct of nouns in other positions it means 'common, ordinary': *fán
rén* 凡 人 'ordinary people.'

It can also be used in front of numerical expressions summing up a
series, 'in all ...'

449. Tiānzǐ yī wèi, gōng yī wèi, hóu yī wèi, bó yī wèi, zǐ nán
tóng yī wèi, fán wǔ děng yě 天 子 一 位 ， 公 一 位 ， 侯
一 位 ， 伯 一 位 ， 子 男 同 一 位 ， 凡 五 等 也

The Son of Heaven was one rank, dukes were one rank, marquises
were one rank, counts were one rank, viscounts and barons were
together one rank. In all there were five grades. (*Mèng* 5B/2)

(c) Jiē 皆 'all,' Jǔ 舉 'all'[54]

Jiē 皆 (EMC kəɨj/kɛːj) and *jǔ* 舉 (EMC kɨǎ') are two members of a word
family with initial *k- which includes also (e) and (f) below, and possibly
other words such as *jiān* 兼 'combine' (EMC kɛm). *Jiē* 皆 is the more
common of the two but it is restricted to adverbial position. *Jǔ* 舉 can be

either adnominal or adverbial. Semantically they seem to be interchangeable. On the analogy of other pairs of particles in which a level tone proclitic contrasts with a rising tone word with freer positional distribution, one would hypothesize that *jǔ* 舉 was more emphatic. It should further be noted that *jiē* 皆 is obviously related to the verb *xié, jiē* 偕 'accompany.'[55] *Jǔ* 舉 is a homophone of a verb 'to lift' written with the same graph, but in this case there is no apparent etymological connection.

The common use of *jiē* 皆 is before a verb or a noun predicate with a plural subject. It behaves very much like modern *dōu* 都 .

> **450.** Bǎi xìng jiē yǐ wáng wéi ài yě. 百 姓 皆 以 王 為 愛 也
>
> The common people all thought Your Majesty stingy. (*Mèng* 1A/7)

In the following example, we find it referring to the object rather than to the subject of the verb it precedes.

> **451.** Jiē shǐ yī shí bǎi yòng, chū rù xiāng yǎn. 皆 使 衣 食 百 用 出 入 相 揜
>
> Ensure that for food, clothing, and all other needs, income and outgo shall cover one another. (*Xún* 10/20)

Note however, that the verb here is *shǐ* 使, the object of which is at the same time subject of another verb following. It seems that *jiē* 皆 has been attracted from its normal position in front of the second verb to stand in front of the auxiliary verb and that it is not a true case of *jiē* 皆 referring to the object.

Less commonly *jiē* 皆, like modern *dōu* 都, can refer to a plural object of a verb, as in:

> **452.** Bǎi hái jiǔ hé liù zāng, gāi ér cún yān, wú shuí yǔ wéi qīn? Rǔ jiē yuè zhī hū? 百 骸 九 竅 六 藏 ， 賅 而 存 焉 。 吾 誰 與 為 親 。 汝 皆 説 之 乎
>
> Of the hundred joints, nine openings, six viscera all present and complete, which should I recognize as more kin to me than another? Are you people pleased with them all? (*Zhuāng* 2/16; Graham 1981:51)

Jǔ 舉 'all' is less frequent than *jiē* 皆 in all Zhōu texts and is not found at all in some (possibly just a matter of chance). It too is more often than not in adverbial position, e.g.,

453. Wáng rú yòng yǔ, zé qǐ tú Qí mín ān? Tiānxià zhī mín jǔ ān. 王 如 用 予 ， 則 豈 徒 齊 民 安 ， 天 下 之 民 舉 安

If the king were to use me, would it be only the people of Qí who would be made content? The people of the whole world would be made content. (*Mèng* 2B/12. Note the emphatic contrast between 'only' and 'all,' supporting the view that *jǔ* 舉 was more emphatic than *jiē* 皆 .)

Jǔ 舉 is not found adnominally in *Mencius* but there are examples in the *Zuǒzhuàn, Mòzǐ, Zhuāngzǐ, Xúnzǐ,* e.g.,

454. Qǐ wéi guǎ jūn, jǔ qún chén shí shòu qí kuàng 豈 惟 寡 君 ， 舉 群 臣 實 受 其 貺

Surely it will be not only our ruler but all his ministers who will receive the benefit of your gift. (*Zuǒ* Zhāo 3/*fù* 2)

(d) Jū 俱 *'both, together'*

Jū 俱 (EMC kuǎ)[56] is always adverbial and is often found when the subject consists of two persons or things.

455. Fù mǔ jū cún, xiōng dì wú gù, yī lè yě 父 母 俱 存 ， 兄 弟 無 故 ， 一 樂 也

That his father and mother are both alive and that among his brothers there is no cause for concern is his first delight. (*Mèng* 7A/20)

It is also found with a subject consisting of more than two persons or things, but usually it is a small number of discrete items rather than an indefinite plural.

456. Rán zé wǒ yǔ ruò yǔ rén jū bù néng xiāng zhī yě 然 則 我 與 若 與 人 俱 不 能 相 知 也

Then I and you and the third person together cannot know (the right answer) for each other. (*Zhuāng* 2/89)

As in this example, *jū* 俱 has an implication of acting in concert, not merely duality or plurality.

457. Suī yǔ zhī jū xué, fú ruò zhī yǐ 雖 與 之 俱 學 ， 弗 若 之 矣

Though he studies along with him, he will not come up to him. (*Mèng* 6A/9)

Jū 俱 is no doubt related etymologically not only to *jù* 具 (EMC guǎ^h) 'to provide' but also to *gòng* 共 (EMC guawŋ^h) 'together; common.' In the *Shījīng*, which does not have *jū* 俱, *jù* 具 is found in the sense of 'all' (not restricted to subjects consisting of a small number).

458. Mín jù ěr zhān 民 具 爾 瞻
The people all look at you. (*Shī* 191/1)

(e) Gè 各 *'each'*
Gè 各 (EMC kak) is always adverbial and referring to the subject in Classical Chinese. It belongs to a set of words ending in *-k which define the subject as individual members of a larger group or the members of such a group taken one at a time. Compare *huò* 或 'someone, something,' *mò* 莫 'none,' and *shú* 孰 'which.'

459. Gè yù zhèng jǐ yě, yān yòng zhàn? 各 欲 正 己 也 ，
焉 用 戰
If each wished [King Wǔ] to correct him, what need was there for fighting? (*Mèng* 7B/4)

(f) Měi 每 *'every (time), always; whenever'*
Měi 每 is mostly adverbial, quantifying the action of the verb rather than the subject or a complement.

460. Shèng rén chóuchú yǐ xīng shì, yǐ měi chéng gōng. 聖 人
躊 躇 以 興 事 ， 以 每 成 功
The sages are hesitant in starting things and so always achieve success. (*Zhuāng* 26/23)
It is frequently found in an initial time clause and is then equivalent in translation to a subordinating conjunction, 'whenever.'

461. Chū, Bózōng měi cháo, qí qī bì jiè zhī yuē … 初 ， 伯
宗 每 朝 ， 其 妻 必 戒 之 曰
Previously, whenever Bózōng went to court, his wife would always warn him …. (*Zuǒ* Chéng 15/*fù*)
Měi 每 may be followed by a time word, as in,

462. Guó měi yè hài yuē, wáng rù yǐ 國 每 夜 駭 曰 ， 王
入 矣
Every night there were alarms in the city that the king had entered. (*Zuǒ* Zhāo 13/3)

(g) *Words of Verbal Origin*

Various words of verbal origin are used adverbially to indicate inclusiveness either of the subject or the predicate. Among them are: *xián* 咸, EMC ɣəim/ɣɛːm 'to unite; unitedly, all (of the subject)'; *jìn* 盡, EMC dzin', 'to exhaust; completely, all (mostly referring to the predicate)'; *xī* 悉, EMC sit, 'thorough; to exhaust or to sum up; all (referring either to the subject or to the predicate)'; *bìng* 並, 竝, 倂, EMC bɛjŋ', 'side by side; equally both,' *bìng* 幷, 倂, EMC pjiajŋʰ, 'together, all' (derived from the verb *bīng* 幷, EMC pjiajŋ, 'combine' — because of the similarity in meaning of these cognates and the graphic overlap, these words are not easy to distinguish); and *bì* 畢, EMC pjit, 'to finish; completely; all (of the object).'

2. Restriction

(a) Wéi 唯 (惟, 維) *'only'*

In the preclassical language, *wéi* 唯 functioned as a copula in noun predication or as an adnominal topicalizing particle with much the same meaning as classical *yě* 也 (III.4). In the classical period, it has the meaning 'only,' but it retains some syntactical peculiarities related to its earlier usage.[57] In the classical period, it is found in the following uses.

(i) Introducing the subject or an exposed element

Regularly in the *Zuǒzhuàn* and *Guóyǔ* and surviving to a limited extent in later texts, the exposed element is recapitualted by a pronoun in front of the verb (see Section VIII.1).

> **463.** Wéi lì zhī qiú. 唯利之求
> They seek only profit. (*Xún* 11/19)

A syntactical peculiarity of such sentences in texts such as *Mencius*, *Mòzǐ*, and *Xúnzǐ* is that one often finds the verb *wéi* 為 'make; be' inserted before the main verb of the sentence.[58]

> **464.** Wú héng chǎn ér yǒu héng xīn zhě, wéi shì wéi néng. 無恆產而有恆心者，惟士為能
> To be without a constant livelihood yet to have a constant mind, only the scholar-gentleman is capable (of that). (*Mèng* 1A/7)

(But compare *Zhuāngzǐ* 17/60, wéi dà shèng zhě, wéi shèng rén néng zhī 為大勝者, 唯聖人能之 : To make a great victory, only a sage is capable of that.)

> **465.** Wéi rén zhī wéi shǒu, wéi yì zhī wéi xíng. 唯仁之為 守, 唯義之為行
>
> Only Benevolence does he cherish, only Righteousness does he put into practice. (*Xún* 3/27)

(ii) Introducing a noun predicate

Final *yě* 也 is often, though not invariably, omitted in such cases.

> **466.** Zhī qí zuì zhě wéi Kǒng Jùxīn. 知其罪者唯孔踞 心
>
> The only one who knows his faults is Kǒng Jùxīn. (*Mèng* 2B/4. Literally: One who knows his faults is only Kǒng Jùxīn.)

> **467.** Wéi jūn suǒ xíng yě. 惟君所行也
>
> It is only for you, sir, to put it into practice. (*Mèng* 1B/4. Literally: It is only what you, sir, put into practice.)

The formula *wéi ... suǒ (yě)* 惟...所 (也) frequently has, as here, a hortatory meaning, 'You should, my lord, just put it into practice.'

(iii) In adverbial position restricting the predicate

> **468.** Cǐ wéi jiù sǐ ér kǒng bú shàn. 此惟救死而恐不贍
>
> In these circumstances they only seek to avoid death and are afraid they will not succeed. (*Mèng* 1A/7)

As the negative of *wéi* 唯 'only' we find mostly *bù wéi* 不唯 in *Zuǒzhuàn*, but twice *fēi wéi* 非唯, evidently a new formation influenced by the fact that *fēi* 非 alone, contracted from *bù wéi* 不唯, had originally been the negative counterpart of *wéi* 唯. In later texts, *fēi wéi* 非唯 replaces *bù wéi* 不唯.

> **469.** Bù wéi Xǔ guó zhī wèi. 不唯許國之為
>
> It is not only for the sake of Xǔ. (*Zuǒ* Yǐn 11/3)

> **470.** Fēi wéi bǎi shèng zhī jiā wéi rán yě. 非惟百乘之家 為然也
>
> Not only did the head of a household of one hundred chariots act thus. (*Mèng* 5B/3)

(b) Dú 獨 *'only'*

A number of words beginning in *d- in Middle Chinese share the meaning 'only' and are presumably based on a common root. *Dú* 獨 (EMC dəwk) occurs as a full adjective meaning 'alone, solitary.' Like other adjectives, it can also be used adverbially in this sense, as in *dú jū* 獨 居 'live alone.' It also functions in adverbial position as a particle restricting the subject as in:

471. Zhū jūn zǐ jiē yǔ Huān yán, Mèngzǐ dú bù yǔ Huān yán. 諸 君 子 皆 與 驩 言 ， 孟 子 獨 不 與 驩 言

The various gentlemen have all spoken with me, Huan. Mencius alone has not spoken with me. (*Mèng* 4B/27)

Fēi dú 非 獨 is used adnominally like *fēi wéi* 非 唯 in:

472. Fēi dú xián zhě yǒu shì xīn yě. Rén jiē yǒu zhī. 非 獨 賢 者 有 是 心 也 ， 人 皆 有 之

It is not only that superior men have this mind. All men have it. (*Mèng* 6A/10)

In Hàn texts we find *wéi dú* 唯 獨 or *dú* 獨 alone used adnominally like *wéi* 唯 .

Dú 獨 is used in rhetorical questions to emphasize the unlikeliness or absurdity of a proposition.

473. Qì jūn zhī mìng, dú shuí shòu zhī? 棄 君 之 命 ， 獨 誰 受 之

If I abandon my ruler's command, who will possibly take it up? (*Zuǒ* Xuān 4/*fù*)

474. Jīn ēn zú yǐ jí qín shòu ér gōng bú zhì yú bǎi xìng zhě, dú hé yú? 今 恩 足 以 及 禽 獸 而 功 不 至 於 百 姓 者 ， 獨 何 與

Now how can it possibly be that your kindness is sufficient to reach birds and animals yet the benefit does not reach the people? (*Mèng* 1A/7)

(A more literal but less idiomatic English translation for *dú* 獨 in such cases would be 'exceptionally.')

(c) *Other Similar Words*

Other similar words in *d- that can be used, adnominally or adverbially or both include: (i) *tú* 徒 (EMC dɔ), 'only; in vain, vainly' (besides its quite separate meanings 'go on foot; follower, disciple; foot soldier; convict;

etc.'); (ii) *tè* 特 (EMC də k) 'only' ('special, particular' as a full word); (iii) *zhí* 直 (EMC drik) 'only' (to be distinguished from the homophonous word 'straight, direct,'); (iv) *dàn* 但 'only' (rare in pre-Hàn texts).

(d) *Restriction by Final Particles*

Restriction can also be expressed by the final phrasal particle *ér yǐ* 而 已 , literally 'then stop,' which may be contracted to *ěr* 耳 . The verbal force of *yǐ* 已 is shown by the fact that *ér yǐ* 而 已 and *ěr* 耳 are frequently followed by the final particleZ *yǐ* 矣 .

475. Yán jǔ sī xīn jiā zhū bǐ ér yǐ. 言 舉 斯 心 加 諸 彼 而 已

It just means to take this mind and apply it to others and that's all. (*Mèng* 1A/7)

476. Zhí hào shì sú zhī yuè ěr. 直 好 世 俗 之 樂 耳
I only like the popular music of the present age. (*Mèng* 1B/1)

477. Zǐ chéng Qí rén ye. zhī Guǎn Zhòng Yànzǐ ér yǐ yǐ 子 誠 齊 人 也 。 知 管 仲 晏 子 而 已 矣

You are truly a man of Qí. You only know Guǎn Zhòng and Yànzǐ. (*Mèng* 2A/1)

For additional examples see **2, 60, 179, 187, 390, 555.**

3. Some, None

(a) Huò 或 *'some one, some'* and Yǒu 有 *'some; sometimes'*

Huò 或 (EMC ɣwək) belongs with other words in *-k which are used adverbially to define the subject as one out of a set (cf. *gè* 各 'each,' *mò* 莫 'none,' *shú* 孰 'which').

478. Huò bǎi bù ér hòu zhǐ, huò wǔ shí bù ér hòu zhǐ. 或 百 步 而 後 止 ， 或 五 十 步 而 後 止

Some (of the soldiers described above) stop after 100 paces, some stop after fifty paces. (*Mèng* 1A/3)

479. Huò gào guǎ rén yuē … 或 告 寡 人 曰
Some one told me … (*Mèng* 1B/16)

480. Sòng rén huò dé yù. 宋 人 或 得 玉
A man of Song obtained a piece of jade. (*Zuǒ* Xiāng 15/*fù* 3 i.e.:
Of the men of Sòng, one obtained a piece of jade.)

Huò 或 is etymologically related to *yǒu* 有 (EMC wuw') 'have.' The construction in which the subject of a relative clause with *zhě* 者 as head appears as a pseudo-subject of *yǒu* 有 (IV.7 above) has a similar partitive implication. Example **480** is roughly equivalent to *Sòng rén yǒu dé yù zhě* 宋 人 有 得 玉 者 'There was a man of Sòng who obtained a piece of jade.' Another example of this is:

481. Sòng rén yǒu mǐn qí miáo zhī bù zhǎng ér yà zhī zhě. 宋 人 有 閔 其 苗 之 不 長 而 揠 之 者
There was a man of Sòng who was concerned that his sprouts were not growing and pulled at them. (*Mèng* 2A/2)

In the following example *zhě* 者 is omitted, so that *yǒu* 有 is in adverbial position and virtually equivalent to *huò* 或 .

482. Xī zhě yǒu kuì shēng yú yú Zhèng Zǐchǎn 昔 者 有 饋 生 魚 於 鄭 子 產
In former times, some one sent a present of a live fish to Zǐchǎn of Zhèng. (*Mèng* 5A/2)

More commonly the partitive implication of *yǒu* 有 in front of a verb phrase without final *zhě* 者 is thrown onto what follows instead of applying to the subject — 'there are cases when; sometimes,' e.g.,

483. Gù jūnzǐ yǒu bú zhàn, zhàn bì shèng yǐ. 故 君 子 有 不 戰 ，戰 必 勝 矣
Therefore the gentleman will sometimes not fight, but if he fights he will certainly win. (*Mèng* 2B/1)

Huò 或 can also be used as a modifier of the predicate with a similar meaning.

484. Yóu jù huò shī zhī. 猶 懼 或 失 之
He is still afraid of failing in some way. (*Zuǒ* Huán 2/6)

In this sense *huò* 或 is often translated as 'perhaps.' The combination *huò zhě* 或 者 is also used in this sense:

485. Tiān qí huò zhě yù shǐ Wèi tǎo Xíng hū 天 其 或 者 欲 使 衛 討 邢 乎

Does Heaven perhaps wish to make Wèi punish Xíng? (*Zuǒ Xī* 19/5. *Qí* 其 here is modal and also has the effect of making the statement a supposition rather than an assertion of fact.)

(b) Mò 莫 *'no one, none'*

Mò 莫 (EMC mak) is related to *wú* 無 (EMC muǎ) 'not have' in the same way that *huò* 或 is related to *yǒu* 有. *Mò* 莫, however, is only used with reference to the subject and does not have adverbial uses like *huò* 或.

486. Jìn guó, tiān xià mò qiáng yān. 晉國，天下莫強焉

No state in the world was stronger than Jìn. (*Mèng* 1A/5.

Literally: The state of Jìn, in the world none was stronger than it.)

    Note the idiom *mò ruò* 莫若 or *mò rú* 莫如 'nothing is better than …' i.e., 'It is best to …'

487. Rú wù zhī, mò rú guì dé ér zūn shì. 如惡之，莫如貴德而尊士

If you hate it, the best thing is to esteem virtue and honour scholars. (*Mèng* 2A/4)

4. Reflexive and Reciprocal Pronominal Adverbs

(a) Zì 自 *'oneself'*

In contrast to the reflexive pronoun *jǐ* 己 (IX.1d) which behaves like other personal pronouns, *zì* 自 always occurs immediately in front of a verb. It may either (1) indicate that the object of a transitive verb is the same as the subject, *wáng zì shā* 王自殺 'the king killed himself,' or (2) if the verb is intransitive or has another object expressed, emphasize the personal participation of the subject in the action, *wáng zì shā zhī* 王自殺之 'the king himself killed him.' Unlike *jǐ* 己, it is always a direct reflexive, referring to the subject of the verb in front of which it stands.

(b) Xiāng 相 *'each other, mutually'*

Like *zì* 自, *xiāng* 相 always occurs immediately in front of a verb although it usually takes the place of the object, e.g.,

488. Shòu xiāng shí, rén qiě wū zhī. 獸相食，人且惡之

Men hate it even when animals eat each other. (*Mèng* 1A/4)

In a case like the following, *xiāng* 相 stands for a locative complement rather than for the object.

> **489.** Yóu xiāng jī è yě. 猶 相 積 惡 也
>
> They are still accumulating evils against each other. (*Zuǒ* Xiāng 30/*fù* 1)

Mutual participation when neither part of the subject is affected by the verb is expressed by *xiāng yǔ* 相 與 'with each other,' not *xiāng* 相 alone as we might expect if *xiāng* 相 and *zì* 自 were completely parallel in their behaviour.

> **490.** Jiē xián rén yě, xiāng yǔ fǔ xiàng zhī. 皆 賢 人 也 ， 相 與 輔 相 之
>
> They were all worthy men; they mutually assisted him and served him as ministers. (*Mèng* 2A/1)

Xiāng 相 is sometimes used when the action is not strictly reciprocal, but there is a mutual bond of some kind between subject and object. Examples, though rare, do occur in pre-Hàn literature, for instance *xiāng cóng* 相 從 meaning '(you) follow me' (*Shū* 16/1010, Pan'geng — see Karlgren 1950b:24). Later it became much more common.

In the preclassical language we find *xū* 胥 used in a similar way to *xiāng* 相. The two words are no doubt etymologically related.

(c) Shēn 身 '*body, person, self*'

Shēn 身 may be used adverbially to emphasize the personal participation of the subject.

> **491.** Bǐ shēn zhī lǚ, qī bì lú, yǐ yì zhī. 彼 身 織 履 ， 妻 辟 纑 ， 以 易 之
>
> He himself wove sandals and his wife twisted threads to exchange for those things. (*Mèng* 3B/10)

(d) Jiāo 交 '*in exchange, mutually*' and Hù 互 '*mutually*'

Mutuality may also be expressed by *jiāo* 交 'to exchange, interchange' used adverbially (see example **415** above). *Hù* 互, which originally meant 'intertwining, crossing' is also used in this way, either alone or with *xiāng* 相, in Hàn and later texts.

XIV. Imperative, Interrogative, and Exclamatory Sentences

1. Imperative Sentences

(a) *Unmarked*

There is no special mark of the imperative as such.

> **492.** Zǐ wèi wǒ wèn Mèngzǐ ... 子 為 我 問 孟 子
> Do you ask Mencius for me ... (*Mèng* 3A/2)

> **493.** Yǐ yáng yì zhī. 以 羊 易 之
> Change it for a sheep. (*Mèng* 1A/7)

In the second example, the subject is deleted, as in an English imperative sentence, but such deletion is no more typical of the imperative than of the declarative in Chinese, as can be seen from the adjacent sentence *gù yǐ yáng yì zhī yě* 故 以 羊 易 之 也 'Therefore I changed it for a sheep.' It is possible that in the spoken language there was a special intonation for the imperative, but only context can serve as a guide as far as the written language is concerned.

(b) Qǐng 請 *'I beg of you, please'*

Qǐng 請 may be inserted parenthetically to turn an imperative sentence into a request. It is placed between the second person subject (if present) and the verb, but its own subject must be understood as first person.

> **494.** Wáng qǐng duó zhī. 王 請 度 之
> I beg Your Majesty to measure it (or) Will Your Majesty please measure it? (*Mèng* 1A/7. Literally: Your Majesty, [I] beg, measure it.)

Qǐng 請 may also be used when both verbs are in the first person, i.e., when the speaker asks permission to do something.

> **495.** Chén qǐng wèi wáng yán yuè. 臣 請 為 王 言 樂
> Let me, I pray, speak to Your Majesty about music. (*Mèng* 1B/1)

(c) *Prohibition*

On *wú* 毋 (無) and *wù* 勿 as negatives of prohibition, see XI.2 above.

(d) *Modal* Qí 其 *in Imperative Sentences*

On modal *qí* 其 in imperative sentences, see XII.4a above.

2. Interrogative Sentences

Questions may be divided into simple questions which ask for information, and rhetorical questions, which imply an answer which is already known and ask for agreement. Both types of questions may be expressed by means of final question particles and/or interrogative pronouns. There are also various adverbial particles which are used in forming different types of rhetorical questions.

(a) *Simple Questions*

(i) The final particle *hū* 乎

The final particle *hū* 乎 turns a statement into a question.

> **496.** Xiàn zhě yì lè cǐ hū? 賢 者 亦 樂 此 乎
> Does a man of virtue also enjoy such things? (*Mèng* 1A/2)

> **497.** Téng, xiǎo guó yě, jiàn yú Qí Chǔ. Shì Qí hū? Shì Chǔ hū?
> 滕，小 國 也 。間 於 齊 楚 。事 齊 乎 。事 楚 乎
> Téng is a small country; it lies between Qí and Chǔ. Should it serve Qí? Or should it serve Chǔ? (*Mèng* 1B/13)

(ii) *Yě hū* 也 乎 , *yú* 與 (歟), *yé* 邪 (耶)

After noun predicates and other types of sentences which end in the particle *yě* 也, the corresponding questions end in *yě hū* 也 乎 in the *Zuǒzhuàn*. In the *Lúnyǔ* and in later forms of Classical Chinese we find the contractions *yú* 與 (歟) or *yé* 邪 (耶) (I.4d; III.1a).

> **498.** Wèi féi gān bù zú yú kǒu yú 為 肥 甘 不 足 於 口 與
> Is it that fat and sweet things are not sufficient for your mouth? (*Mèng* 1A/7)

> **499.** Tiān zhī cāng cāng, qí zhèng sè yé, qí yuǎn ér wú suǒ zhì jí yé? 天 之 蒼 蒼 ，其 正 色 邪 ，其 遠 而 無 所 至 極 邪
> Is the blue of the sky its true color or is it that it is distant and without limit? (*Zhuāng* 1/4, 5)

(iii) *Zhū* 諸

Zhū 諸 at the end of a sentence is a contraction of *zhī hū* 之 乎. Thus, *yǒu zhū* 有 諸 (= 有 之 乎). 'Is it so?' in example **112** above.

(iv) *Fǒu* 否

On *fǒu* 否 '(or) not,' forming alternative questions, see XI.1b above.

(v) Interrogative pronouns

Interrogative pronouns are treated in IX.3. Note that sentences which contain an interrogative pronoun may or may not also have a final interrogative particle.

(b) *Rhetorical Questions*

Simple questions formed as in (a) above may, in context, imply or favour one answer rather than another. There are, however, a number of special ways to indicate such implications.

(i) Negative questions requiring affirmative answers

As in English, a negative particle in a question commonly implies an affirmative answer.

> **500.** Wén wáng jì mò, wén bú zài zī hu? 文 王 既 沒 ， 文 不 在 兹 乎
>
> King Wén having passed away, has not (the cause of) civilization (*wén*) been lodged here (in me)? (*LY* 9/5)

> **501.** Xiān shì hòu dé, fēi chóng dé yě yú? 先 事 後 得 ， 非 崇 德 也 與
>
> To put duty first and achievement last, is that not to exalt virtue? (*LY* 12/21)

There are exceptions, however:

> **502.** Xìn hū, fū zǐ bù yán, bú xìao, bù qǔ hu? 信 乎 ， 夫 子 不 言 、 不 笑 、 不 取 乎
>
> It is true that your master does not speak, does not laugh, and does not take? (*LY* 14/13)

(Note the presence of the preliminary phrase, 'Is it true?' Without it the sentence would have presumably meant: 'Does not your master speak, does he not laugh, does he not take?')

In the above example, 'not speaking,' 'not laughing,' and 'not taking' denote positive qualities, not merely the absence of a certain activity. This is an unusual meaning of negation with verbs but is quite normal with adjectives. *Bú shàn* 不善 normally means 'wicked,' not merely 'not good' in a neutral sense. This is probably why there is a special formula *bú yì ... hū* 不亦 ... 乎 for making rhetorical questions with adjectives.

503. Yǒu péng zì yuǎn fāng lái, bú yì lè hū? 有朋自遠方來，不亦樂乎

Is it not enjoyable to have friends come from afar? (*LY* 1/1)
(Without *yì* 亦, *bú lè hū* 不樂乎 would likely mean 'is it disagreeable?')

504. Mín yǐ wéi xiǎo, bú yì yí hū? 民以為小，不亦宜乎

Was it not natural that the people considered it small? (*Mèng* 1B/2)
This is a common construction found in all texts of the classical period.
We have *yì bú* 亦不 instead of *bú yì* 不亦 in:

505. Yì bù zú diào hū? 亦不足弔乎

Is he not worthy to receive condolences? (*Mèng* 3B/3)
When the adjective is modified by an adverb of degree we find *yì* 亦 omitted, presumably because there is then no possibility of ambiguity through interpreting 不 + Adj. as meaning the contrary rather than the negative.

506. Sān yuè wú jūn zé diào, bù yǐ jí hū? 三月無君則弔，不以急乎

Was it not overly hasty to send condolences to someone who was three months without a ruler (i.e., unemployed)? (*Mèng* 3B/3) 以 = 已 'very,' see XII.1c above. Compare also *bù yǐ tài hū* 不以泰乎 in *Mèng* 3B/4.)

507. Bù yóu yù hū? 不猶愈乎

Would it not be still better? (*Zuǒ* Xuān 12/3 and Xiāng 13/*fù* 3)
The function of *yì* 亦 in questions, apart from the formula *bú yì* + Adj. *hū* 不亦 + Adj. 乎, needs further study. For example, in

508. Gài (= hé) yì fǎn qí běn yǐ? 蓋 (盍) 亦反其本矣

Why not return to the fundamentals? (*Mèng* 1A/7)
we find it in a rhetorical question formed with an interrogative pronoun and

negative particle (combined into one syllable 盍 = 胡 不) which is
equivalent in meaning to an exhortation. The same sentence is repeated later
in the passage without *yì* 亦.

We also find it implying an affirmative answer in questions with no
negative particle:

509. Sǒu bù yuǎn qiān lǐ ér lái. Yì jiāng yǒu yǐ lì wú guó hū?
叟不遠千里而來，亦將有以利吾國乎

You sir have come without considering a thousand *li* too far.
Surely you must have something to benefit my country. (*Mèng*
1A/1)

(ii) *Qí* 其 in rhetorical questions
The modal particle *qí* 其 is used to introduce a common type of rhetorical
question requiring an affirmative answer.

510. Shǐ zuò yǒng zhě, qí wú hòu hū? 始作俑者，其無
後乎

Surely he who first made tomb figures must have no posterity.
(*Mèng* 1A/4)

511. Kǒng zǐ yuē, wéi cǐ shī zhě, qí zhī dào hū? 孔子曰，
為此詩者，其知道乎

Confucius said, 'He who made this poem surely understood the
Way.' (*Mèng* 2A/4)

As we see in the first example, the scope of *qí* 其 includes a negative
particle following it, so that the negative proposition is affirmed by the
rhetorical question. In the following example, on the other hand, the
negative particle before *qí* 其 merely reinforces the rhetorical effect.

512. Cái nán, bù qí rán hū? 才難，不其然乎

Is it not true that talent is difficult (to discover)? (*LY* 8/20)

For *qí zhū... yú* 其諸 … 與 as an equivalent rhetorical question formula
for noun predicates, see XIII.1a above.

(iii) *Qǐ* 豈
The particle *qǐ* 豈 introduces rhetorical questions requiring a negative
answer (like Modern Chinese *nán dào* 難道 or Latin *num*).

513. Suī yǒu tái, chí, niǎo, shòu, qǐ néng dú lè hū? 雖有臺
池鳥獸，豈能獨樂乎

Though he had towers, ponds, birds and animals, how could he enjoy them alone? (*Mèng* 1A/2)

514. Qǐ yǐ rén yì wéi bù měi yě. 豈 以 仁 義 為 不 美 也

Surely it is not that they regard benevolence and righteousness as bad. (*Mèng* 2B/2)

The subject, if it is expressed, is normally placed in front of *qǐ* 豈.

515. Ér wáng qǐ wèi shì zāi? 而 王 豈 為 是 哉

But how could it be that Your Majesty would do it for these reasons? (*Mèng* 1A/7)

However, *qǐ wéi* 豈 唯, *qǐ tú* 豈 徒, etc., 'it is only …' precede the subject.

516. Wáng rú yòng yǔ, zé qǐ tú Qí mín ān? Tiān xià zhī mín jǔ ān 王 如 用 予 ，則 豈 徒 齊 民 安 。天 下 之 民 舉 安

If the king were to use me, would it be only the people of Qi who would be made content? The people of the whole world would be made content. (*Mèng* 2B/12)

Qǐ 豈 can also be used with a noun predicate.

517. Cǐ qǐ shān zhī xìng yě zāi? 此 豈 山 之 性 也 哉

Is this the nature of the mountain? (*Mèng* 6A/8; implying that it is not)

In such cases, final *yě* 也 may be omitted.

518. Shì qǐ shuǐ zhī xìng zāi? 是 豈 水 之 性 哉

Is this the nature of water? (*Mèng* 6A/2)

Note that, as shown in several of the above examples, *qǐ* 豈 is often followed by the final exclamatory particle *zāi* 哉. The question particle *hū* 乎 is also sometimes found or there may be no final particle to mark the question.

The negative particle *bù* 不 when following *qǐ* 豈 may be limited in scope, affecting only the verb or adjective it precedes, or may apply to the whole predicate converting the expectation from a negative to an affirmative answer. The first case is found in:

519. Shǐ rén qǐ bù rén yú hán rén zāi? 矢 人 豈 不 仁 於 函 人 哉

Is the arrow-maker less kind-hearted than the maker of defensive armor? (*Mèng* 2A/7)

The second is found in such a case as:

> **520.** Zǐsī zhī bù yuè yě, qǐ bù yuē … 子思之不悅
> 也，豈不曰…
>
> When Zǐsī was displeased, did he not say … (*Mèng* 5B/7)

It should be noted that there are also occasional examples in which *qǐ* 豈 expects an affirmative answer, e.g.,

> **521.** Jūn qǐ yǒu dǒu shēng zhī shuǐ ér huó wǒ zāi. 君豈有斗
> 升之水而活我哉
>
> Surely you have a gallon or even a pint of water to keep me alive.
> (*Zhuāng* 26/8)

(iv) *Yōng* 庸, *jù* 詎 (鉅, 距, 巨, 遽), *qú* 渠, *yōng jù* 庸遽, etc. These particles alone or in combination with each other or other question particles are used like *qǐ* 豈 in rhetorical questions expecting a negative answer. *Yōng* 庸, which means 'use; usual, ordinary,' as a full word (related to *yòng* 用), is here an adverb with modal implications. *Jù* 詎 (EMC giǎ', with variants in other tones) may be related etymologically to *qí* 其 (EMC gi).

(v) *Wú* 毋 (無) in rhetorical questions

Like the ordinary p-negatives, *bù* 不 and *fēi* 非, the modal negative *wú* 毋 is used in rhetorical questions implying an affirmative answer. The effect of using *wú* 毋 instead of *bù* 不 is similar to that of modal *qí* 其 in that it indicates a degree of uncertainty on the part of the speaker, giving the rhetorical question the effect of suggesting rather than positively asserting a proposition. This usage is found mainly in comparatively early texts like the *Zuǒzhuàn*.

> **522.** Yǒu jī wú huài, wú yì shì wù hū? 有基無壞，無亦
> 是務乎
>
> To have a foundation (for the state) and not let it collapse, should
> one not strive for that? (*Zuǒ* Xiāng 24/*fù* 1)

Note the presence of the particle *yì* 亦. More common is the formula *wú nǎi* 無乃, as in *wú nǎi bù kě hū* 無乃不可乎 'Would it not be improper?' which occurs several times in the *Zuǒzhuàn*. The function of *yì* 亦 or *nǎi* 乃 is probably mainly to prevent ambiguity by excluding the possibility of interpreting *wú* 無 in the sense of 'not have, be without.' *Wú bù kě hū* 無不可乎 would be a simple question, 'Is there no impropriety?' Note the following example in which *bù yǒu* 不有 is used, rather than *wú* 無 'not have,' to make a rhetorical question.

523. Bù yǒu bó yì zhě hū? 不有博弈者乎
Are there not the games of *bó* and *yì*? (*LY* 17/20)

We find *wú níng* 無寧 'would it not be preferable' used when two alternatives are presented.

524. Qiě yǔ yǔ qí sǐ yú chén zhī shǒu yě wú níng sǐ yú èr sān zǐ
zhī shǒu hū? 且予與其死於臣之手也，無寧死
於二三子之手乎

Moreover would I not rather die surrounded by my disciples than surrounded by ministers? (*LY* 9/12)

(vi) *Fú* 夫 'is it not?'
As a final particle, *fú* 夫 is probably a fusion of *bù* 不 + *hū* 乎.[59] It adds a tag question 'is it not?' expecting agreement (French *n'est-ce pas*), as in *bēi fú* 悲夫 'Sad, is it not?' added as a comment to a tragic story.

525. Wú sǐ yǐ fú? 吾死矣夫
Am I not as good as dead? (*Mèng* 4B/24)

(vii) Rhetorical questions with interrogative pronouns
The distinction between rhetorical and simple questions when interrogative pronouns are used requires further study. Note, however, the following observations:
    (a) When *hé* 何 is used adverbially in the sense of 'why' or 'how' (as opposed to its use as object of the verb), it is generally rhetorical, implying that there is no acceptable reason for what is referred to.

526. Hé bì yuē lì? 何必曰利
Why must you say 'profit'? (*Mèng* 1A/1)

527. Wú hé ài yī niú? 吾何愛一牛
Why should I grudge one ox? (*Mèng* 1A/7)
Yān 焉 'how?' is also used in this way.

528. Yān dé rén rén ér jì zhī? 焉得人人而濟之
How could he take them all across one after the other? (*Mèng* 4B/2)
    (b) The generalizing initial particle *fú* 夫 in front of an interrogative pronoun has the effect of making it rhetorical:

529. Fú shuí yǔ wáng dí? 夫 誰 與 王 敵

Who will be a match for Your Majesty? (*Mèng* 1A/5)

(Compare this with English 'whoever, who in the world.')

(viii) *Kuàng* 況 'how much the more'

As a full word *kuàng* 況 means 'to compare with, be equal to,' as in:

530. Chéng míng kuàng hū zhū hóu. 成 名 況 乎 諸 侯

Established a name comparable to a feudal lord. (*Xún* 6/17)

More commonly, however, it is used to make a rhetorical comparison, as in

531. Guǎn Zhòng qiě yóu bù kě zhào, ér kuàng bù wéi Guǎn Zhòng zhě hu 管 仲 且 猶 不 可 召 ， 而 況 不 為 管 仲 者 乎

If even Guǎn Zhòng could not be summoned (by his prince), how much less could one who is not a Guǎn Zhòng? (*Mèng* 2B/2)

3. Exclamatory Sentences

(a) Zāi 哉

The final particle *zāi* 哉 is a mark of exclamation which may be added either to a declarative statement or to a question.

532. Kuàng ān zhái ér bú jū, shě zhèng lù ér fú yóu, āi zāi 曠 安 宅 而 不 居 ， 舍 正 路 而 弗 由 ， 哀 哉

How sad it is to vacate the tranquil dwelling (of benevolence) and not dwell in it, to abandon the proper road (of righteousness) and not follow it. (*Mèng* 4A/11)

533. Shì chéng hé xīn zāi? 是 誠 何 心 哉

What sort of mind was this really? (*Mèng* 1A/7)

In this example, final *yě* 也 is omitted but one can also have *yě zāi* 也 哉 and *hū zāi* 乎 哉 .

534. Shì qǐ shuǐ zhī xìng yě zāi? 是 豈 水 之 性 也 哉

Is this the nature of water? (*Mèng* 6A/2)

535. Ruò guǎ rén zhě kě yǐ bǎo mín hū zāi? 若 寡 人 者 可 以 保 民 乎 哉

Can someone like me protect the people? (*Mèng* 1A/7)

(b) *Inversion of Subject and Predicate*

In exclamatory sentences there may be inversion of the normal word order. That is, the predicate is placed before the subject.

> **536.** Shàn zāi wèn yě 善 哉 問 也
>
> An excellent question! (*Mèng* 1B/4. For: wèn yě shàn zāi 問 也 善 哉)

> **537.** Wū zài qí wéi mín fù mǔ yě 惡 在 其 為 民 父 母 也
> Wherein lies his being father and mother of the people? (*Mèng* 1A/4. For: qí wéi mín fù mǔ yě wū zài 其 為 民 父 母 也 惡 在).

Note the following example in which a final particle is retained at the end of the sentence in spite of inversion of the predicate and subject.

> **538.** Wáng yuē, dà zāi yán yǐ 王 曰 ，大 哉 言 矣
> The king said, 'Great is that saying!' (*Mèng* 1B/3. For: yán dà yǐ zāi 言 大 矣 哉).

XV. Complex Sentences

1. Parataxis and Hypotaxis

As noted above in Section V.5, simple sentences can be linked together to form longer units without any overt indication of the connections between them. In the following example, four verbs, which all have the same subject, are arranged in a sequence that corresponds to the temporal order of events and there is a clear implication that what is prior explains in some way what is posterior, but the exact nature of the relationship is not expressed.

> **539.** Téng Wén gōng wéi shì zǐ, jiāng zhī Chǔ, guò Sòng ér jiàn Mèngzǐ. 滕文公為世子，將之楚，過宋而見孟子。 (*Mèng* 3A/1)

This could be translated literally: Duke Wén of Téng was crown prince, was about to go to Chǔ, passed through Sòng, and saw Mencius. Alternatively one could show the subordination of the first three verbs to the final, main verb by using -ing forms: Duke Wén of Téng, being crown prince, and being about to go to Chǔ and passing through Sòng, saw Mencius. The particle *ér* 而 inserted before the final verb, etymologically related to words meaning 'like' and hence having a root meaning of something like 'thus' or 'so,' is little more than an empty connective indicating that the end of the sequence has been reached. It may be translated as 'and,' but it differs from English 'and' in that it can only link verbs, or more exactly predicates, since verbless noun predicates are occasionally found in such series.

More idiomatic English renderings would use a combination of subordinating (hypotactic) and coordinating (paratactic) constructions. For example, one might say: When Duke Wén of Téng was crown prince, he saw Mencius while he was passing through Sòng on his way to Chǔ, or: When Duke Wén of Téng was crown prince, he passed through Sòng on his way to Chǔ and saw Mencius.

Where English and many other languages use hypotactic constructions, with relationships of subordination explicitly marked by conjunctions and verbal morphology, Chinese very often uses parataxis, leaving the semantic relationships to be inferred from the context. In the above example even the particle *ér* 而 , which has the effect of tying the sequence together, is not obligatory (see V.5). Chinese does, however, have the means to make hypotactic relationships explicit, as will be shown below.

The same general rules of word order apply to subordinate and main clauses that apply within simple sentences. That is, modifier precedes modified. Apparent exceptions to the rule can occur when what is semantically the real, main, predicate is followed by another predicate that adds a restriction or explanation, for example *ér yǐ* 而 已 'only' (XIII.2d). However, even in such cases the surface structure is governed by the formal rule. *Ér yǐ* 而 已 is literally 'then stop,' *yǐ* 已 being the final verb in a series.

Subordination between clauses may be indicated by (a) a particle in the first clause, (b) a particle in the second clause, or (c) particles in both clauses. Thus an 'if' clause may be marked by a particle such as *rú* 如 or *gǒu* 苟, or may be implied by the particle *zé* 則 introducing the conclusion, or may have both kinds of markers.

2. Conditional Clauses

(a) *Parataxis*
As with temporal and causal relationships, conditionals are often expressed paratactically, simply by juxtaposing two simple predicates.

540. Bù duó bù yàn. 不奪不饜
If they are not snatching, they are not satisfied. (*Mèng* 1A/1.
Literally: not snatch not satisfied.)

There is nothing but the sense to tell us that we should translate in this way rather than as two coordinate clauses: They do not snatch and are not satisfied.

541. Bù néng gēng míng, dōng xǐ, yóu wù zǐ zhī shēng. 不能更鳴，東徙，猶惡子之聲
If you cannot change your cry, when you move east, they will still hate your voice. (*Shuōyuàn* 16.164. Literally: Cannot change cry, move east, still hate your voice.)

The subordination of the first two clauses is again implied rather than expressed and, if the context permitted, we could translate: You cannot change your voice. You will move east. They will still hate your voice.

(b) *Subordination by a Particle in the If-Clause*

(i) *Ruò* 若, *rú* 如, *ér* 而

These three words meaning 'if' are grouped together because they are etymologically related. The choice between *ruò* 若 (EMC ɲiak) and *rú* 如 (EMC ɲiǎ) seems to be at least partly a matter of dialect — *ruò* 若 in the *Zuǒzhuàn* and *Guóyǔ*, *rú* 如 in *Lúnyǔ* and *Mencius* — but the exact history of these words still needs study.[60] *Ér* 而 (EMC ɲɨ) is comparatively rare in this sense.

> **542.** Ruò jué dì jí quán, suì ér xiāng jiàn, qí shuí yuē, bù rán?
> 若闕地及泉，隧而相見，其誰曰，不然
> If you dig into the earth and reach the Yellow Springs, and then make a subterranean passage where you can meet each other, who can say that your oath has been violated? (*Zuǒ* Yǐn 1/3, Legge p.6)

> **543.** Rú yù píng chí tiān xià, dāng jīn zhī shì, shě wǒ qí shuí yě?
> 如欲平治天下，當今之世，舍我其誰也
> If Heaven wished to bring peace and good order to the world, in the present generation who is there except me (to bring it about)?
> (*Mèng* 2B/13)

In the *Zuǒzhuàn* there is a clear distinction between *ruò* 若 'if' and *rú* 如 'like.' *Ruò* 若 is also used exclusively in the construction *ruò* X *hé* 若 X 何 'what is to be done about X' (IV.8g above), in which *ruò* 若 can be interpreted as a causative: 'make X to be like what?' This suggests that *ruò* 若 'if' is also in origin a causative construction: 'let it be so.' Compare the use of *shǐ* 使 and *líng* 令 to introduce suppositions (see (ii) below). In the Lǔ dialect (*Lúnyǔ* and *Mencius*) the causative and non-causative meanings are not formally distinguished and both *rú* 如 and *ruò* 若 are used for 'if' as well as 'like.'

If this interpretation is correct, *ruò* 若 and *rú* 如 govern the 'if' clause as object and are themselves impersonal, i.e., have no subject. The particle should therefore precede the subject of the 'if' clause. This is what we find in such cases as:

> **544.** Ruò Zhào Mèng sǐ ... 若趙孟死
> If Zhào Mèng dies ... (*Zuǒ* Xiāng 31/*fù* 1)

> **545.** Rú zhī zhě yì xíng qí suǒ wú shì ... 如知者亦行其
> 所無事

If your wise men would also carry out what they do not need to
make a problem of ... (*Mèng* 4B/26)
It is also possible, however, for the subject of the 'if' clause to be placed in
front of the particle, as if the latter were an adverb.

546. Zǐ ruò miǎn zhī, yǐ quàn zuǒ yòu, kě yě. 子 若 免 之 ，
以 勸 左 右 ， 可 也
If you spare him so as to encourage those about you, it will be
well. (*Zuǒ* Zhāo 1/3)

This is the usual word order with *rú* 如 'if' in the *Lúnyǔ* and *Mencius*,
e.g.,

547. Wáng rú zhī cǐ ... 王 如 知 此
If Your Majesty knows this ... (*Mèng* 1A/3)

Ér 而 , which is closely related to *rú* 如 , is occasionally found in the
sense of 'if' in both the *Zuǒzhuàn* and Lǔ texts. It invariably follows the
subject of the clause, if present, and may be regarded as an unemphatic,
enclitic form.

548. Zǐchǎn ér sǐ, shuí qí sì zhī. 子 產 而 死 ， 誰 其 嗣 之
If Zǐchǎn dies, who will succeed him? (*Zuǒ* Xiāng 30/*fù* 6. A
textual variant has *ruò* 若 instead of *ér* 而)

549. Yān yǒu rén rén zài wèi, wǎng mín ér kě wéi yě? 焉 有 仁
人 在 位 ， 罔 民 而 可 為 也
How is there a benevolent man on the throne if entrapping the
people can be practiced? (*Mèng* 1A/7. With inversion of the main
clause and subordinate clause in an exclamatory sentence — see
XIV.3).

(ii) *Shǐ* 使 , *Líng* 令 , etc., 'supposing'
The causative auxiliaries *shǐ* 使 and *líng* 令 can be used impersonally
(i.e., without a definite subject) to introduce suppositions: 'Let it be that
...' = 'Suppose that ...' (compare modern *jiǎshǐ* 假 使). This usage is rare
in texts of the classical period but becomes common in the late Warring
States period and in Hàn.

550. Nǎng zhě shǐ rǔ gǒu bái ér wǎng, hēi ér lái 曩 者 使 女
狗 白 而 往 ， 黑 而 來
Supposing just now your dog had gone away white and come back
black ... (*HF* 23, p. 138)

551. Jiē hū, líng dōng yuè yì zhǎn yī yuè, zú wú shì yǐ 嗟
乎，令冬月益展一月，足吾事矣

Alas, if winter had extended for one more month, it would have
sufficed for my business. (*Shǐjì* 122.3148)

Other verbs that can be used impersonally to introduce suppositions
include *jiǎ* 假 'borrow, simulate, pretend' and *shè* 設 'set up, establish.'

552. Jiǎ zhī yǒu rén ér yù nán wú duō ér wù běi wú guǎ 假之
有人而欲南無多而惡北無寡

Supposing there is a man who desires to go south no matter how
often and hates to go north no matter how seldom. (*Xún* 22/68.
Literally: 'suppose it, there is a man, he desires ... he hates ...'
The use of *zhī* 之 as a dummy object after *jiǎ* 假, with the
following clause in apposition, may be compared to the use of *zhī*
之 after *wén* 聞 'to hear': 'I have heard it that ...')

553. Shè Qín dé rén, rú hé? 設秦得人，如何

Supposing Qín had obtained men, what would they have done
about it? (*Yángzǐ Fǎyán* 10, p. 30)

(iii) *Gǒu* 苟

As a verb *gǒu* 苟 means 'be careless of.'

554. Wú yuē gǒu yǐ 無曰苟矣

Do not say, 'I do not care.' (*Shī* 256/6; Karlgren 1950a)

555. Jūn zǐ yú qí yán, wú suǒ gǒu ér yǐ yǐ. 君子於其言，
無所苟而已矣

In his speech there is just nothing the superior man is careless
about. (*LY* 13/3)

From this comes an adverbial use in the sense of 'carelessly,' with
idiomatic extensions 'without regard to principle, by any means; by
chance.' Compare the expression *gǒuqiě* 苟且 'careless, without
foresight.' The most frequent use of *gǒu* 苟 in texts of the classical period
is introducing 'if' clauses, where its meaning is originally 'if, by chance,
...' but is often quite attenuated.

556. Gǒu wéi shàn, hòu shì zǐ sūn bì yǒu wàng zhě yǐ. 苟為
善，後世子孫必有王者矣

If, perchance, he does good deeds, in later generations among his
descendants there will be one who will be King. (*Mèng* 1B/14)

557. Gǒu yǒu qí bèi, hé gù bù kě? 苟 有 其 備 ， 何 故 不
可

If you are prepared for it, why should it not be possible? (*Zuǒ
Zhāo* 5/*fù* 1)

A word with similar meaning that comes to mean 'if' is *tǎng* 儻 (also
written 倘 ,黨). In its earliest use it is an adverb meaning 'accidentally, by
chance':

558. Guài xīng zhī tǎng xiàn … 怪 星 之 黨 見

The occasional appearance of strange stars … (*Xún* 63, 17/30)

It is rarely, if ever, found in the sense of 'if' in pre-Hàn texts but becomes a
regular particle with this meaning in later *wényán*.

(iv) *Chéng* 誠 , *Xìn* 信

The adverbs *chéng* 誠 'truly, really' and *xìn* 信 'truly,' used in 'if'
clauses, serve to emphasize the suppositious character of the proposition
(since a statement that is self-evidently true does not need strengthening by
such words!). They thus come to serve as grammatical markers for
conditional sentences. Compare modern *rú guǒ* 如 果 'if' (literally, 'if
really').

559. Chéng rú shì yě, mín guī zhī yóu shuǐ zhī jiù xià … 誠 如
是 也 , 民 歸 之 猶 水 之 就 下

If he is really so, the people will turn to him as water goes
downward … (*Mèng* 1A/6)

560. Xìn néng xíng cǐ wǔ zhě, zé lín guó zhī mín, yǎng zhī ruò
fù mǔ yǐ. 信 能 行 此 五 者 ， 則 鄰 國 之 民 ， 仰 之
若 父 母 矣

If he can really carry out these five things, the people of
neighbouring countries will look up to him as to their parents.
(*Mèng* 2A/5)

The literal force of the adverb 'truly' is sometimes more attenuated than in
these examples.

(v) *Jí* 即

In addition to its use in the sense of 'then' in a main clause (see 2c.iii)
below), *jí* 即 is sometimes found as a particle introducing an 'if' clause. In
this sense it is probably to be derived from the verb *jí* 即 'approach, come

to' used impersonally, 'coming to the point that.' Compare this to *jí* 及 'come to' in the sense of 'when.'

> **561.** Zhòng fù jiā jū yǒu bìng. Jí bú xìng ér bù qǐ, zhèng ān qiān zhī? 仲父家居有病。即不幸而不起，政安遷之
>
> You, Father Zhòng, are confined to your house by illness. If, by misfortune, you do not recover, to whom shall I transfer the government? (*HF* 10, p. 51)

(vi) *Fēi* 非 'unless'

A noun predicate negated by *fēi* 非 can stand as a conditional clause to a following main predicate. The particle *yě* 也 which accompanies an independent noun predicate is then omitted. The predicate negated by *fēi* 非 may be a noun or a verbal phrase treated as a noun.

> **562.** Fēi wǒ zú lèi, qí xīn bì yì. 非我族類，其心必異
>
> If he is not of our clan, his mind will certainly be different. (*Zuǒ* Chéng 4/7)

> **563.** Jīn rén zhǔ zhī yú chí yì rán. Fēi bù zhī yǒu kǔ, zé ān yù chí qí guó. Fēi rú shì, bù néng tīng shèng zhì ér zhū luàn chén 今人主之於治亦然。非不知有苦，則安欲治其國。非如是，不能聽聖知而誅亂臣
>
> A ruler's attitude to government should also be like this. Unless he ignores the suffering it entails, how can he be willing to govern his country. If it is not like this, he cannot heed sage wisdom and punish disorderly subjects. (*HF* 34 p. 247. In the first case, the particle *zé* 則 also marks the preceding clause as conditional.)

(vii) *Wéi* 微 'if it were not for'

The m- negative of nouns, *wéi* 微, mostly occurs in contrary to fact conditions. See examples **394** and **438** above.

(c) *Subordination by a Particle in the Main Clause*

(i) *Zé* 則 'then'

A frequent way of marking a conditional sentence is to use the particle *zé* 則 'then' to introduce the second or main clause. The if-clause may or may not be marked by one of the particles discussed above.

564. Hénèi xiōng, zé yí qí mín yú Hédōng … 河 內 凶 ， 則
移 其 民 於 河 東

If there is a bad harvest in Hénèi, I move people from there to
Hédōng … (*Mèng* 1A/3)

565. Yǐ wǔ shí bù xiào bǎi bù, zé rú hé? 以 五 十 步 笑 百
步 ， 則 何 如

If, on the basis of having run fifty paces, they laugh at those who
have run one hundred paces, how will it be? (*Mèng* 1A/3)

The force of *zé* 則 in this usage is closely related to its use to mark a noun
as topic (see Section VIII.3). That is, the if-clause presents a situation that
defines the circumstances under which the statement in the main clause
applies and, by implication, contrasts it with other situations. It is thus like
a topic for the main clause.

(ii) *Sī* 斯 'then'

The pronoun *sī* 斯 'this' is used as an alternative to *zé* 則 in the *Shījīng*,
Lúnyǔ, and *Mencius*. It is quite rare in other texts such as the *Zuǒzhuàn* and
Guóyǔ.

566. Guān guò, sī zhī rén yǐ. 觀 過 ， 斯 知 仁 矣

If one examines a man's faults, then one will know if he is
virtuous. (*LY* 4/7)

567. Wáng wú zuì suì, sī tiān xià zhī mín zhì yān. 王 無 罪
歲 ， 斯 天 下 之 民 至 焉

If Your Majesty will not blame the harvest, then the people of the
whole world will come to you. (*Mèng* 1A/3)

(iii) *Jí* 即 'then'

In its earliest use, *jí* 即 is a verb meaning 'approach, go to,' as in *jí wèi*
即 位 'ascend the throne,' *jí shì* 即 世 'pass away, die.' From this can be
derived a number of its uses as a grammatical particle, including its use in
introducing conditional clauses (see XV.2b.v above). In phrases like *jí rì*
即 日 'on the very day' (literally, 'going to the day') it has the idea of
immediacy and it can also be used independently as an adverb meaning
'immediately, forthwith.'

568. Yuán sān rì jí xià yǐ. 原 三 日 即 下 矣
Yuán will fall in three days. (*HF* 32 p. 213. Literally: Yuán in
three days forthwith will have fallen.)

In this sense it can occur at the beginning of a main clause preceded by a
'when' clause.

569. Jí Wèi zhāo zhī, jí fǎn wèi Wèi shǒu Fēng. 及 魏 招
之 ，即 反 為 魏 守 豐
When Wei summoned him, he immediately revolted and guarded
Feng for Wei. (*Shǐjì* 8.352)

Besides this usage, however, which does not seem to be found in pre-Hàn
texts, *jí* 即 sometimes occurs in earlier texts as a variant of *zé* 則 'then,'
without any connotation of 'immediately.'

570. Zhù zhī shì tīng zhě zhòng, zé qí suǒ wén jiàn zhě yuǎn yǐ
... Zhù zhī dòng zuò zhě zhòng, jí qí jǔ shì sù chéng yǐ 助 之
視 聽 者 眾 ，則 其 所 聞 見 者 遠 矣 ⋯ 助 之 動 作
者 眾 ，即 其 舉 事 速 成 矣
If those who assist him to look and listen are many, then his
hearing and seeing will be far-reaching ... If those who help him to
act are many, then his undertakings will be swiftly accomplished.
(*Mò* 12/67-68)

In such cases *jí* 即 (EMC tsik) is probably a particle of pronominal origin,
related to *zī* 兹 (EMC tsɨ) 'this,' quite unrelated to the verb 'go to.' It is
presumably the same word as *jí* 即 when used as a particle to introduce
noun predicates (see III.1b).

3. Concessive Clauses

Whereas an if-clause states a condition under which a proposition is true and
implies that it is not or may not be true under other conditions, a
concessive clause asserts that a given condition does *not* affect the truth of
the proposition stated in the main clause.

(a) Suī 雖 *'although, even if'*

The main particle of concession in Classical Chinese is *suī* 雖. *Suī* 雖 is
closely related to the preclassical copula *wéi* 惟 'is,' being very likely an
old causative formation with the Sino-Tibetan *s- prefix: 'let it be ...,'
hence 'even if it be ...' Because of its origin as a copula, *suī* 雖 can be

followed either by a noun or by a sentence standing for a noun. In this it resembles *fēi* 非 and *wéi* 微 'if not, unless.'

571. Suī dà guó bì wèi zhī yǐ. 雖 大 國 必 畏 之 矣

Even great countries will certainly be in awe of him. (*Mèng* 2A/4. Literally: Even if they are great countries …)

572. Suī bù dé yú, wú hòu zāi. 雖 不 得 魚 ， 無 後 災

Even though he does not catch a fish, he will have no disaster afterwards. (*Mèng* 1A/7)

If the subject of the clause is expressed, *suī* 雖, like *ruò* 若 and *rú* 如, is often moved into the adverb position between the subject and the verb.

573. Qí guó suī biǎn xiǎo, wú hé ài yī niú? 齊 國 雖 褊 小 ， 吾 何 愛 一 牛

Though Qí is narrow and small, how should I begrudge one ox? (*Mèng* 1A/7)

The phrase *suī rán* 雖 然 'though it is so' should be noted. It may be used as a connective between sentences, equivalent to 'nevertheless, however.' In Classical Chinese, however, it must always be given its full value as a clause and is not, as in the modern language, simply a particle meaning 'although.'

(b) Suī … ér 雖 … 而

The conclusion of a *suī* 雖 clause may be introduced by *ér* 而, which then has an adversative meaning, 'yet.'

574. Suī zhí ér bú bìng. 雖 直 而 不 病

Though he may be outspoken, he will not be blamed. (*Zhuāng* 4/22)

(c) Fēi … ér 非 … 而

Fēi 非, which like *suī* 雖 is derived from the preclassical copula, can sometimes be used as the negative of *suī* 雖, i.e., 'even if not …'

575. Wǒ fēi ài qí cái ér yì zhī yǐ yáng yě. 我 非 愛 其 財 而 易 之 以 羊 也

Even though I did not begrudge the cost, yet I changed it for a sheep. (*Mèng* 1A/7)

The adversative *ér* 而 'yet' helps to make clear the concessive meaning.

(d) Zòng 縱

Zòng 縱, which as a verb means 'to relax, let go, allow,' can be used to introduce a concessive clause.

> **576.** Wú yī fù rén ér shì èr fū, zòng fú néng sǐ, qí yòu xī yán?
> 吾一婦人而事二夫，縱弗能死，其又奚言
> I, being one woman, have served two husbands. Even though I could not die (with my first husband), how could I again speak?
> (*Zuǒ* Zhuāng 14/3)

4. Temporal Clauses

(a) *Verbs in Series*

Verbs in series are normally arranged in order corresponding to the temporal sequence of events and this may be sufficient indication of time relationships without explicit markers. (See the example **539** in Section XV.1.)

(b) *Aspect Particles in the First Clause*

The aspect particles *jì* 既 'already' and *wèi* 未 'not yet' in the first clause indicating completed or uncompleted action, may be used to show relationships of before and after (XII.1a, b).

> **577.** Yáo Shùn jì mò, shèng rén zhī dào shuāi 堯舜既沒，聖人之道衰
> After Yáo and Shùn passed away, the way of the sages declined.
> (*Mèng* 3B/9. Literally: Yáo and Shùn having passed away …)

> **578.** Wèi zàng, Kǒngzǐ wén zhī, shǐ Zǐgòng wǎng shì shì yān.
> 未葬，孔子聞之，使子貢往侍事焉
> Before he was buried, Confucius heard of it and sent Zǐgòng to go and assist at the funeral. (*Zhuāng* 6/63. Literally: not yet having been buried)

Note that final *yě* 也, which is normal with *wèi* 未 in an independent main clause, is omitted in such cases.

(c) Jí 及 *'when'*

Jí 及, which as an independent verb means 'to arrive at, reach,' is used impersonally as a coverb introducing a temporal clause: 'coming to, when.'

579. Jí xiàn yú zuì ... 及 陷 於 罪

When they fall into crime ... (*Mèng* 1A/7)

If the verb following *jí* 及 has a subject expressed, the phrase is nominalized with *zhī* 之 or *qí* 其. Like other nominalized clause objects, a clause introduced by *jí* 及 may be followed by *yě* 也.

580. Jí jūn zhī sì yě ... 及 君 之 嗣 也

When Your Lordship succeeded to the throne ... (*Zuǒ* Chéng 13/4)

581. jí qí wéi tiān zǐ yě 及 其 為 天 子 也

When he became Son of Heaven ... (*Mèng* 7B/6)

Jí 及 followed by a noun may also be semantically equivalent to a temporal clause, as in:

582. Jí guǎ rén zhī shēn ... 及 寡 人 之 身

When I came to the throne ... (*Mèng* 1A/5; literally: Coming to my person,...)

Jí 及 is the most regular and frequent coverb used in this sense. Other verbs of similar meaning that can be used in the same way include *zhì yú* 至 于 or *zhì yú* 至 於 'arrive at,' *bì* 比 'be side by side,' and *dài* 逮 'reach; up to, until.'

583. Zhì yú Yí Wáng ... Zhì yú Lì Wáng ... Zhì yú Yōu Wáng ... Zhì yú Huì Wáng ... Zhì yú Líng Wáng ... 至 于 夷 王 ⋯ 至 于 厲 王 ⋯ 至 于 幽 王 ⋯ 至 于 惠 王 ⋯ 至 于 靈 王

Coming to the time of King Yí ... Coming to the time of King Lì ... Coming to the time of King Yōu ... Coming to the time of King Huì ... Coming to the time of King Líng ... (*Zuǒ* Zhāo 26/7)

584. Bì qí fǎn yě ... 比 其 反 也

When he returns ... (*Mèng* 1B/6)

585. Xī dài wǒ Xiàn Gōng jí Mù Gōng xiāng hào, lù lì tóng xīn 昔 逮 我 獻 公 及 穆 公 相 好 ，戮 力 同 心

Formerly when our Duke Xiàn and (your) Duke Mù were on terms of friendship, they strove with all their might to be of one mind. (*Zuǒ* Chéng 13/4)

Dài 逮 may introduce a clause containing the aspect negative *wèi* 未, in which case it may be translated as 'while' or 'before.'

586. Yuàn jūn dài Chǔ Zhào zhī bīng wèi zhì yú Liáng, jí yǐ shǎo gē shōu Wèi. 願君逮楚趙之兵未至於梁，亟以少割收魏

I wish that, while the troops of Chǔ and Zhào have not yet reached Liáng, you would quickly offer to make peace with Wèi for a small piece of territory. (*Shǐjì* 72.2326)

Dài 迫 'come to, reach,' which is used in much the same way as *dài* 逮 in the *Shījīng* and occasionally in other texts, was cognate but not identical in Old Chinese.

(d) *Simultaneity* — Dāng 當, Fāng 方, ... shí 時

Simultaneity can be expressed by *dāng* 當 'be at.'

587. Dāng zài Sòng yě ... 當在宋也

When I was in Song ... (*Mèng* 2B/3)

More frequently *dāng* 當 in this sense is followed by *shí* 時 'time' (or a word of similar meaning such as *shì* 世 'age') modified by a noun, pronoun, or noun clause, e.g.,

588. Dāng Yáo zhī shí ... 當堯之時

In the time of Yao ... (*Mèng* 3A/4, 3B/9)

589. Dāng jīn zhī shì ... 當今之世

In the present age ... (*Mèng* 2B/13)

590. Dāng Yān zhī fāng míng fèng fǎ shěn guān duàn zhī shí ... 當燕之方明奉法審官斷之時

At the time when Yān was clearly upholding the laws and scrutinizing officials' decisions ... (*HF* 19, p. 91)

Fāng 方 'just now, just then,' which is more commonly an adverb (as in the above example), can also be used like *dāng* 當 as a coverb (see example **429** above).

The noun *shí* 時 'time' can be used by itself, without a preceding coverb, to mark the end of a temporal clause, like modern ... *de shíhou* ... 的時候.

591. Lǔ Mù Gōng zhī shí ... 魯穆公之時

At the time of Duke Mù of Lǔ ... (*Mèng* 6B/6)

592. Sūn Shū'áo wéi yīng ér zhī shí ... 孫叔敖為嬰兒之時

When Sūn Shú'áo was a child ... (*Xīnxù* 1.2)

(e) *Topic Phrases in* Yě 也 *as Time Clauses*

A topic phrase nominalized by *zhī* 之 and followed by *yě* 也 can be semantically equivalent to a temporal clause.

593. Xī, Huán gōng zhī bà yě ... 昔，桓公之霸也

Formerly, when Duke Huan was hegemon ... (*HF* 35, p.255)

(f) Ér hòu 而 後, Rán hòu 然 後

The time sequence between two clauses may be indicated by *ér hòu* 而 後 or *rán hòu* 然 後 'afterwards' introducing the second or main clause.

594. Huò bǎi bù ér hòu zhǐ, huò wǔ shí bù ér hòu zhǐ 或 百 步 而 後 止，或 五 十 步 而 後 止

Some go a hundred paces before they stop, some go fifty paces before they stop. (*Mèng* 1A/3. Literally: Some, going a hundred paces, afterwards stop ...)

595. Yì wáng xīng jiǎ bīng, wéi shì chén, gòu yuàn yú zhū hóu, rán hòu kuài yú xīn yú? 抑 王 興 甲 兵，危 士 臣，搆 怨 於 諸 侯，然 後 快 於 心 與

Or is it that Your Majesty must take up arms, endanger your subjects, and incur resentment among the other feudal lords before you feel pleasure in your heart? (*Mèng* 1A/7. Literally: ... take up arms ... and afterwards feel pleasure ...)

Note that in both these examples the idiomatic English translation makes the *second* clause into a subordinate clause. This is because the first clause is in each case semantically the main predicate, conveying the most new information. The Chinese syntax must, however, conform to the rule that modifier precedes modified, so that the final verb is the main verb as far as the surface syntax is concerned. Compare ... *ér yi* ... 而 已 'only,' which according to surface syntax is the final verb of a sequence of verbs in series but is equivalent to a final particle placed *after* the main verb and is translated as if it were adverbial to the main verb.

5. Cause, Reason

(a) *The Coverb* Yǐ 以

The coverb *yǐ* 以 governing a nominalized clause as its object may be equivalent to English 'because.'

596. Sòng yǐ qí shàn yú Jìn hóu yě, pàn Chǔ jí Jìn. 宋 以 其 善 於 晉 侯 也 ，叛 楚 即 晉

Sòng, because of having made friends with the Marquis of Jìn, revolted against Chǔ and went over to Jìn. (*Zuǒ* Xī 26/7)

Note that, as in the examples with *jí* 及 'when,' etc., the nominalized clause is marked off by final *yě* 也 . *Wèi* 為 'for' can be used similarly.

(b) Gù 故 *'reason'*

Gù 故 'reason' may be used at the end of a 'because' clause introduced by *yǐ* 以 in much the same way that *shí* 時 'time' is used at the end of a temporal clause.

597. Jūn yǐ nòng mǎ zhī gù ... 君 以 弄 馬 之 故

The ruler, because of his fondness for the horses ... (*Zuǒ* Dìng 3/*fù* 2)

More frequently, *gù* 故 is used by itself as a connective introducing a main clause (or a separate sentence) in the sense of 'therefore,' of which many examples have been given (see examples **17**, **41**, **47**, etc.) Note also *shì gù* 是 故 '(for) this reason,' used in the same way.

(c) *Explanatory Noun Predicate after a Main Clause*

A reason or explanation may be provided by an additional noun predicate added after a main clause (see VII.2a.ii, XII.3c).

Notes

1 Downer 1963.

2 See Downer 1959 for an extensive classified list of such departing tone derivates. The theory that the departing tone is derived from *-s was first proposed by Haudricourt (1954). See also Pulleyblank 1962, 1973a, b.

3 Pulleyblank 1973a, 1989.

4 Pulleyblank 1965, 1973a, 1989. The vowel /ə / can be analyzed as a phonological null in Chinese, inserted epenthetically by rules of syllabification. This means that when /a/ alternates with /ə/ as the root vowel, it can be regarded as infixation of the same morpheme that occurs as a prefix in (b).

5 Pulleyblank 1973a, 1989, 1991a.

6 On the equivalence of *yú* 與 and *yěhū* 也乎 see Graham 1957. On the dialectal difference between *yú* 與 and *yé* 邪 see Karlgren 1926.

7 For a fuller discussion see Pulleyblank 1994.

8 On the related contrast between reference to presupposed information and additon of new information in *shí wéi* 是為 X as opposed to *shí* X *yě* 是 X 也 in *Mencius* and other Warring States texts see Pulleyblank 1960:51-52. In the *Shījīng*, such presupposition was indicated by inserting a demonstrative pronoun, either *shí* 時 or *shí* 實 (寔), in front of the copula *wéi* 維 . In the *Zuǒzhuàn* and *Guóyǔ*, *shí* 實 (寔) alone, sometimes with *wéi* 為 but often alone without any copula and never with final *yě* 也, is used for this purpose (pp. 57, 45-46). The role of presupposed versus new information in Classical Chinese syntax needs more study.

9 For fuller discussion see Pulleyblank 1959, 1994.

10 On the distinction between *kě* 可 and *kě yǐ* 可以 in pre-Hàn Chinese, see Section V.4a and Chou Fa-kao 1950, with further precisions.

11 For a useful analysis of passive constructions in Classical Chinese, see Cikoski 1978.

12 Compare Pulleyblank 1987. See also Gassmann 1982.

13 See Chou Fa-kao 1950, Section 6, 'Kě hé kě yǐ 可和可以'

14 On the differences between *yú* 于 and *yú* 於 see Karlgren 1926, Pulleyblank 1986.

15 Yang Shuda (1954), *Ciquan* 9/1, remarks about this example that it is unnecessary to follow commentators who have assumed that a verb has dropped out in front of 於 .

16 For a discussion of the phonology see Pulleyblank 1986.

17 In the preclassical language, *rú* 如 'like' had a similar syntax to *yú* '(go) to' and *yú* '(be) in.' Along with *wéi* 惟 'be' and some others, it belonged in a special class of copula-verbs which were not followed by the object pronoun *zhî* and which, on the other hand, were followed rather than preceded by interrogative pronouns. Thus, in the *Shijing*, *rú hé* 如 何 means 'is like what?' In the language of *Mencius*, *rú* 如 conforms to the word order of normal transitive verbs, so that the equivalent phrase is *hé rú* 何 如 . See Pulleyblank 1991a.

18 On the development of classifiers see Wang Li 1957-58, v. 2, ch. 34.

19 For a fuller discussion of the issues discussed in the following section see Robert H. Gassmann 1982. Though my analysis has been developed independently over many years, it has many points of contact with that of Gassmann.

20 The function of *yě* 也 in nominal predicates and related functions after nominalized verbal predicates are discussed in Gassmann 1980. He sums up his conclusions in the formula: "Das grammatische Morphem *yě* 也 weist im Nominalsatz und in der Grundform eingebetteter Komplementensätze, d.s. Komplemente vom Typ ZHI 知 'wissen', eine prädikativiernede oder prädikatsanzeigende Funktion auf" ("In the nominal sentence and the basic form of embedded complement sentence the grammatical morpheme *yě* 也 performs a predicativizing or predicate marking function.") This seems to me quite insightful, though points of detail remain disputable.

21 There is a comprehensive survey of pronouns in Classical Chinese in Chou Fa-kao 1959.

22 The graph 朕 is phonetic in 媵 EMC jiŋ^h and its other *xiesheng* derivatives are of the same pattern as those of 余 and 予. Compare *tú* 塗 EMC dɔ, *chú* 除 EMC drɨǎ, *shū* 舒 EMC ɕiǎ; *téng* 滕 EMC dəŋ, *shēng* 勝 EMC ɕiŋ, etc. Forms in dr- probably had a prefix. The original root initial in such *xiesheng* series is difficult to determine with certainty. My first assumption (1962) was that it was Sino-Tibetan *l but it is now clear that there are other possible sources of Middle Chinese j- (Type B syllables) and d- (Type A syllables), including *ɣ, *ɥ, and *ŋ^j, as well as *x^j (with a voicing prefix) (Pulleyblank 1991b). No Tibeto-Burman cognates to this Old Chinese first person singular pronoun have been identified.

23 Old Chinese *ŋá and *ŋálʔ, cognate to Tibeto-Burman forms such as Tibetan ŋa 'I,' ŋed 'I, we (elegant),' Burmese ŋa 'I,' etc. (Benedict 1972:93, 65).

24 Chen Mengjia 1956:94-96.

25 This was pointed out to me by David Hawkes.

26 The controversy about *wú* 吾 and *wǒ* 我 began with Karlgren (1920), who supposed that they were the relics of an original case system with *wú* 吾 as nominative/genitive and *wǒ* 我 as accusative. Kennedy (1956) argued that the contrast was not one of case but between a stressed form, *wǒ* 我 ,

appearing freely in any position in the sentence, and an unstressed form, *wú* 吾 , which could not appear before a pause. Graham (1969) argues strongly against the theory that the difference between *wú* 吾 and *wǒ* 我 had anything to do with stress.

27 On *jué* 厥 see Karlgren 1933, Bodman 1948.

28 The basic study of *yān* 焉 is that of George Kennedy 1940, with a supplementary note, 1953. See also Pulleyblank 1991a.

29 Kennedy 1953.

30 For the textual variant 諱 instead of 謂 see Graham 1983:36. Graham translates *yún* as 'to say it' but there is nothing in the preceding discourse for 'it' to refer to.

31 According to Graham (1983), who seems to have been the first to identify the semantic import of this pattern, it is confined to the Lǔ dialect, that is *Lúnyǔ*, *Mèngzǐ*, the *Gōngyángzhuàn* and the *Gǔliángzhuàn*.

32 On the specialized uses of *shì* 是 in the technical language of logical disputation developed by the Later Mohists see Graham 1978.

33 On the dialectal distribution of *sī* 斯 'this' and *sī* 斯 'then' see Karlgren 1926.

34 Pulleyblank 1960.

35 In spite of the difference in initials, *fú* 夫 (<*b-) as a pronoun must surely be related etymologically to *bǐ* 彼 (<*p-). One possibility is that, since *fú* 夫 as a pronoun seems to have become obsolete at quite an early period, its reading in the literary tradition was confused with that of the introductory particle *fú* 夫 (see VIII.5d), from which it is semantically quite distinct. The introductory particle, which often has a generalizing force, seems to be related to *fán* 凡 EMC buam 'all' and is probably etymologically unrelated to the pronoun. The distinction between these morphemes needs more study.

36 Pulleyblank 1988, 1991a.

37 Kennedy (1940) drew a parallel with Modern Chinese *nǎ* 哪 'what' and *nà* 那 'that' and also with *jǐge* 幾個 , which can either mean 'how many' or 'some, a few.' The latter comparison seems the more appropriate. Alternation between interrogative and indefinite pronouns is found in many languages. Compare also Mandarin 甚麼 'something' as well as 'what?' Derivation of an interrogative pronoun from deictic pronoun with a definite reference seems less likely. The deverbal derivatives in -n in Classical Chinese, *yān* 焉 , *rán* 然 , *yún* 云 , *yuán* 爰 , may have originally had an indefinite reference, 'in something,' 'like something,' etc., which acquired a definite, anaphoric meaning in context. Some of the uses of *yún* 云 retain this original indefinite meaning. See example **276** above.

38 Yang Shuda (1954:399) cites Zhèng Xuán's 鄭玄 commentary to the Tán Gōng 檀弓 section of the *Lǐjì* for the equivalence of *wū hú* 惡乎 to *yú hé* 於何 and argues that *hū* 乎 is here a preposition, equivalent to *yú* 於 ,

placed after its object [as if it were an ordinary verb]. This will not do. *Wū* 惡 alone is not found as a free pronoun occuring, like *hé* 何 , in front of other verbs or prepositions and as an interrogative word it always has the same meaning as the combination *wū hū* 惡 乎 , of which it appears to be a contraction. It is much more likely that *wū hū* 惡 乎 (EMC ʔɔ ɣɔ) is somehow derived from *yú hé* 於 何 (EMC ʔiă ɣa) (or, perhaps, *yú hú* 於 胡 EMC ʔiă ɣɔ) by a change in prosody from Type B, with accent on the first mora of the syllable to Type A, with accent on the second mora. The issues are complex, however, and must be left aside here.

39 These are actually 'literary' readings borrowed in premodern times from northern Chinese. The particle of simple verbal negation in Cantonese and several other southern dialects is the syllabic nasal [m̩]. Since Tibeto-Burman generally has negative particles beginning with m-, the northern Chinese forms with p- may be an innovation. There does not appear to be any evidence available at present, however, to show how such forms could have developed out of forms in *m-.

40 Takashima 1988, Graham 1983, Pulleyblank 1991a. For a summary of the controversy over the etymology and meaning of *fú* 弗 see Pulleyblank 1991a and Grahams's reply in the same volume.

41 Pulleyblank 1959.

42 See Lyu Shuxiang 1955.

43 Karlgren 1957, no. 742 a-f; Graham 1961:174-176, quoting Yang Bojun 1958:26.

44 Pulleyblank 1994.

45 Pulleyblank 1959.

46 Pulleyblank 1978.

47 Graham 1983, Pulleyblank 1991a.

48 See the analysis in Li and Thompson 1981.

49 Chao 1968.

50 For further discussion of the points raised here see Pulleyblank 1994.

51 There is by now an extensive literature on *qí* 其 on the oracle bone inscriptions. Takashima 1994 sums up previous studies as well as presenting his own most recent views. In my opinion to link modal *qí* 其 as it appears on the inscriptions with the later pronoun *qí* 其 remains unconvincing, as do attempts to relate modal *qí* 其 to *qí* 期 'a stipulated time, set a time for.' For a study of *qí* 其 in the *Zuǒzhuàn* see Malmquist (1981).

52 Karlgren compares the force of *gài* with the German adverb *ja* 'truly, indeed' (1964, Gloss no. 533).

53 The phonology of these derivatives remains uncertain in a number of ways but I suggest the following analysis: (1) The simplest form of the root was no doubt just *tV, that is, the consonant *t syllabified by a default vowel, which gave rise to the reading pronunciation of *zhī* 之 (EMC tɕɨ) and has

survived as Mandarin *de* 的 . Some words in this Old Chinese rhyme group ended in a velar glide, partly derived from earlier *-ɥ but it is very likely that this grammatical particle had no underlying final consonant. I suspect an etymological connection with the Tibetan demonstrative *de* 'that'; (2) The forms *zhū* 諸 and *zhě* 者 has the vowel *a added to the root consonant and thus are examples of ə/a, i.e., zero/a , ablaut. The problem of a final velar fricative or glide in the *yú* 魚 rhyme group to which they belong is similar to that of the *zhī* 之 rhyme group. Again I think it likely that there was no underlying consonantal final in these grammatical words. The difference in between *zhū* 諸 and *zhě* 者 (apart from the glottal stop in the latter giving rise to the Middle Chinese rising tone) is a further unsolved problem of Old Chinese phonology. I suspect that the Type B words like *zhě* 者 in this rhyme group that gave rise to EMC -ia instead of the more usual -ɪǎ had long vowels in Old Chinese but have no way of independently testing this hypothesis at present. Modern *dōu* 都 'all' is no doubt a Type A variant of *zhū* 諸 .

54 He Leshi 1994 has an exhaustive study of these and other quantifiers in the *Zuǒzhuàn*.

55 The modern reading *xié* for 偕 'accompany' is not found in the *Guǎngyùn* which reads the graph as a homophone of *jiē* 皆 'all.' It is tempting nevertheless to see the modern reading as a survival of a distinct reading for the verb.

56 This word is now commonly read *jù*. There is, however, no ancient authority for this and I suspect that it is analogical, based on the reading of the phonetic part of the graph, *jù* 具 . The *Guǎngyùn* gives only a level tone reading and the same is true of the *Jíyùn* and the *Kāngxī zìdiǎn*, which cites only these two earlier authorities.

57 Pulleyblank 1960.

58 This should, perhaps, be correlated with the use of the copula-verb *wéi* 為 rather than verbless noun predication when the predicate refers to something presupposed rather than new information. See Note 7 above. Further study is needed.

59 On the meaning see Graham (1955) who interprets it as equivalent to French 'n'est-ce pas?' Following a suggestion by W. Simon, Graham suggested that *fú* 夫 was a fusion of *fēi hū* 非 乎 . This seems unlikely since *fú* 夫 is regularly a tag question after verbal, not nominal, predicates. According to Y. R. Chao (1968), modern *ba* 吧 , which may be compared with final *fú* 夫 in meaning, is a fusion of *bù* 不 + *a* 啊 . The voicing of the initial of *fú* 夫 (EMC bɔ) probably comes from the voiced initial consonant of *hū* 乎 (EMC ɣɔ). Compare *pǒ* 叵 (EMC pʰa') = *bù kě* 不 可 , in which the contracted form has acquired the aspiration of the initial consonant of the second initial.

60 Karlgren 1926; see also Pulleyblank 1988.

Sources of Examples

Chūnqiū 春秋 , cited according to *Chūnqiū jīngzhuàn yǐndé* 春秋經傳引得 (Combined Concordances to Ch'un-Ch'iu, Kung-yang, Ku-liang and Tso-chuan), Harvard-Yenching Institute Sinological Index Series, Supplement No. 11. Peiping: Yenching University Press, 1937. Reprint, Taipei: Ch'eng-wen Publishing Co., 1966.

Gōngyáng zhuàn 公羊傳 (*Gōng*), cited according to *Chūnqiū jīngzhuàn yǐndé* 春秋經傳引得 (Combined Concordances to Ch'un-Ch'iu, Kung-yang, Ku-liang and Tso-chuan), Harvard-Yenching Institute Sinological Index Series, Supplement No. 11. Peiping: Yenching University Press, 1937. Reprint, Taipei: Ch'eng-wen Publishing Co., 1966.

Guǎnzǐ 管子 (*Guǎn*), cited according to *Guǎnzǐ jiàozhèng* 管子校正 . Edition of Zhūzǐ jíchéng 諸子集成 . Beijing: Zhonghua shuju, 1954.

Guóyǔ 國語 (*GY*). Punctuated edition of the Shanghai Guji chubanshe, 1978.

Hán Fēizǐ 韓非子 (*HF*), cited according to *Hán Fēizǐ jíjiě* 韓非子集解 , ed. of Zhūzǐ jíchéng 諸子集成 . Beijing: Zhonghua shuju, 1954.

Lúnyǔ 論語 (LY), cited according to Lúnyǔ yǐndé 論語引得 (A Concordance to the Analects of Confucius), Harvard-Yenching Institute Sinological Index Series, Supplement No. 16. Peiping: Yenching University Press, 1940. Reprint, Taipei: Ch'eng-wen Publishing Co., 1966.

Mèngzǐ 孟子 (Mèng), cited according to Mèngzǐ yǐndé 孟子引得 (A Concordance to Mêng Tzu), Harvard-Yenching Institute Sinological Index Series, Supplement No. 17. Peiping: Yenching University Press, 1941. Reprint, Taipei: Ch'eng-wen Publishing Co., 1966.

Mòzǐ 墨子 (Mò), cited according to Mòzǐ yǐndé 墨子引得 (A Concordance to Mo Tzu). Peiping: Yenching University Press, 1948. Reprint, Tokyo: The Japan Council for East Asian Studies, 1961.

Quán Jìn wén 全晉文 . In Yán Kějūn 嚴可均 , Quán Shànggǔ Sāndài Qín Hàn Sanguó Liùcháo wén 全上古三代秦漢三國六朝文 . Reprint, Beijing: Zhonghua shuju, 1958.

Shǐjì 史記 , cited according to the punctuated edition of Gù Jiégāng 顧頡剛 and others. Beijing: Zhonghua shuju, 1959.

Shījīng 詩經 (Shī) , cited according to Máo Shī yǐndé 毛詩引得 (A Concordance to Shih Ching). Peiping: Yenching University Press, 1934. Reprint, Tokyo: Japan Council for East Asian Studies, 1962.

Shūjīng 書經 (Shū), cited according to Shāngshū tōngjiǎn 商書通檢 . Peiping, 1936. Reprint, Taipei, 1966.

Shuōyuàn 説苑 , cited according to Shuōyuàn zhúzì suǒyǐn 説苑逐字索引 (A Concordance to the Shuoyuan). Hong Kong: Commercial Press, 1992.

Xúnzǐ 荀子 (Xún), cited according to Xúnzǐ yǐndé 荀子引得 (A Concordance
    to Hsun Tzu), Harvard-Yenching Institute Sinological Index Series,
    Supplement No. 22. Peiping: Yenching University Press, 1950. Reprint,
    Taipei: Ch'eng-wen Publishing Co., 1966.
Yángzǐ Fǎyán 揚子法言, by Yáng Xióng 揚雄 cited in the edition of Zhūzǐ
    jíchéng 諸子集成. Beijing: Zhonghua shuju, 1954.
Zhànguó cè 戰國策 (ZGC), cited according to Zhànguó cè zhúzì suǒyǐn 戰國
    策逐字索引 (A Concordance to the Zhanguoce). Hong Kong:
    Commercial Press, 1992.
Zhuāngzǐ 莊子 (Zhuāng), cited according to Zhuāngzǐ yǐndé 莊子引得 (A
    Concordance to Chuang Tzu), Harvard-Yenching Institute Sinological Index
    Series, Supplement No. 20. Peiping: Yenching University Press, 1947.
    Reprint, Cambridge, MA: Harvard University Press, 1956.
Zuǒzhuàn 左傳 (Zuǒ), cited according to Chūnqiū jīngzhuàn yǐndé 春秋經傳
    引得 (Combined concordances to Ch'un-Ch'iu, Kung-yang, Ku-liang and
    Tso-chuan), Harvard-Yenching Institute Sinological Index Series,
    Supplement No. 11. Peiping: Yenching University Press, 1937. Reprint,
    Taipei: Ch'eng-wen Publishing Co., 1966.

Bibliography

Benedict, Paul K. 1972. *Sino-Tibetan: A Conspectus*. Contributing editor: James A. Matisoff. Cambridge: Cambridge University Press.

Bodman, Nicholas C. 1948. 'The Functions of *Jywé* (厥) in the *Shàng-shū*' *Journal of the American Oriental Society* 68:52-60.

Chao, Yuen Ren. 1968. *A Grammar of Spoken Chinese*. Berkeley and Los Angeles: University of California Press.

Chen Mengjia 陳夢家 . 1956. *Yīnxū bǔcí zòngshù* 殷虛卜辭綜述 . Beijing: Kexue chubanshe.

Chou Fa-kao 周法高 .1950. 'Shànggǔ yǔfǎ zhájì 上古語法札記 ' (Notes on Ancient Chinese Grammar). *Bulletin of the Institute of History and Philology, Academia Sinica* 22:171-207.

——. 1959. *Zhōngguó gǔdài yǔfǎ, chēngdài biān* 中國古代語法：稱代編 (A Historical Grammar of Ancient Chinese, Part III: Substitution). Taipei: Academia Sinica.

——. 1961. *Zhōngguó gǔdài yǔfǎ, zàojù biān (shang)* 中國古代語法：造句編 （上） (A Historical Grammar of Ancient Chinese, Part I: Syntax, Chapters 1-4). Taipei: Academia Sinica.

——. 1962. *Zhōngguó gǔdài yǔfǎ, gouci bian* 中國古代語法：構詞編 (A Historical Grammar of Ancient Chinese, Part II: Morphology). Taipei: Academia Sinica.

Cikoski, John S. 1978. 'An Analysis of Some Idioms Commonly Called Passive in Classical Chinese,' *Computational Analyses of Asian and African Languages* 9:133-208.

Downer, Gordon, B. 1959. 'Derivation by Tone Change in Classical Chinese,' *Bulletin of the School of Oriental and African Studies* 22: 258-90.

——. 1963. 'Traditional Chinese phonology,' *Transactions of the Philological Society*, 127-142.

Gabelentz, Georg von der. *Chinesische Grammatik*. Leipzig: T.O. Weigel. Reprint 1953. Berlin: Deutsche Verlag der Wissenschaften.

Gassmann, Robert H. 1980. *Das grammatische Morphem Ye* 也 . Bern & Frankfurt am Main: Peter Lang.

——. 1982. *Zur Syntax von Einbettungsstrukturen im klassischen Chinesisch*. Bern & Frankfurt am Main: Peter Lang.

Graham, Angus C. 1955. 'The Final Particle *Fwu* 夫 ' *Bulletin of the School of Oriental and African Studies* 17:120-132.

——. 1957. 'The Relation between the Final Particles *Yu* 與 and *Yee* 也 ' *Bulletin of the School of Oriental and African Studies* 19:105-123.

——. 1961. 'The Date and Composition of Liehtzyy 列子' *Asia Major* 8: 139-198.

——. 1969. 'The Archaic Chinese Pronouns' *Asia Major* 15:17-61.

——. 1978. *Later Mohist Logic, Ethics and Science.* Hong Kong and London: Chinese University Press and School of Oriental and African Studies.

——. 1981. *Chuang-tzǔ: The Seven Inner Chapters and Other Writings from the Book of Chuang-tzǔ.* London: Allen and Unwin.

——. 1983. '*Yún* 云 and *Yuē* 曰 as Verbs and Particles' *Acta Orientalia Havniensia* 44:33-71.

Harbsmeier, Christoph. 1981. *Aspects of Classical Chinese Syntax.* Scandinavian Institute of Asian Studies Monograph Series, No. 45. London and Malmö: Curzon Press.

——. 1989. 'The Classical Chinese Modal Particle *I* 已 ' In *Proceedings of the Second International Conference on Sinology, December 29-31, 1986. Section on Linguistics and Paleography.* Taipei: Academia Sinica, pp. 471-504.

Haudricourt, André G. 1954. 'Comment reconstruire le chinois archaïque,' *Word.* 10:351-364.

He Leshi 何樂士 . 1994. *Zuǒzhuàn fànwéi fùcí* 左傳範圍副詞 . Yuèlù shūshè: Changsha.

Karlgren, Bernhard. 1920. 'Le Proto-chinois langue flexionelle' *Journal Asiatique* 15:205-233.

——. 1926. 'The Authenticity and Nature of the Tso-chuan' *Göteborgs Högskolas Årsskrift* 32:1-65.

——. 1933. 'The Pronoun *Küe* (厥) in *Shu King' Göteborgs Högskolas Årsskrift* 39(2):29-37.

——. 1950a. *The Book of Odes.* Reprinted from *Bulletin of the Museum of Far Eastern Antiquities*, 16 and 17.

——. 1950b. *The Book of Documents.* Reprinted from *Bulletin of the Museum of Far Eastern Antiquities*, 22.

——. 1951. 'Excursions in Chinese Grammar' *Bulletin of the Museum of Far Eastern Antiquities* 23:107-133.

——. 1957. *Grammata Serica Recensa.* Reprinted from *Bulletin of Far Eastern Antiquities* 29:1-332.

——. 1964. *Glosses on the Book of Odes.* Reprinted from *Bulletin of the Museum of Far Eastern Antiquities* 14 (1942), 16 (1944) and 18 (1946).

Kennedy, George A. 1940. 'A Study of the Particle *Yen*' *Journal of the American Oriental Society* 60:1-22, 193-207. Reprinted in Kennedy 1964:27-78.

——.1953. 'Another Note on *Yen*' *Harvard Journal of Asiatic Studies*, 16:226-36. Reprinted in Kennedy 1964:199-212.

———.1956. 'Zai lun wu wo' (The Classical pronoun forms *ngo* and *nga*) *Bulletin of the Institute of History and Philology, Academia Sinica* 28: 273-281. Reprinted in Kennedy 1964:434-442.

———.1964. *Selected Works of George A. Kennedy*. Ed. by Li Tien-yi. New Haven, Conn.: Far Eastern Publications Yale University.

Lyu Shuxiang 呂 叔 湘 . 1955. *Hànyǔ yǔfǎ lùnwén jí* 漢 語 語 法 論 文 集 . Beijing: Kexue chubanshe.

Malmqvist, Göran. 1981. 'On the Functions and Meanings of the Graph 其 *Chyi* in the Tzuoojuann' In *Proceedings of the International Conference on Sinology, August 15-17, 1980. Section on Linguistics and Paleography.* Taipei: Academia Sinica, pp. 365-89.

Pulleyblank, Edwin G. 1959. '*Fei* 非 , *Wei* 唯 and Certain Related Words.' In S. Egerod and E. Glahn, eds., *Studia Serica Bernhard Karlgren dedicata*. Copenhagen: Munksgaard, pp. 178-89.

———. 1960. 'Studies in Early Chinese Grammar, Part I' *Asia Major* 8:36-67.

———. 1962. 'The Consonantal System of Old Chinese' *Asia Major* 9:58-144, 206-265.

———. 1965. 'Close/open Ablaut in Sino-Tibetan' In G. B. Milner and E. J. A. Henderson, eds., *Indo-Pacific Linguistic Studies* (= *Lingua* 14). Amsterdam: North Holland, pp. 230-240.

———. 1973a. 'Some New Hypotheses Concerning Word Families in Chinese,' *Journal of Chinese Linguistics* 1:111-125.

———. 1973b. 'Some Further Evidence Regarding Old Chinese -*s* and its Time of Disappearance,' *Bulletin of the School of Oriental and African Studies* 36:368-73.

———. 1978. 'Emphatic Negatives in Classical Chinese.' In David T. Roy and Tsuen-hsuin Tsien, eds., *Ancient China: Studies in Early Civilization*. Hong Kong: Chinese University Press. pp. 115-136.

———. 1986. 'The Locative Particles *Yü* 于 , *Yü* 於 , and *Hu* 乎 ' *Journal of the American Oriental Society* 106:1-12.

———. 1987. 'Some Embedding Constructions in Classical Chinese,' *Wang Li Memorial Volumes: English Volume*, ed. by the Chinese Language Society of Hong Kong. Hong Kong: Joint Publishing Company, pp.359-356.

———. 1988. 'Jo chih ho 若 之 何 → nai ho 奈 何 ' *Bulletin of the Institute of History and Philology, Academia Sinica* 59:339-351.

———. 1989. 'Ablaut and Initial Voicing in Old Chinese Morphology: *a as an Infix and Prefix.' In *Proceedings of the Second International Conference on Sinology. Section on Linguistics and Paleography.* Taipei: Academia Sinica, pp. 1-21.

———. 1991a. *Lexicon of Reconstructed Pronunciation in Early Middle Chinese, Late Middle Chinese and Early Mandarin*. Vancouver: University of British Columbia Press.

———. 1991b. 'Some Notes on Morphology and Syntax in Classical Chinese' In Henry Rosemont, ed., *Chinese Texts and Philosophical Contexts: Essays Dedicated to Angus C. Graham*. La Salle, Illinois: Open Court. pp. 21-45.

———. 1994. 'Aspects of Aspect in Classical Chinese' to appear in the Proceedings of the International Symposium on Classical Chinese Grammar, University of Zürich, February 1994.

Takashima, Kenichi. 1988. 'Morphology of the Negatives in Oracle-bone Inscriptions' *Computational Analyses of Asian and African Languages*, 30:113-133.

———. 1994. 'The Modal and Aspectual Particle *Qi* in Shang Chinese' Paper for the International Symposium on Ancient Chinese Grammar, University of Zürich, 21-25 February, 1994.

Waley, Arthur. 1938. *The Analects of Confucius*. London: Allen and Unwin

Wang Li 王力. 1957-58. *Hànyǔ shǐgǎo* 漢語史稿, 3 vols. Beijing: Kexue yuan.

Yang Bojun 楊伯峻. 1958. *Lúnyǔ yìzhù* 論語譯注. Beijing: Zhonghua shuju.

Yang Shuda 楊樹達. 1954. *Cíquǎn* 詞詮. Beijing: Zhonghua shuju.

Index of Chinese Vocabulary Items

Grammatical words discussed in the text are indexed as well as their occurrences in the examples (indicated in bold type). Also indexed are content words written with the same graphs, except for proper names.

ān 安 'peaceful, content' 4, 8, 25, **39**, **40**, **209**, **453**, **516**, **532**; 'how?, where?' 4, 8, 81, 91, 96, **277**, **561**, **563**; 'then' 81, **273**

àn 案 'then' 81

áng 卬 preclassical first person pronoun 76

bèi 被 'receive, undergo, suffer' 36

bǐ 彼 far demonstrative 'that, other' 79, 87, 88, **106**, **139**, **158** and throughout

bǐ 比 'beside; by the time that' 57, 160, **215**, **584**

bì 必 'necessarily' 18, 71, 72, 94, 99, 121, **18**, **22**, **148**, and throughout

bì 畢 'to finish; completely; all (of the object)' 131

bīng 并 'combine' 131

bìng 并, 併 'together, all' 131, **219**

bìng 並, 竝, 併 'side by side; equally both' 131

bìxià 陛下 78

bù 不 general particle of negation 'not' 16, 23, 84, 103, 104, **3**, **6** and throughout. See also fǒu

bù gǔ 不穀 'unworthy; I (of a ruler)' 77

bù kě 不可 contracted to pǒ 叵 106

bù rú 不如 'is not as good as' **218**, **283**

bù wéi 不唯 'not only' 132, **239**,

469; source of fēi 非 (?) 22, 106

bú yì ... hū 不亦 ... 乎 'is it not X' rhetorical question formula 141, **503**, **504**

céng 曾 119, **421**. See also zēng 曾

cháng 嘗 'once' mark of past tense 119, 121, **77**, **218**, **418**, **419**. See also wèi cháng 未嘗

chéng 乘 'ride (in a chariot)' 11

chéng 誠 'really' 18, **19**, **206**, **477**, **533**; in 'if' clauses 153, **297**, **559**

chóu 疇 93

chū 初 'at the beginning, previously' 118, 121, **432**, **461**

cǐ 此 near demonstrative 'this' 17, 72, 85, 86, 88, 90, **11**, **12**, **24** and throughout

cóng 從 'follow' **233**; 'from' 52, **170**

cóng shì 從事 'apply oneself to matters' **235**

dài 殆 'dangerous; is in danger of; almost, maybe' 18, 124, **271**

dài 迨 'reach; up to, until, while' 160

dài 逮 'reach; up to, until, while' 159, **585**, **586**

dàn 但 'only' 134

dāng 當 'correspond to, match; confront' **256**; 'in, at (of time)' 160, **434, 543, 587-590**

dé 得 'to get' 68, **120**, and throughout

dé (ér) 得 (而) 'get to (do something)' 46, 122, **124, 134-136, 292, 303, 310, 448, 528**

dì zǐ 弟子 'disciple; your disciple, I' **361**

diàn xià 殿下 'your highness' 78

dū 都 127

dú 獨 'only, alone' 133, **315, 330, 391, 471, 513**; 'one footed' **244**; in rhetorical questions **473, 474**. See also fēi dú 非獨

duó 奪 verb with two objects 'rob, deprive' 32, 108, **76, 204, 301, 389, 540**

è 惡 'bad' 11, **155, 489**. See also wū 惡, wù 惡

ér 而 'you' 77, **263, 264**; connective for verbs in series 'then' 44, 45, 148, **4, 17** and throughout; 'if' 150, 151, **548, 549**. See also suī … ér 雖 … 而, fēi … ér 非 … 而

ér hòu 而後 'and afterwards' 161, **41, 62, 93, 153, 234, 259, 364, 478, 594**

ér yǐ 而已 'only' 20, 46, 134, 149

ěr 耳 'ear' **171**; contraction of ér yǐ 而已 134, **179**

ěr 爾 'you' 11, 77, **42, 174, 289** and throughout; 'so, thus' 78, 90, **279, 317, 318**. See also yún ěr 云爾

fán 凡 'all' introducing a noun phrase 74, 127, **448, 449**; 'ordinary' 127, **274**

fǎnqiè 反切 5

fāng 方 'square' **186**; 'direction, region' **503**; 'method, device' **92**; 'just now, just then' 121, 160, **428, 429, 590**

fēi 非 negator for nouns and noun phrases 12, 16, 22, 23, 71, 110, **5, 6, 9, 207, 212, 238, 244, 260, 318, 501**; introducing an exposed noun phrase 72, **242**; 'if not, unless' 106, 154, **381, 562, 563**; 'wrong' 86, 106, **298**; 'call wrong, deny' **382**

fēi dú 非獨 'not only' 133, **472**

fēi … ér fēi … 而 157, **575**

fēi wéi 非唯 'not only' 132, **470**

fēi 匪 preclassical for fēi 非 106

fēi 棐 preclassical for fēi 非 106

fǒu 否 (不) 103, 140 'no' **147, 372**; 'or not?' **373**; 'not' (verb understood) **374, 376**; 'if not' **375**. See also pǐ 否

fū 夫 'man, male person' 89, **239**. See also dà fū 大夫, pǐ fū 匹夫, zhàng fū 丈夫

fū rén 夫人 'lady of high rank, wife of a nobleman' **110**

fū zǐ 夫子 'the master' 77, **160, 419, 446, 502**; 'you (honorific)' 78, **16, 237, 400, 502**

fú 夫 demonstrative pronoun 'that one, he' 89, **294, 315, 316**; final question particle 'is it not' 17, 104, 146, **11, 525, 545**; generalizing initial particle 74, **9, 94, 254, 256, 257, 281, 431**; with interrogative pronouns 147, **258, 529**. See also ruò fú 若夫

fú 弗 (EMC put) 'not' aspectual contrast with bù 不 in

preclassical and early classical language 85, 105, **379, 380**; later interpreted as incorporating a third person pronoun object 79, 104, **268, 377, 532, 576**; post-Hàn 105-106

gài 蓋 'cover' **182**; modal particle 'probably' 124, **441**; introducing a final explanatory predicate 'for' **442**; graph used for hé 盍 'why not' **508**

gǎn 敢 'dare' 40, 122, **106, 256, 430, 442**

géxià 閣下 'your excellency' 78

gè 个 count word for arrows 59

gè 各 'each' 92, 130, 134, **342, 459**

gǒu 苟 'be careless of' 153, **554, 555**; 'if' 150, 153, **556, 557**

gǒuqiě 苟且 'careless, without foresight' 152

gōng 公 'duke' **449**; term of address 'lord' 78

gòng 共 'together, common' 130

gū 孤 'orphan; self designation for a ruler' 77

gǔ 古 'old (noun), ancient times' 118, **17, 21, 116, 154, 217**

gǔ zhě 古者 'formerly, of old' 74, 118, **330**

gù 固 18, 99

gù 故 'ancient' (adjective) **226**; 'affairs, troubles' **411, 455**; 'reason' **307**; 'so, thus, therefore' 162, **17, 41, 47, 58, 212, 287, 303, 362, 483**; 'deliberately' **116**; at the end of a 'because' clause 162, **597**. See also wèi ... gù 為 ... 故

guǎ jūn 寡君 'our ruler' (humble form) **87, 241, 454**

guǎ rén 寡人 humble self designation for a ruler 77, **179, 233, 479, 535, 582**

hài 害 'injure, harm' **116, 222**, preclassical interrogative pronoun, used for hé 曷 95

hé 何 'what?' 91, 93, 94, 145, **213, 262, 265, 307, 474**; attributive to a noun or noun phrase **234, 340, 533**; 'why? how?' **191, 267, 279, 422, 448, 526, 527**; follows a copula or locative coverb, **334, 335, 336**; follows rú 如 'is like' in preclassical language **337**. See also nài hé nài hé 奈何, rú hé 如何, rú zhī hé 如之何, ruò zhī hé 若之何, yún hé 云何

hé gù 何故 'for what reason, why' 94, **557**

hé rú 何如 'is like what? how would it be?' 94, **123, 142, 565**

hé shí 何實 what? as subject of a verb 95, **341**

hé wèi 何謂 94

hé yǐ 何以 'by what? how?' 223

hé yóu 何由 'from what?, how?' **169, 214**

hé 曷 'what, when, how, why' 91, 95, 96

hé 盍 'why not' 10, 96, 107, **342, 508**

hū 乎 final question particle 8, 16, 79, 140, 144, **33, 42** and throughout; variant of yú 於 'in, at, etc.' 53, 54, 55, 56, **79, 156, 174, 446**. See also bù yì ... hū 不亦 ... 乎,

qí ... hū 其 ...乎 , *wū hū* 惡
乎 , *yě hū* 也乎 , *yú shì hū* 於
是乎

hū zāi 乎 哉 exclamatory question
146, **262, 535**

hú 胡 interrogative pronoun
'why?' 10, 91, 95, 96, 107,
142; in a proper name **78**

hù 互 137

huò 或 'some, someone,
something, perhaps' 92, 130,
134, 135, 136, **79, 80, 156,
478, 479, 480, 484, 594**

huò zhě 或 者 'perhaps' 135,
485

jī 其 preclassical question particle
337. *See also* qí 其

jí 及 'reach' 29, **57, 262, 474**;
'up to, till; when' 57, 154,
159, 162, **116, 184, 428,
569, 579, 580, 581, 582**;
'and' (with nouns) 61, **199,
200, 585**

jí 即 'approach, come to' **596**;
'immediately, forthwith' 155,
568, 569; 'if' 154, **561**;
specifier of a noun predicate
'it was that ...' 17, **17**; 'then'
(like zé 則) **570**

jǐ 己 reflexive personal pronoun
'self' 83, 136, **280, 281,
282, 283, 284, 351, 459**

jì 既 'to complete' 113, **398**;
perfective marker 'already'
109, 112, 113, 114, **399,
400, 406**; 'when, after' 113,
115, 158, **401, 404**

jì ér 既 而 113, **402**

jì yǐ 既 已 115, **412**

jì ... yòu ... 既 ··· 又 ··· 'having
... also ...' 113, **403**

jiǎ 假 'borrow, simulate, pretend;
supposing that' 152, **552**

jiǎshǐ 假 使 'supposing' 151

jiān 兼 'combine' 127

jiàn 見 'see; meet' 11, **1, 56, 131**
and throughout; mark of the
passive 35, **90-95, 100**. *See
also* xiàn 見

jiāng 將 'bring; lead an army' 120;
modal adverb of futurity 'about
to, be going to, intend to'
119, 120, 122, **55, 96, 131**
and throughout; introducing a
preposed element 71, 72, 120,
239, 425, 426; 'approximately' 58, **189**

jiāo 交 'to cross, exchange, have
relations with' **67**; 'with each
other, mutually' 137, **415**

jiē 皆 pronominal adverb 'all' 17,
128, 129, **14, 28, 36** and
throughout

jīn 今 'now, today' 53, **21, 116,
180** and throughout; empty
introductory particle 'now'
118, **189, 278, 474, 543,
563**

jīn yě 今 也 'now (contrastive)'
74, 118, **382**

jīn zī 今 茲 'now at this time, now'
311, 341

jìn 盡 'to exhaust' 101, **179**;
'completely, all' 101, 131, **9**

jū 俱 'together, both, all' 7, 129,
130, **380, 455, 456, 457**

jǔ 舉 'lift' 35, **122, 475**;
'undertake' **570**; 'all' 128,
129, **453, 454, 516**

jù 具 'provide; all' 130, **458**

jù 詎 (鉅 , 距 , 巨 , 遽) in rhetorical
questions 144

jué 厥 preclassical possessive
pronoun 80

jūn 君 'ruler, lord' 9, **22, 43, 44**
and throughout; 'your
lordship, you' 78, **224, 467,**

521, 580, 586. *See also* guǎ
jūn 寡君
jūn zǐ 君子 'gentleman, superior
    man; gentlemanly' 9, 26, **24,
    63, 249, 310, 404, 409,
    471, 483**

kě 可 'is possible, permissible' as
    predicate 23, 24, 122, 144,
    **169, 214, 291, 325, 364,
    376, 546, 557**; with
    passive verb as complement
    23, 42, **94, 117, 125** and
    throughout; with an active
    verb followed by zhī 之 43,
    123, 124; hortatory 'should'
    43, 122, **127, 128, 276**.
    See also bù kě 不可, pǒ 叵
kě dé (ér) 可得 (而) 46, **134,
    135, 136**
kě yǐ 可以 'is possible' with
    active verb as complement 21,
    23, 42, 43, **121, 406, 448,
    535**
kě yǐ wéi 可以為 'can be (with
    nouns and adjectives)' 21, 23,
    24, **28, 33, 260**
kěn 肯 'be willing to' 40, 122
kuàng 況 'to compare with, be
    equal to' 146, **530**; 'how
    much the more' 146, **531**

le 了 19, 116
liàng 輛 count noun for carriages
    59
líng 令 'to order' 41, **110**; 'make,
    cause' 41, **114, 116**;
    'supposing, if' 150, 151,
    551
luò tuo 駱駝 'camel' 9

měi 每 'every (time), always;
    whenever' 130, **460, 461,
    462**

mǐ 靡 preclassical negative
    particle 110, **395**
miè 蔑 'destroy,' perfective
    negative particle, same as mò
    末 85, 110, **396**
mǒu 某 'some (one), a certain' 97,
    98, **349, 350**
mò 末 'end, tip'; perfective
    negative particle (same as miè
    蔑) 110, 111, **397**
mò 莫 'none, no one, nothing'
    referring to the subject 85, 92,
    109, 130, 134, 136, **49, 63,
    290, 296, 486**; post-
    classical 'do not' 109
mò rú 莫如 'nothing is as good
    as, it is best to' 136, **487**
mò ruò 莫若 'nothing is as good
    as, it is best to' 136

nǎi 乃 'you, your' preclassical 77;
    'then' 45, 119, **171**; focusing
    on new information 75, **257,
    260, 264**; introducing a
    noun predicate 17, **15, 16**.
    See also wú nǎi 無乃
nǎi ruò 乃若 topic marker 75,
    260
nǎi 迺 old form of nǎi 乃 'then' 78
nài 奈 contraction of ruò zhī 若
    之 34
nài hé 奈何 same as ruò zhī hé
    若之何 79
nán 難 'difficult' 42, 122, **119,
    512, 242**. *See also* nàn 難
nán dào 難道 Modern Chinese
    equivalent of qǐ 豈 142
nàn 難 'difficulty, trouble; to make
    trouble for' 58
néng 能 'can, be capable' 6, **207,
    212, 223, 247, 311, 464**;
    with a noun or pronoun object
    40, 132, **107, 108**; with a

clause object having the same subject 40, 46, **40**, **105**, **114** and throughout

níng 寧 'quiet, peaceful' **379**; 'rather' 124, **443**, **444**. *See also* wú níng 無寧

nǚ 女 'woman' 8, **128**; nǚ zǐ 女子 'daughter' **251**

pǐ 匹 count noun for horses 59, **195**

pǐ fū 匹夫 'common fellow' **256**, **285**

pǐ 否 'bad, evil' 104. *See also* fǒu 否

pǒ 叵 contraction of bù kě 不可 **105**

pú 僕 'servant, slave; I' 77

qí 其 pronoun substitute for N + zhī 之 62, 80, **4**, **10**, **22**, **62**, and throughout; as a mark of nominalization 37, 39, 41, 50, 64, 80, 159, **17**, **30**, **89** and throughout; weak demonstrative 'the' 80, **268**; instead of zhī 之 after a demonstrative pronoun 88, **306**, **307**; modal particle 122, 142, 144, **429**, **434**, **435**, **436**, **437**, **438**, **512**, **542**, **543**, **548**, **576**; softening an imperative 123, 139, **439**. *See also* jì 其

qí ... hū 其 ... 乎 rhetorical question expecting an affirmative answer 123, 126, 142, 143, 144, **308**, **394**, **433**, **510**, **511**

qí zhū ... yú 其諸 ... 與 126, **446**, **447**

qǐ 豈 introduces a rhetorical question expecting a negative answer 142, **94**, **162**, **225**,

248, **303**, **453**, **454**, **513**-**521**, **534**

qiě 且 'moreover' 116, **524**; 'and' with adjectives 39, **103**, 157; 'even' **488**, **531**; adverbial particle of futurity 'going to, about to' 120, **101**, **427**. *See also* gǒuqiě 苟且

qiè 妾 'concubine, slave' humble self-designation for a woman 77

qiè 竊 'steal; private' humble self designation 77

qīng 卿 'minister' 78, **25**, **148**

qǐng 請 'to request; I beg, please' 138, **37**, **494**, **495**

qū 驅 'drive' construction with ér 而 46, **136**

rán 然 'be thus, so' equivalent to rú zhī 如之 10, 79, 81, 90, **11**, **36**, **374**, **470**, **512**, **542**, **563**; closing an expression introduced by rú 如 or ruò 若 83, **278**; suffix forming descriptive adverbs 102, **48**, **130**, **210**, **228**, **320**, **367**-**370**, **402**. *See also* suī rán 雖然

rán hòu 然後 'afterwards' 81, 118, 161, **138**, **430**, **595**

rán zé 然則 'if so then' 81, **400**, **417**, **450**

rén 人 'man, person' **9**, **14**, **19** and throughout; 'some one, other(s)' 98, **53**, **94**, **109**, **184**, **203**, **281**, **313**, **330**, **351**, **381**, **407**, **446**, **456**; 'each' 98, **352**. *See also* fán rén 凡人 , guǎrén 寡人

rénrén 人人 'every one' 98, **353**, **528**

róng 戎 a non-Chinese people

232, 443; 'you' preclassical 78

rú 如 '(is) like' 10, 18, 34, 78, 81, 90, 94, **373, 559, 563**; introducing a descriptive complement 56, 99, **181, 182, 404**; 'if' 149, 150, 151, 157, **437, 453, 487, 516, 543, 545, 547**; suffix for an expressive adverb 102. *See also* bù rú 不 如 , hé rú 何 如 , mò rú 莫 如

rú guǒ 如 果 'if' (Modern Chinese) 153

rú hé 如 何 'is like what?' preclassical 94, **337**; as an abbreviation of rú zhī hé 如 之 何 95, **553**

rú zhī hé 如 之 何 'what is to be done about it?' 35, 94, **89, 397**

rú 如 X hé 何 'what is to be done about X?' 34

rǔ 女 used for rǔ 汝 'you' 77, 78, **294, 550**. *See also* nǔ 女

rǔ 汝 'you' 8, 11, 77, **199, 277, 452**

ruò 若 'agree, accord with, conform to' 90; 'that sort of' 91, **319**; 'is like, is equal to' 11, 18, 34, 77, 83, 90, **18, 361, 380, 535**; 'is not as good as ..., it would be better to ...' **352**; 'if' 150, 157, **213, 236, 542, 544, 546, 548** (variant); introducing a descriptive complement 99, **17, 278, 560**; 'you' 77, 78, **101, 456**

rùo fú 若 夫 'as for' 75, **34, 259, 260**

ruò X hé 若 X何 'what is to be done about X?' 34, 150, **86, 87**

ruò zhī hé 若 之 何 'what is to be done about it?' 34, 35, 79, **88**

sàn 三 'thrice' 101, **274, 364**

shā mén 沙 門 'Buddhist monk' 9

shàn 善 'good' 141, **77, 138, 182, 260, 324, 362, 536, 557**, 'be good at' 44, **130**, 'make friends with' **596**

shè 設 'set up, establish; supposing' 152, **553**

shēn 身 'body, person; self' 84, 137, **285, 375, 491, 582**

shēng 生 'be born, live, alive' 10

shèng 乘 count word for chariots 11, 59, **22, 230, 470**

shí 實 'full, real'; demonstrative pronoun 'this' referring to the subject 72, 89, **241, 242, 313, 315, 426, 454**. *See also* hé shí 何 實

shízì 實 字 'full word, content word' 12

shí 時 'time, season' **3, 143, 300, 301, 385, 389**; closing a time clause 160, 162, **588, 590, 591, 592**; preclassical demonstrative pronoun 'this, that' 89, **314**

shí 寔 alternative form of shí 實 as a pronoun 72, 89

shǐ 使 'send; employ' **98, 184, 421, 578**; 'make, cause' 33, 41, 43, 46, 81, **89, 109, 113, 125, 146, 181, 209, 210, 216, 244, 303, 451, 485**; 'supposing, if' 57, 128, 150, 151, **550**. *See also* jiǎshǐ 假 使

shǐ 始 'begin; for the first time, at first' 63, 64, 121, **180, 211, 430, 510**. *See also* wèi shǐ 未 始

shì 是 anaphoric demonstrative

pronoun 'this, that,' 14, 85,
86, 89, **30, 105, 162**, 235,
**246, 266, 279, 326, 361,
515, 518, 533, 534, 559,
563**; attributive, **239, 472**;
introducing a noun predicate
17, **6, 13, 15, 23, 113,
207, 208, 209, 403**;
recapitulating a preposed
object 50, 70, **152, 232,
233, 240, 425, 522**;
recapitulating a preposed
subject 72, **243, 244**; 'right'
85, 106, **297, 298**; modern
Chinese copula 16. *See also* yǐ
shì 以 是 , yú shì 於 是
shì gù 是 故 'for this reason,
therefore' 86, 162
shì yǐ 是 以 sentence connective
'because of this, therefore' 50,
86, **129**
shì zǐ 世 子 Crown Prince **131**
shū jī 庶 幾 'almost; probably; I
hope' 9, 124, **440**
shú 孰 'which, who' 91, 92, 130,
134, **156, 157, 290, 327,
328, 329**; referring to things
93, 95, **330, 331, 332**; as
object 93, **333**
shuài 率 'lead' with ér 而 46,
137, 299
shuí 誰 'who' 91, 92, 94, **26,
153, 258, 320-326, 434,
452, 473, 529, 542, 543,
548**
sī 斯 'this' 17, 88, **89, 308,
309, 310, 349, 475**; 'then'
155, **123, 270, 566, 567**
sǐ 死 'die' 17, 49, **89, 164,
213, 236, 249, 252, 356,
377, 403, 411, 468, 524,
524, 544, 548**; 'die for
someone' 27, **49, 576**; 'the
dead' **113**

suī 雖 'although, even if' 22, 156,
157, **132, 259, 315, 380,
387, 437, 457, 513, 572,
573**; 'even (if it is)' with a
noun 157, **442, 571**
suī ... ér 雖 … 而 'although ...
yet' 157, **574**
suī rán 雖 然 'even if it is so' 81,
157
suǒ 所 'place' 68; relative pronoun
standing for the object or
destination of an embedded
verb or coverb 16, 37, 39, 64,
68, **8, 20, 31, 32, 56, 224,
226, 260, 272, 317, 319,
416, 417, 555, 570**;
standing for a locative
complement **225, 499, 545**.
See also wéi ... suǒ 為 … 所 ,
wéi ... suǒ (yě) 惟 … 所 (也)
suǒ yǐ 'that by which' 所 以 49,
93

tā 他 Modern Chinese pronoun
'he, she, it' 80. *See also* tuō
他
táng láng 螳 螂 9
tǎng 儻 (also written 倘 , 黨)
'accidentally, by chance; if'
153, **558**
tè 特 'special, particular; only'
134
tiān zǐ 天 子 Son of Heaven **285,
303**
tú 徒 'followers' **399**; 'only' 134,
453, 516
tuō 他 'other' 7, 97, **167, 224,
291, 347, 348**
tuó tuó 橐 駝 'camel' 9

wáng 亡 109
wáng 王 78
wǎng 罔 'net; catch, entrap' **549**;
preclassical negative 'not

have, there is no' 109

wéi 唯 (隹, 惟, 維) preclassical
copula 22, 106, 110, 157,
158, 334; classical '(is)
only' 22, 131, 132, **31, 32,
129, 454, 464, 466**;
adverbial 'only' **98, 468**;
introducing an exposed or
topicalized element 71, 72,
74, 120, 131, **239, 253,
463, 465**. *See also* bù wéi 不
唯, fēi wéi 非 唯, wěi wéi 唯

wéi dú 唯 獨 'only' 133

wéi suǒ (yě) 惟 所 (也) hortatory
'it is only what ...' 132, **467**

wéi 為 'do, make' 22, **6**; copula or
equational verb 'be' 20, 23,
36, **25, 26, 27, 28, 44**;
with an indirect object 33,
81, 82; in passive
construction 36, 37, **96, 97,
98, 100**; with adjectives 24,
25, **33, 36**. *See also* wèi 為;
yǐ 以 X wéi 為 Y

wéi (...) suǒ 為 (...) 所 passive
construction 37, 38, **99, 101**

wéi 微 'small, minute; secret; if it
were not for' 7, 110, 154,
157, **394, 438**

wěi 唯 'yes' 22

wèi 未 aspectual negative 'not yet,
never' 23, 24, 109, 112, 114,
116, 117, 118, **4, 62, 147,
228, 295, 311, 393, 405,
406**; 'before' 114, 158, **164,
404, 407, 578, 586**

wèi cháng 未 嘗 'not yet, never
yet' 119, **116, 310, 420,
442**

wèi shǐ 未 始 'not yet' 121, **431**

wèi 謂 'say, tell, call' 33, 34, 42,
43, 71, **83, 84, 85, 123,
126, 226, 237, 238, 260,
276, 285, 303, 308, 408**.

See also hé wèi 何 謂

wèi zhī hé 謂 之 何 'what does one
call it' 95

wèi 為 '(is) because of, for' 51,
90, **163**

wèi ... gù 為 ... 故 'for the sake of,
on behalf of' **194**

wèn 問 'ask' 33, **79, 80, 156,
367, 392, 430, 492, 536**

wén 聞 'hear' 32, 152, **77, 78,
136**, and throughout

wényán 文 言 4

wǒ 我 first person pronoun 'I, me,
we, us' 11, 76, **5, 42, 65**, and
throughout

wū 惡 'how' 91, 96, **106, 256,
304, 316, 346, 537**

wū hú 惡 乎 'how' 96, 97, **345**

wū 烏 'crow' **97**; 'how' (= wū 惡)
96, 97

wú 无 (see wú 無) 107

wú 無 'not have' 30, 107, 109,
110, 136, **17, 29, 61**, and
throughout; 'do not' (= 毋)
79, 84, 107, 108, 124, 138,
**35, 104, 283, 289, 291,
383, 384, 385, 386, 387,
554, 567**; in rhetorical
questions 144, **522**

wú nǎi 無 乃 'would it not be' 144

wú níng 無 (毋) 寧 'would it not
be preferable to' 125, 145,
524

wú yǐ 無 以 'have no means to'
31, 49

wú 毋 'do not' (see wú 無) 107,
114, **114**

wú 吾 first person pronoun 'I, my,
we, our' 10, 76, **16, 30, 49**,
and throughout

wúzǐ 吾 子 'you, sir' honorific 78,
156, 328, 439

wù 勿 'do not' 79, 85, 108, 110,
124, 138, **317, 388, 389**,

390

wù 惡 'hate' 11, **294, 317, 487, 488, 541, 552**

X zhǐ yú 之 於 Y 56, 73, **41, 94, 179, 180, 249, 250, 275, 563**

xī 昔 'formerly' 118, **585, 593**

xī zhě 昔 者 'formerly' 74, 118, **59, 482**

xī 悉 'thorough; to exhaust or to sum up; all' 131

xī 奚 'where, how' 91, 95, **424, 576**

xī shuài 蟋 蟀 9

xiān shēng 先 生 78

xián 咸 'to unite; unitedly, all' 131

xiàn 見 'appear' 11, **348, 558**

xiāng 相 pronominal adverb 'each other, one another' 136, **451, 456, 488, 489**

xiāng yǔ 相 與 'mutually, together' 137, **490**

xié, jiē 偕 'accompany, together with' 128, **154**

xìn 信 'trust, believe, good faith; true' **31, 180, 502,** 'really, (if) really' 99, 153, **560**

xìng 姓 10

xìng 性 10

xūyú 須 臾 9

yān 焉 equivalent to *yú zhī 於 之 'in it, to it, etc.' 10, 30, 31, 55, 56, 69, 79, 80, **41, 54** and throughout; 'then' 81, **272**; mark of an expressive adverb 102; interrogative pronoun 'where, how' 81, 91, 96, **343, 344, 459, 528, 549**

yé 邪 (耶) question particle

equivalent to yě hū 也 乎 10, 16, 94, 139, **10, 499**

yě 也 mark of noun predication 12, 16, 52, **5-8** and throughout; after a final explanatory clause 63, 124, **442**; omitted 19, 132, 143, 154, 158, **22, 31, 32, 466**; after nominalized phrases as topic 20, 65, 73, 131, **30, 94, 104, 179** and throughout; as time clauses 161, **593**; after embedded clauses 20, 50, 57, 64, 159, **35, 88, 89, 116, 184, 214, 215, 218, 220, 351, 355, 383, 444, 524, 580, 581, 584, 587, 596**; after proper nouns 73, **82, 252, 418**; after the complement of the adjectives kě 可, zú 足, nán 難, yì 易 **119, 120, 135, 262, 549**; mark of continuing state 20, 109, 112, 114, 116, 117, 118, **4, 62, 116, 147, 228, 295, 393, 397, 405, 416, 420, 441**. *See also* jīn yě 今 也, wéi suǒ (yě) 惟 所 (也)

yě hū 也 乎 10, 16, 139

yě yǐ 也 已 19, 118

yě yǐ yǐ 也 已 矣 19, 118, **24, 397**

yě yú 也 與 17, **501**

yě zāi 也 哉 146, **534**

yī 一 'one' 76, **122, 191, 256, 300, 321, 381, 407, 449, 527, 551, 573, 576**; 'first' **455**; 'unite' **329**; 'once' 101, **365**

yī 伊 postclassical third person pronoun 80

yí 台 preclassical first person pronoun 76, 77

yí 宜 'fitting, proper, right' 44,

122, **129, 504**

yǐ 以 'use, employ' 42, 47, **139, 437**; 'with, by means of' 47, **17, 71, 72, 93, 124, 140-144**, and throughout; anaphoric with object zhī 之 omitted 'thereby, therewith, in order to' 32, 48, 79, 86, **47, 73, 75, 125, 145, 146, 193, 217, 359, 399, 423, 460, 491, 546**; recapitulating a preposed object 70, **236, 282**; 'because' 49, 57, 162, **596**. *See also* hé yǐ 何 以 , kě yǐ 可 以 , kě yǐ wéi 可 以 為 , shì yǐ 是 以 , suǒ yǐ 所 以 , wú yǐ 無 以 , yǒu yǐ 有 以 , zú yǐ 足 以

yǐ lái 以 來 48, **147**

yǐ shì 以 是 'because of this' 49, 86, **220**

yǐ X wéi Y 以 X 為 Y 'regard X as Y' 49, **150, 151, 157, 305, 327, 409, 450, 504, 514**

yǐ 以 X zhī gù 之 故 'because of X' 162, **597**

yǐ xià 以 下 48, **148**

yǐ 已 'stop' 101, 114, **386, 408**; 'already' 19, 58, 101, 112, 116, **188, 410, 411**; 'very' 101, 115, **409, 506**; aspect particle combining the functions of yě 也 and yǐ 矣 19, 118, **23, 387, 417**. *See also* yě yǐ 也 已 , yě yǐ yǐ 也 已 矣 , ér yǐ 而 已 , jì yǐ 既 已

yǐ ér yǐ 已 而 'afterwards' 115, **413**

yǐ 矣 final particle of perfect aspect 19, 20, 23, 24, 112-116, **2, 27, 48** and throughout. *See also* yě yǐ yǐ

也 已 矣

yì 亦 'also' 18, 99, **13, 208, 496, 563**; 'surely' 141, 144, **2, 60, 149, 233, 508, 509, 522**. *See also* bú yì ... hū 不 亦 ... 乎

yì 易 'change' **17, 491, 493, 575**; 'easy' 42, 122, **120, 278**

yōng 庸 particle in rhetorical questions 144

yòng 用 'use, need' **90, 171, 192**, and throughout; 'sacrifice' **163**; preclassical coverb 'using, with' 50

yōu 攸 'place' preclassical reflexive pronoun 68

yóu 由 'to follow along (a road)' 52, **166, 532**; 'from' 52, 79, **167, 168, 169, 197, 214**; used for yóu 猶 57, **183, 320**

yóu 猶 'still, yet' 18, **151, 164, 259, 484, 489, 507, 531, 541**; 'like' 18, 55-57, **21, 132, 183, 250, 559**

yǒu 有 'have' 30, **2, 60, 103**, and throughout; 'there is, are' 13, 30, **4, 62, 64, 65**, and throughout; 'some' 31, 135, **483**; preclassical prefix for proper names **127**. *See also* yòu 有

yǒu sī 有 司 'officer' **49, 224**

yǒu yǐ 有 以 'have the means to' 49, **149, 435, 509**

yòu 又 'again, also, moreover' 18, 99, **235, 265, 358, 576**. *See also* jì ... yòu 既 ... 又

yòu 有 'and' with numerals 60, **197**

yú 于 'go (to); to, at, in' 53, 56, 94, **127, 175, 235, 432**. *See also* zhì yú 至 于

yú 余 first person pronoun 'I, my'

76, **240**, **263**, **274**, **288**

yú 於 'in, at, to, from' 10, 28, 29,
   30, 32, 33, 36, 53, 54, 94,
   25, **58**, **65**, **171**, and
   throughout; 'than' 24, **35**,
   104, **321**, **383**; 'by' with a
   passive verb 28, 36, **53**, **92**,
   94, **135**. *See also* X zhī yú
   之 於 Y, zhì yú 至 於

yú shì 於 是 'thereupon, then' 55,
   81, 86

yú shì hū 於 是 乎 'thereupon,
   then' 86

yú 與 (歟) question particle
   equivalent to yě hū 也 乎 10,
   16, 126, 139, **9**, **108**, **118**,
   266, **278**, **308**, **326**, **406**,
   474, **498**, **595**. *See also* qí
   zhū ... yú 其 諸 ⋯ 與 , xiāng
   yǔ 相 與 , yě yú 也 與 , yǔ 與 ,
   yù 與

yǔ 與 'accompany' 50, **152**, **153**;
   'give' 23, **68**, **71**, **290**,
   317, **329**; 'with' 50, 68, **30**,
   52, **154**, and throughout; in
   comparisons 50, 93, 124,
   156, **157**, **223**, **328**, **331**,
   332, **444**, **524**; 'and' with
   nouns 51, 61, **75**, **158**, **159**,
   198, **456**. *See also* yú 與 , yù
   與

yǔ 予 first person pronoun 'I, me'
   76, **111**, **199**, **261**, **316**,
   412, **422**, **453**, **516**, **524**

yù 與 'participate in' 50, **437**. *See
   also* yú 與 , yǔ 與

yúan 爰 'there; then, thereupon'
   56

yuē 曰 'say' introducing direct
   quotation 10, 79, 81, 82, **24**,
   30 and throughout ; 'is called'
   21, 34, 94, **29**, **30**, **84**

yún 云 'say so, say it' 10, 79, 81,
   274, **275**; 'speak' 82, **276**;

closing a quotation 82, **277**

yún ěr 云 爾 'say thus' closing a
   quotation of imagined speech
   83, 90, **279**

yún hé 云 何 94, **338**, **339**

zāi 哉 final particle of exclamation
   143, 146, **94**, **106**, **162** and
   throughout

zài 再 'twice, again' 101, **274**,
   364

zé 則 'then' introducing the
   conclusion of an if-clause
   119, 149, 155, **35**, **40**, **47**
   and throughout; marking the
   subject or another element as
   contrastive 72, 155, **139**,
   206, **245-248**, **260**, **312**,
   414, **416**

zēng 曾 'just, even' 119, **422**. *See
   also* céng 曾

zhān 旃 contraction of zhī yān 之
   焉 10, 79

zhāng 張 10

zhàng 帳 10

zhàng 脹 (漲) 10

zhàng fū 丈 夫 'male person, man'
   251, **267**

zhě 者 pronominal substitute for
   the head of a noun phrase 'that
   which, one who' 16, 31, 62,
   64, 66-68, 74, 126, 127, 135,
   4, **7**, **11** and throughout; in
   time expressions 74, 118. *See
   also* gǔ zhě 古 者 , huò zhě 或
   者 , xī zhě 昔 者

zhī 之 'go to' 29, 94, **55**, **66**,
   131, **138** and throughout;
   demonstrative 'that' 79, **265**;
   object pronoun 'him, her, it,
   them' 9-10, 14, 32, 34, 37,
   41, 48, 49, 55, 69, 79, **17**,
   30 and throughout; genitive
   marker 24, 61-62, **9**, **12** and

throughout; mark of nominalization 15, 37, 39, 50, 54, 64-66, **8**, **90** and throughout. *See also* rú zhī hé 如 之 何 , ruò zhī hé 若 之 何 , wèi zhī hé 謂 之 何 , X zhī yú 之 於 Y, yǐ 以 X zhī gù 之 故

zhèn 朕 preclassical first person pronoun 'I, my' 76, 77

zhí 直 'direct, straight' **152**, **574**; 'only' 99, 134, **187**, **476**

zhì 至 'arrive; arrive at, reach' **11**, **120**, **270**, **310**, **350**, **430**, **499**, **567**, **586**; 'to the utmost' **436**

zhì yú 至 于 coverb 'until, when' 159, **583**

zhì yú 至 於 coverb 'until, when' 57, 159, **168**, **197**

zhū 諸 'the class of, all' 126, **201**, **445**, **471**; contraction of zhī hū 之 乎 (question) 9, 54, 79, **112**, **408**; contraction of zhī hū 之 乎 (= zhī yú 之 於) 9, 54, 56, 79, 140, **291**, **475**. *See also* qí zhū … yú 其 諸 … 與

zhū hóu 諸 侯 'feudal lord(s)' 126, 87, **193**, **304**, **341**, **530**, **595**

zhuó zhuó 濯 濯 9

zī 茲 'this, here' 72, 88, 156, **245**, **311**, **312**, **341**, **500**

zǐ 子 'son, child' 9, **9**, **43**, **66**, **134**, **182**, **210**, **236**, **343**, **355**; 'master' 78, **198**, **351**; 'you' polite 78, **9**, **19**, **26** and throughout. *See also* dì zǐ 弟 子 , fū zǐ 夫 子 , jūn zǐ 君 子 , nǚ zǐ 女 子 , shì zǐ 世 子 , tiān zǐ 天 子 , wú zǐ 吾 子

zì 自 'follow' 52, **164**; 'from' 52, **116**, **147**, **165**, **175**, **272**, **379**, **503**; pronominal adverb 'self' 83, 136, **128**, **157**, **178**, **273**, **416**

zòng 縱 'to relax, let go, allow; even though' 158, **576**

zú 足 'foot' 178; 'sufficient, worth' 42, 122, **118**, **122**, **278**, **279**, **305**, **445**, **498**, **505**, **552**

zú yǐ 足 以 **474**

zú xià 足 下 respectful term of address for an equal 78

zuò 作 'arise, appear, act; cause to arise, create, make' 27, **368**, **510**, **570**; 'make; perform a role, be' (Modern Chinese) 20

General Index

Only the main occurrences of grammatical terms are indexed.

ablaut 11
active 23, 27, 42, 43, 44, 122
adjective 9, 12, 13, 14, 23, 24-26, 27, 28, 36, 39, 42-44, 55, 62, 99, 100, 101
adnominal 71, 72, 97, 122, 125, 127, 130
adverb 9, 14, 58, 99, 100, 101, 115, 120, 121, 126, 141, 144, 151, 153, 155, 157, 160
adverbial 31, 63, 88, 90, 93, 95, 97, 99-102, 109, 112, 118, 118, 121, 122, 125-134, 136, 137, 139, 145, 152, 160
adverbial use of nouns 99
agent 24-28, 35-37, 41, 43
agent of a passive verb 28
Analects 3
Ancient Chinese 5
Anyáng 安陽 3
Archaic Chinese 5
aspect 10, 19, 20, 21, 23, 24, 53, 80, 82, 105, 108, 109, 111-118, 158

Bodman, N.C. 164 n. 27
Book of Changes 3
Book of Documents 3
Book of Odes 3
bound compound 9

Cantonese 6, 81, 103
causative 12, 25-28, 34, 40, 41, 50, 63, 150, 151, 156
Chao, Y.R. 166 n.49, 167 n.59
Chen Mengjia 164 n.24
Chou Fa-kao 163 n.10, n.13, 164 n.21
Chǔ 楚 3

Chǔcí 76
Cikoski, John S. 163 n.11
Cíyuán 辭源 6
Classical Chinese (definition) 3
classifier 59
clause object 39-41, 57, 66, 122, 159
clerical style 8
colloquial 7, 17, 66, 77, 80, 103, 120, 127
comparative degree 24
Confucius 3
content word 12
contraction 9, 79, 95, 104, 106, 107, 139, 140
coordination 39, 45, 51, 61
copula 16, 17, 20-22, 23, 24, 58, 74, 85, 86, 91, 93, 94, 106, 110, 131, 156, 157
copula verb 20, 23, 24, 25, 36, 91
coverb 12, 20, 24, 28, 30, 33, 35, 38, 47-57, 61, 65, 68-70, 78, 91, 93, 94, 95, 96, 100, 121
coverbs as subordinating conjunctions 57, 158-162

dà zhuàn 大篆 8
Dai Kanwa Jiten 大漢和辭典 6
declarative 13, 14, 103, 138, 146
denominative 25, 26
departing tone 6, 10, 11, 60, 123
descriptive complement 18, 57
direct object 29, 31, 68
double object construction 33
Downer, G.B. 163 n.1, n.2
durative 80, 112

Early Mandarin 5
Early Middle Chinese 5

empty words 12
exclamatory 14, 145
existential negative 109, 114
existential verb 30, 31
expletive 13
exposed position 14
exposure 69 ff.
expressive adverbs 102

fǎnqiè 反切 5, 6
Former Hàn 前漢 8
full words 12

Gassmann, Robert H. 163 n.12,
 164 n.19, n.20
Graham, A.C. 121, 129, 163 n.5,
 164 n.26, 165 n.30, n.31,
 n.32, 166 n.40, 43, 47, 167
 n.59
gǔ wén 古文 8
Guǎngyùn 廣韻 6
Guóyǔ 國語 3

Hán Fēi zǐ 韓非子 3
Hàn 漢 3, 8, 9, 17, 36, 37, 44,
 59, 66, 92, 97, 103, 105,
 106, 121, 127, 133, 137, 151
Haudricourt, A. 163 n.2
Hawkes, David 164 n.25
He Leshi 167 n.54
homophone 4
huì yì 會意 8
hypotactic 147

imperative 13, 14, 123, 137
impersonal 13, 30, 43, 151
inclusion 126 ff.
indefinite 13, 27, 28, 67, 97
indirect object 27, 31, 33
infix (or prefix) *r 11
interrogative pronoun object 14,
 20
intransitive 11, 12, 23, 26 ff., 36,
 105, 136
inversion 28, 146

jiǎjiè 假借 8

kǎishū 楷書 8
Kāngxī zìdiǎn 康熙字典 6
Karlgren, Bernhard 5, 50, 89, 94,
 114, 137, 152, 163 n.5, 163
 n.14, 164 n.26, 165 n.27,
 n.33, 166 n.43, n.52, 168
 n.60
Kennedy, George A. 164 n.26,
 165 n.28, n.29, n.37
King Xuān 宣 of Zhōu 周 8

Large Seal 8
Late Middle Chinese 5
Later Hàn 後漢 5
Li and Thompson 166 n.48
Lí Sāo 離騷 3
Lǐ Sī 李斯 8
lìshū 隸書 8
Literary Chinese 4
loanwords 9
locative complement 28, 29, 32,
 33, 54 ff., 96, 99, 137
Lǔ 魯 3
Lúnyǔ 論語 3
Lù Fǎyán 陸法言 6
Lyu Shuxiang 166 n.41

Malmqvist, Göran 166 n.51
marked nominalization 64 ff.
measure words 59
Mencius 3
Mèngzǐ 孟子 3
Middle Chinese 6
modal particles 80, 116, 139,
 142, 144
modality 112, 122 ff.
modifier 14, 24, 48, 62, 66, 99,
 149, 161
mood 112
Morohashi 6
morpheme 9, 10
morphology 10 ff.

neuter 11
nominalization 12, 16, 37, 62 ff., 80, 127
non-perfective 80
noun phrase 12
noun 12
noun suffix 10
nouns of status 26
nouns used as verbs 25
numerical expressions 58, 101

object 14, 16, 20
object position 27
Old Chinese 5
omission of the coverb in locative complements 55
oracle bones 3

paratactic 147
passive 27, 35
patient 27
Pekingese 6
perfect 116
perfective 116
personal name (míng 名) used as self-designation 77
pivot construction 33, 40
possessive 14
post-Hàn 36, 80, 90, 106
pre-Hàn 8, 106, 121, 134, 137, 153, 156
preclassical 3
predicate 13, 14
prefix *s 11
prepositions 12
pronominal adverb 126
pronoun object 14
proper names 73, 74
pseudo-subject 30
pǔtōnghuà 普通話 7
pīnyīn 拼音 7

Qièyùn 切韻 5, 6
Qín 秦 3
questions 16

Records of the Historian 4
reduplication 9
reflexive personal pronoun 83
reflexive pronominal adverb 52, 83
relative clause 14, 16, 31
restriction 125
rhetorical questions 139

sentence adverb 18, 19
sentential aspect 115
serial verb construction 45
Shāng 商 3
Shěn Yuē 沈約 6
Shījīng 詩經 3, 5
shízì 實字 12
Shǐjì 史記 4
Shūjīng 書經 3
Shuōwén jiězì 說文解字 7
sì shēng 四聲 6
Simon, Walter 167 n.58
Small Seal 8
Sòng 宋 6
sound 4
speech-act 112
subject 13, 14
subject position 27
subordination 61
suffix *-s 10
superlative 25
symbol 7
synonym 4

Taiwan 7
Takashima Kenichi 166 n.40, n.51
Tán Gōng 檀弓 165 n.37
Táng 唐 6
tense 112
tones 6
topicalization 14, 69
transitive 11, 12, 23, 27, 29
transitive verbs with two objects 31

unmarked nominalization 16, 62

verb 14
verbal aspect 112
verbless noun predicate 16, 66
verbs 12
verbs as adverbs 100
verbs in series 44, 157
verbs of location 29
verbs of motion 28
voiced initial 11

Wang Li 164 n.18
Warring States 3
wényán 文言 4
word classes 12
word families 10
word order 14

xiàng xíng 象形 7
xiǎo zhuàn 小篆 8

xiéshēng 諧聲 8
xíng shēng 形聲 7
Xiōngnú 匈奴 9
xūzì 虛字 12
Xǔ Shèn 許慎 7
Xúnzǐ 荀子 3

Yang Bojun 166 n.43
Yang Shuda 163 n.15, 165 n.38
Yìjīng 易經 3
yǔ qì cí 語氣詞 116
Yuán 元 5

Zhèng Xuán 鄭玄 165 n.38
zhǐ shì 指事 7
Zhōu 周 3
Zhòu 籀 8
zhuǎn zhù 轉注 8
Zhuāngzǐ 莊子 3
Zuǒzhuàn 左傳 3

Set in Times, IPATimes, and Fang Song by E.G. Pulleyblank

Printed and bound in Canada by Friesens

Copy-editor: Ann Webb

Proofreader: Stacy Belden